Restructuring and Quality: Issues for Tomorrow's Schools

The worldwide restructuring of education is causing major difficulties at both the systemic level and for individual schools. This book seeks to look at the linkages between this restructuring movement and the qualitative improvements that it promised to bring.

The book contains a series of essays which consider the issues related to this change, from conceptual, policy and practical points of view. It also considers the problems and possibilities facing schools in the next decade, if all of the current trends are followed through to their logical conclusion.

The chapter writers are all leaders in their field and bring together a blend of research, policy and practice to discuss what might be the most crucial reform initiative for education.

Tony Townsend is currently the Director of the South Pacific Centre for School and Community Development at Monash University. He has worked with principals, teachers, parents and education and community agencies promoting school-based community development, and has presented papers to international meetings in more than twenty countries. He has published several articles and is the author of *Effective Schooling for the Community: Core Plus Education*.

Educational management series
Series editor: Cyril Poster

Restructuring and Quality: Issues for Tomorrow's Schools

Edited by Tony Townsend

London and New York

First published 1997
by Routledge
11 New Fetter Lane, London EC4P 4EE

Transferred to Digital Printing 2004

Simultaneously published in the USA and Canada
by Routledge
29 West 35th Street, New York, NY 10001

Typeset in Garamond by Routledge

British Library Cataloguing in Publication Data
A catalogue record for this book is available from the British Library

Library of Congress Cataloguing in Publication Data
Restructuring and quality: issues for tomorrow's schools/edited by
Tony Townsend. (Educational management series) Includes
bibliographical references. 1. School management and organization –
Case studies. 2. Educational change – Case studies. 3. School
improvement programs – Case studies. I. Townsend, Tony. II. Series.
LB2805.R456 1997   96–47827
371.2–dc21   CIP

ISBN 0–415–13338–6 (hbk)
ISBN 0–415–13339–4 (pbk)

To my children Paul, Cindy and Ben, who have passed through the state school system, and Jenni, who is still passing through, and to other children like them, who are suffering from the traumas their teachers, parents and schools are facing as they deal with what might be seen in hindsight as the greatest attack on public schools in over a hundred years.

Contents

Illustrations

Contributors

David Aspin is Professor of Education and former Dean of the Faculty of Education at Monash University, where he has published extensively in the areas of philosophy of education, and particularly as it applies to Education Organisation and Administration, Professional and Academic Leadership and Management and Diplomacy. Prior to his appointment at Monash, Professor Aspin held senior positions at Macquarie University, King's College at the University of London and at the University of Manchester. He has consulted extensively in Australia, the United Kingdom, New Zealand, Indonesia, Thailand, Hong Kong and South Africa. Recent publications include *Quality Schooling: A Pragmatic Approach to Some Current Problems, Trends and Issues* (with Judith Chapman), *Creating and Managing the Democratic School: Experiences of Educational Reform in Australia and Russia* (edited with Judith Chapman and Isak Froumin).

Judith Chapman is Professor of Education at the University of Western Australia. After teaching and administrative experience in secondary schools in Australia and Europe, she undertook postgraduate study in the USA, returning to Australia in 1979. Since that time she has undertaken research and development work on behalf of a number of international, national and state authorities. At the international level her work includes: for OECD – 'Learning: Realizing a Life-Long Approach for All', 'The Effectiveness of Schooling and of Educational Resource Management', 'Decentralisation and School Improvement', and 'The Curriculum Re-defined'; for UNESCO – 'Institutional Management in Asia and the Pacific' and 'Micro Level Planning and Management'. She has also directed a number of management training programmes on behalf of the Indonesian Ministry of Education with the support of the World Bank and IDP. At the national level she has directed four Projects of National Significance, including the 'Selection and Appointment of Australian School Principals', and 'A Descriptive Profile of Australian School Principals'. Prior to accepting the Chair of Education at UWA she was Director of the School Decision-Making and Management Centre at Monash University. Judith is a Fellow of the Australian College of

Education and the Australian Council of Educational Administration. Recent publications include *Quality Schooling: A Pragmatic Approach to Some Current Problems, Trends and Issues* (with David Aspin), *Creating and Managing the Democratic School: Experiences of Educational Reform in Australia and Russia* (edited with Isak Froumin and David Aspin) and *Educational Administration in Australia* (edited with Colin Evers).

Judy Codding is Director of the National Alliance for Restructuring Education, a programme of the US National Center on Education and the Economy. The Alliance is a consortium of states and local school districts that are at the cutting edge of efforts fundamentally to rethink and restructure state and local education systems so that all students can achieve at high levels. As Alliance Director, Dr Codding is responsible for working with national, state and local education leaders to develop and implement strategic plans for restructuring their education systems, developing programmes to create new tools and strategies to support restructuring efforts, and ensuring that the procedures and lessons learned from these efforts are available nationally. Dr Codding has been principal of Pasadena High School (California), a large urban comprehensive high school serving predominantly low-income African-American and Latino students, and of Bronxville High School (New York), a suburban public high school serving mainly high-income Anglo students. She has been an Associate in Education at the Harvard Graduate School of Education, and received the 1992 California Harvard Educator of the Year Award. She has been a contributing author of several books, has written numerous articles, and has participated on many national education panels and task forces. She has also served as an education consultant to the US Department of Defense schools and to the Ministry of Education of the People's Republic of China.

Peter Cuttance is Professor of Education at the University of Sydney and was recently the Assistant Director-General (Quality Assurance) for the NSW Department of School Education. He has been a teacher in schools, TAFE and universities. He has worked in universities in a number of countries and has published a number of research papers on the performance of education systems and the management of quality in the public sector. From 1989–92 he was the founding director of the Education Review Unit in the South Australian Education Department. From 1992-96 he was responsible for developing and implementing a programme of quality assurance reviews of schools and for the evaluation of programmes and service delivery in the NSW Department of School Education. The author of many reports, journal articles and conference papers, he is also the joint editor (with David Reynolds) of *School Effectiveness: Research, Policy and Practice.*

Dean Fink is an independent leadership consultant. A former superinten-dent with the Halton Board of Education in Ontario, Canada, he has completed thirty-five years as an educator. He has taught at all levels of education, from primary to graduate school. He has been a principal and vice-principal in secondary and public schools and has taught in a number of Canadian universities. As well as extensive consulting work in Canada, he has conducted workshops and made presentations in fourteen other coun-tries. He has published numerous articles on school effectiveness, change theory and invitational education and leadership. He is co-author, with Louise Stoll, of a book entitled *Changing Our Schools: Linking School Effectiveness and School Improvement*, published by the UK's Open University Press in 1996. He is on the Advisory Council of the Alliance for Invitational Education, and is a member of the editorial board for the journal *School Effectiveness and School Improvement*.

Barry McGaw is Director of the Australian Council for Educational Research. He also holds honorary positions as Professor of Education at Monash University and Professorial Associate in Psychology at the University of Melbourne. He is a fellow of the Academy of the Social Sciences in Australia, the Australian College of Education and the Australian Psychological Society. Professor McGaw completed his BSc and BEd (Hons) at the University of Queensland and MEd and PhD at the University of Illinois. His research interests are in educational and psycho-logical measurement. He has had extensive involvement in issues of assessment at the end of secondary schooling and selection for higher educa-tion. His most recent involvement in this area has been as author of a government Green Paper on the Higher Schools Certificate in New South Wales.

Joseph Murphy is Professor and Chair in the Department of Educational Leadership at the Vanderbilt University in Nashville, Tennessee. He is also a Senior Research Fellow for the National Center for Educational Leadership and an Investigator for the John F. Kennedy Center for Research on Human Development. He has served on several national commissions related to promoting in excellence education and has published widely in the areas of school improvement and educational leadership. Recent books include *Rethinking School-Based Management* and *The Role of Ethics in Educational Leadership: An Expanding Focus* (with L. Beck), *Reshaping the Principalship: Insights from Transformational Reform Efforts* (edited with K. S. Louis), and *Preparing Tomorrow's School Leaders: Alternative Designs*.

Ken Rae is a Senior Policy Analyst with the Education and Management Section of the New Zealand Ministry of Education. His major areas of interest are school governance and management, school reporting and accountability and teacher development and professional education. Prior to his current appointment he was a teacher, Deputy Principal, Assistant General Secretary of the New Zealand Post-Primary Teachers' Association and a Senior Education Officer in a number of regional offices. He is an active member and past national secretary of the New Zealand Educational Administration Society, has presented conference papers in Australia, Hong Kong and Kenya, and has been published in the New Zealand Journal of Educational Administration as well as BEMAS and the Commonwealth Council for Educational Administration.

David Reynolds is Professor of Education at the University of Newcastle upon Tyne. He has published widely on school effectiveness and improvement, the sociology of the school and on educational policy. His recent books include *Merging Traditions: The Future of Research on School Effectiveness and School Improvement* (edited with J. Gray, C. Fitz-Gibbon and D. Jesson, 1996), *Making Good Schools: Linking School Effectiveness and Improvement* (with R. Bollen and B. P. M. Creemers, in press), *Dilemmas of Decentralisation: Quality, Equality and Control* (edited with J. Chapman, B. Boyd and R. Lander, 1996) and *Advances in School Effectiveness Research and Practice* (with B. P. M. Creemers, S. Stringfield and C. Teddlie). He is on the editorial board of numerous journals and is the former chair of the International Congress for School Effectiveness and Improvement. His current research includes work with the International School Effectiveness Research Project (ISERP), a study of schools that change their effectiveness over time, and a study of 'High Reliability Schools'.

Kathryn Riley is Professor of Education and the Director of the Centre for Educational Management at the Roehampton Institute, London. She has wide-ranging experience in education and local government and has worked extensively with senior managers in schools and local authorities. Her current research interests include Effective School Leadership, the Role and Effectiveness of the LEA, and the Implications for Education of the Shift from Local Government to a System of Local Governance. Her recent publications include *Quality and Equality: Promoting Opportunities in Schools*, and *Managing for Quality in an Uncertain Climate*.

David Rowles is a Principal Lecturer at the Centre for Educational Management at the Roehampton Institute, London. His work involves him in managerial training for school senior staff management teams and running whole-day In Service Training for staff on management and teacher appraisal. He has also been involved, in conjunction with the National Association of Head Teachers, in a national programme of preparation for inspection for groups of headteachers. He is an OFSTED-trained inspector and takes part in inspections of both primary and secondary schools, and was previously Senior Inspector of Schools with the London Borough of Merton. He has also been involved with international teacher exchange programmes.

Louise Stoll is Coordinating Director of the International School Effectiveness and Improvement Centre (ISEIC) at the Institute of Education, University of London. She works with schools in all phases of development and has set up the School Improvement Network with a group of associates. Her research includes action studies on school improvement and improving school effectiveness for the Scottish Office Education Department. Previously she was a primary school teacher, researcher and coordinator of the Halton Effective Schools Project in Canada. She has presented and consulted throughout the world and is an active member of the International Congress for School Effectiveness and Improvement. Her publications include *School Matters* and *Changing Our Schools: Linking School Effectiveness and School Improvement* (with Dean Fink), and she is on the board of the international journal *School Effectiveness and School Improvement*.

Sam Stringfield is a principal Research Scientist at the Johns Hopkins University Center for The Social Organization of Schools (CSOS), where he serves as co-director of the Systemic and Policy Studies section of the Center for Research on Education of Students Placed At Risk (CRESPAR). Stringfield has authored over fifty articles, chapters and books. His two most recent projects concern methods for improving programmes within schools (*The Special Strategies Studies*, Stringfield et al. 1996) and whole schools (*Bold Plans for School Restructuring: The New American Schools Designs*, Stringfield, Ross and Smith 1996). Prior to coming to Johns Hopkins, Stringfield worked as a teacher, a programme evaluator, a Tulane University faculty member, and coordinator of the Denver office of Northwest Regional Educational Laboratory. As a Kellogg Fellow, he studied the politics and economics of school improvement in the US, Asia, Africa and Europe. Stringfield has served as the chairman of the School Effectiveness and Improvement special interest group of the American Educational Research Association, and is an executive committee member at large of the International Congress for School Effectiveness and Improvement (ICSEI). Dr Stringfield's charming wife Kathleen valiantly struggles against long odds to improve his dancing and gardening skills.

Tony Townsend is an Associate Professor in the Faculty of Education, and Director of the South Pacific Centre for School and Community Development, at Monash University in Melbourne. He has brought the research interests of community education and school effectiveness together in his work for the International Community Education Association (where he has been the elected Director of the Pacific region since 1987) and the International Congress for School Effectiveness and Improvement (where he serves on the editorial board of the journal *School Effectiveness and School Improvement* and was conference manager for ICSEI's 1994 Conference in Melbourne). He has published widely in school management and community education journals, and is the author of *Effective Schooling for the*

Community: Core Plus Education and editor of the forthcoming publication *The Australian Primary School: Responding to Change.* He has conducted workshops and seminars for principals, teachers, parents and community members in over twenty countries in the Pacific, Asia, North America and Europe.

Preface

In the past decade, in countries around the world, educational authorities have embarked upon an exercise that has come to be known as the restructuring of education. Major examples of changes to how schools are managed and organised have occurred in school systems as diverse as those of England and Wales, Canada, the USA, New Zealand, Hong Kong and Australia. It could be argued that the original efforts in restructuring came from the idea of an education voucher system, which was first attempted in the United States in the early 1970s, where the US Office of Economic Opportunity first undertook feasibility studies in Gary, Indiana, San Francisco and Seattle, and then funded a voucher system in Alum Rock School District in San Jose, California, in 1972. However, the movement really took shape in the early 1980s, where major reports in many places, but especially the United States and the United Kingdom, called upon schools to play a greater role in the economic development of their countries. However, not all the movement of power was in the direction of the school, nor was the movement consistent in all countries.

There have been shifts in decision-making to schools for some elements of organisation, but they seem to happen simultaneously with increases in centralised decision-making powers and influence for others. There seems to be a general trend towards centralised control over areas such as the development and assessment of school curriculum, but increasing responsibility at the school level, through finance and staffing decisions, for the structuring of learning activities to achieve those goals. But these general trends, which suggest the acceptance of the devolution of educational management in almost all parts of the world, disguise some underlying features which bear closer scrutiny.

The literature that is being produced about efforts to restructure schools seems to indicate a common claim by any system that has undergone this form of restructuring that it will improve student achievement or the quality of education, yet there has been no research able to show substantial causal links between devolution and improved student outcomes. Some of the concerns underpinned by these factors become the central focus of this book.

The first section of the book looks at some of the broader issues that helped to initiate recent restructuring efforts. The international research in such disciplines as school effectiveness and school improvement, which is often used as the justification for many of the restructuring activities, the movement towards school-based management as the most common implementation strategy, and the concept of quality, are all considered in some depth.

Barry McGaw, in Chapter 1, provides an overview of the key issues of restructuring within two contexts, the economic and the educational. He suggests that, while there has been a recovery of faith in the impact of schooling, there are expressed doubts about the impact of resources. This has led to the critical argument that standards can be raised simultaneously with the reduction of funding. He also uses Galbraith's argument of the loss of commitment to the common good as a means of explaining how, while the public policy has been to reduce education expenditure, the people implementing that policy send their own children to the most expensive schools. This chapter provides an excellent overview that will be both a concern and a challenge to those involved in public education.

In Chapter 2, Louise Stoll and David Reynolds review the impact of the school effectiveness and school improvement research on school systems in the past decade. They point out that, although the two disciplines started from different places, there has become a realisation that each requires the other if a complete understanding of school development is to emerge. They discuss a number of principles upon which such a merger of disciplines might take place and demonstrate how a number of school improvement or school effectiveness projects in different countries have contributed substance to each of the principles. They also indicate a number of continuing challenges that must be addressed if we are to develop a better understanding of what make schools work.

Joseph Murphy considers the introduction of school-based management as one of the major forms of the recent drive to restructure schools. In Chapter 3, he provides an overview of the history and rationale for restructuring, pointing to a number of concerns, such as the need to develop economic competitiveness and the developing concern for social inequities, that have produced the need to look at education from a new conceptual framework. He also considers the various dimensions of school-based management, such as the devolution of decisions related to school goals, budget, staffing, curriculum and administration, and provides a balanced account of some of the negative impacts that this form of restructuring can have. He considers some of the implications that restructuring might have for various agents in the education process: policymakers, regional administrators, principals and teachers. Finally, he provides a list of necessary conditions that will help facilitate the successful implementation of school-based management, and lists some concerns about the way in which the restructuring activity is being implemented.

Judith Chapman and David Aspin consider some of the conceptual issues related to the notion of quality in Chapter 4. They argue that, despite the lack of consensus about a particular definition of 'quality', the use of the term in education brings with it a general agreement on certain values that are generally accepted by those that use it. Only when some agreement about what the term implies is reached can we concern ourselves with the implementation of a 'quality' education. They then consider different ways in which a quality education might be implemented, and how restructuring might occur, based upon various ideological views of the world, from the notion of education as a commodity in a market-place to the notion of education as a public good. They argue that any autonomy that schools receive must be balanced by a mutuality based upon common benefit. They establish an agenda for reform that will lead to a system where schools operate in harmony while maintaining their autonomous decision-making base.

The second section of the book considers various strategies used by school systems in England and Wales, Australia and New Zealand to improve the quality of education by restructuring their education systems. Chapter 5, written by Kathryn Riley and David Rowles, analyses the impact of the introduction of a new national inspection system in England and Wales and examines the changing role of the local system – the local education authority (LEA) – in relation to school quality. The analysis draws on a study of the LEA's role in quality conducted in seven English local authorities in 1993, on a follow-up study conducted in 1995, and on seminars and work-shops conducted with over 1,000 headteachers in some thirty locations during 1993–94. The chapter illustrates how the system has been modified in response to a range of pressures such as the growing diversity in the activities of LEAs, but also the scope they still retain to exercise their discretion and develop evaluative systems which respond to local circumstances.

In Chapter 6, Peter Cuttance discusses the relationship between quality improvement and quality assurance, business terminologies that have taken on major significance for schools and school systems. He provides a broad view of the concepts and how they might be applied to school systems. He uses the notion of Total Quality Management (TQM) as a strategy for school improvement and discusses how quality assurance reviews within the New South Wales (Australia) school system have been used to promote improved school performance and development. He argues that a significant degree of community participation in the review process, and the use of school-based data to lead to recommendations for future development, have been well received by school communities as a means of providing future directions to schools.

Ken Rae, in Chapter 7, provides a theoretical basis for restructuring, from such diverse sources as public choice theory, principal-agent theory and managerialism theory, as a background to a discussion of the changes to the

New Zealand education system. These saw the rapid abandonment of the various layers of bureaucracy, leaving just the centre as policy maker and the school as the site of delivery of educational services. He discusses the impacts that five changes have had on various aspects of education provision. These include the new curriculum framework, national education guidelines, an education review office, new accreditation procedures and issues related to the new Public Finance Act. He argues that the system should be seen as one in evolution, rather than one that has been fully transformed, a state which can be said for all of the systems discussed in this book.

The third section of the book looks at specific programmes that may provide a better understanding of the effects that the implementation of restructuring has on schools and at the school system level in the USA, Canada and Australia. In Chapter 8, Sam Stringfield discusses the notion of 'high reliability schools', schools which seem to have unusually high success rates and characteristics that seem to ward off failure. He uses four longitudinal case studies of 'successful' American schools, schools that have succeeded when the demographic conditions suggest they shouldn't, and explores the common elements that they appear to have. The case studies provide the reader with an excellent set of characteristics which, if purposefully applied, may improve student outcomes, in any school, in any country. He discusses fourteen characteristics of high-reliability organisations, organisations where any failure of the system is seen as a major catastrophe, and applies these characteristics to each of the case study schools. The conclusion he reaches is significant for all educators. Despite seemingly different methods and strategies, underneath this variation lies an order and a structure that is very similar. Each of the highly successful schools contained all or most of the characteristics of highly reliable organisations. These can perhaps be seen as a guide to future school development.

In Chapter 9, we follow through with the American example by looking at a detailed case study of one American High School. Judy Codding provides an excellent overview of the American reform agenda and shows how one school, Pasadena High School, has responded to its underlying principles. The American reform agenda, similar to others in other countries, has been based upon a desire to attain high standards for all students, to redesign learning environments to respond to the future rather than the past, to provide support for families and children to ensure that all children succeed, to adopt an organisation that focuses on results, and to engage parents and the public fully in the restructuring effort. These issues are discussed in detail within the context of a particular school that had changed dramatically in a short period of time, due to demographic changes, from one of the more successful schools to one that was less successful. Codding discusses the processes used to turn the school around and provides a series of useful 'lessons learned' for school staff and administrators who wish to do the same.

In Chapter 10, Dean Fink and Louise Stoll describe their 'odyssey' over nearly a decade in Halton, Canada, as they establish a school system that responded to, and supported, individuals and schools in their quest for change. They discuss the need for changing from the traditional learning paradigm, where children, curriculum and schools are divided into neat and hierarchical packages to be dealt with in some perceived appropriate order, to a new learning paradigm where neither children, learning nor organisations can be considered predictable and therefore subject to external control. They argue the case for a new form of management that incorporates both anticipation and commitment, weaving these two components together to achieve school goals.

Tony Townsend, in Chapter 11, provides another view of a restructured school system, this one from Victoria, Australia. He argues that the *Schools of the Future* programme was designed as a comprehensive view of school management, from both the systemic and the individual school perspective. Similar in style to the United Kingdom and New Zealand restructuring exercise, but perhaps pushing the boundaries of decentralisation even further, Townsend describes the key features of the system. These include accountability to both the local community and to the state through the development of a school charter, the implementation of curriculum frameworks and their standardised testing, and the single-line budget allocation to schools called the Schools Global Budget, which provides for decisions about how the school's budget is to be spent to be made at the local level. He considers the efforts of the school system to provide access for students to the new technologies and the structures provided to support the staff of schools. He argues that, despite there being many positive features that have attracted school and community support, there are still a number of issues to be resolved before the programme can verify its claim of improving the quality of education for all Victorian students.

In an Afterword, Tony Townsend reviews the key issues related to the restructuring activity. He identifies some of the difficulties that are caused by different understandings of what a quality education entails, and some of the gaps between the rhetoric of the current proponents of restructuring and the reality of what is happening in schools. He then provides some thoughts as to the direction that research and practice might take in the years ahead if the promise of quality through restructuring is to be achieved.

Acknowledgements

I wish to express my gratitude to Helen Fairlie at Routledge, both for her encouragement to produce the book and for her patience when it took longer than expected, and to each of the contributors who have made the book what it is. When you try to get the best people in their fields, they are invariably busy on their own projects and writings. I appreciate their support on this project. I also wish to express my thanks to the staff of the Faculty of Education at Monash, particularly the Dean, Dick White, and my Head of School, Jeff Northfield, for their continued support of my ideas and activities. Finally, I am indebted to my wife, Juli, who has invariably been there when time has become tight or things have become tough, to allow me the space and time I have required to be involved in the things I do.

Tony Townsend
January 1997

Part I

Restructuring for quality in schools

Chapter 1

Quality and equality in education
Central issues in the restructuring of education

Barry McGaw

Management of education systems changes in ways that reflect new insights into education and management but also in ways that reflect ideology. Some highly centralised systems, like those in the Australian states, have devolved authority to regional structures on the basis of claims that regional culture and context should be given expression in education. More recently, some of these systems have gone further in devolving responsibility to schools. In some cases, the justification advanced involves local community ownership and responsibility, and the local structure involves school councils with a strong community voice. New Zealand is an example. In other cases, the justification involves local professional leadership, particularly by the principal, and is based on the view that decentralised management with local discretion yields more professional engagement and greater efficiency. Within schools, the most complete delegation grants local control over resource allocation. The Australian State of Victoria presents itself as an example, and is discussed in Chapter 11.

There are some important countervailing trends which are evident in attempts to develop national, or at least state or provincial, goals for education. This is evident in long-standing devolved systems, like those of the USA and England and Wales, and in systems which are at the same time devolving responsibility in other respects, like some of the Australian states. In England and Wales, where there are no state or provincial governments between the national government and local school authorities, the national government has been able to develop a national curriculum framework and to introduce associated programmes to assess student learning. In the USA, where the federal system interposes state authorities between the national government and local school authorities, there have been strengthening state prescriptions and also emerging national specifications of goals and specific curriculum standards. In Australia, where education is the responsibility of the states and not the national government or local authorities, there has been unprecedented cooperation among states in recent years in the development of broad national goals and more detailed curriculum statements and associated specifications of anticipated student learning outcomes.

On the face of it, all of these changes represent attempts to improve the quality of education. Shifts in responsibility to the local level are expected to locate decision-making where it can be best informed and have the greatest purchase. Specification of national or state goals is expected to improve performance by setting higher benchmarks for many who might be blinkered by limited local experience in setting their expectations. Where all of these changes occur in a context of fiscal restraint, the surrounding rhetoric adds the concept of efficiency to that of effectiveness, but it often seems as though the goal is economy – not efficiency or effectiveness – in reaching quality outcomes. The result can then be such differential outcome achievement that equality is in no sense assured.

ECONOMIC CONTEXT

The economic context in which contemporary reforms in education are being undertaken in many countries can be characterised as reflecting a recovery of faith in the impact of schooling but a loss of faith in the impact of resources; a concern about national outcomes but a loss of commitment to common good; and belief in the efficacy of market forces in yielding efficient strategies for obtaining high-quality outcomes but primarily pursuit of economy, at least in public provision.

Recovery of faith in the impact of schooling

Key participants probably never lost faith in the efficacy of schooling. What they had to contend with, however, were consistent research findings that challenged their conventional, practical wisdom. There was never a claim that schooling made no difference in comparison with no schooling, only that differences among schools appeared to make no difference to student outcomes. A major US study of educational opportunity, commissioned to identify school characteristics that produced a difference in order to suggest how to improve impoverished and ineffective schools, reached the conclusion that schools made no difference (Coleman et al., 1966). Extensive re-analyses of Coleman's data, and further investigation, did nothing to shift this disappointing conclusion over the next decade. Jencks et al. (1972) concluded that 'the evidence suggests that equalizing educational opportunity would do very little to make adults more equal' (p. 255).

In England, the Plowden Report (Central Advisory Council, 1967) had proposed intervention in areas of educational disadvantage in the expectation that educational action could make a difference. A major programme of action research, designed to change districts and schools in ways recommended by the Plowden Report, reached somewhat more optimistic conclusions than the US research, suggesting that both pre-schools and community schools could raise educational standards in disadvantaged areas

(Halsey, 1972). What they concluded was that differences in home and cultural background had very much more effect than differences in schools.

More radical interpretations of the general finding of a low level of impact of schools, however, reinforced the pessimistic interpretation of Coleman and Jencks. Bowles and Gintis (1976) in the US found that, far from being impotent, schools 'play a central role in the reproduction of the social order' (p. 246). In the Australian context, Connell (1977) and Connell *et al.* (1982) argued similarly that schooling legitimated and reproduced existing social structures with their patterns of advantage and disadvantage.

The critics, like Bowles, Gintis and Connell, who saw the failure of schooling to alleviate disadvantage not as impotence but as complicity, did not abandon all hope that schools might contribute to social reform. They did, however, perceive the task as more substantial than the 1960s reformers did, and saw the need for educational reform not to be viewed in isolation from more general social reform.

More recent research on school effectiveness and school improvement has weakened the argument about impotence somewhat, and established new ground for belief that schools have an impact beyond that of home and family background. How much this impact can be harnessed to remove or reduce social inequities remains a rather open question, but one that should remain at the forefront in research on school reform and in policy development.

Two methodological developments have yielded these more optimistic interpretations from both new data and re-analyses of old data, illustrated in the work and findings of Mortimore *et al.* (1988) and Hill *et al.* (1993). One is a focus on progress, measured as change in levels of achievement during a period of schooling, rather than on status, measured as the student's level of achievement at a particular time. Differences between schools and classrooms are more strongly related to changes occurring while the students are in those schools and classrooms than they are to the performance level students have reached at the end of the period of study. The final status is influenced by initial status, as well as by the characteristics of school and classroom that make a difference.

The second methodological advance is the development of data analysis methods that take account of the structure of the samples of students investigated, with students clustered in classrooms in schools, and do not impose the unjustified assumption that a simple random sample of students is being used. These new methods take account of the fact that students within classrooms and schools tend to be somewhat like one another and permit classroom and school effects to be estimated in ways that take account of this clustering of the students. Using these methods of analysis, the effects of differences among schools are generally shown to be stronger than they appear to be from analysis assuming a simple random sample structure in the data (see, for example, Aitken *et al.*'s, 1981, re-analysis of the data from Bennett, 1976).

Doubts about the impact of resources

At a time when the research evidence has restored some of the ground for faith in the efficacy of schooling, it is perhaps disappointing that a case has been built to support the view that differences in resource levels make no difference. The original Coleman study was commissioned to identify the most effective ways in which resources might be deployed to make a difference in the educational outcomes for disadvantaged students. Its conclusion that differences among schools made little difference to outcomes undermined the case for differential provision, though it did not stop it. By the time the case that differences among schools do make a difference had been re-established, other evidence had been produced to show that the crucial differences among schools were apparently not dependent on differential resource levels.

Most Western countries committed substantially increased resources per student to school programmes in the 1970s and early 1980s, but little systematic evidence was gathered about the benefits of those increased resources. By the mid-1980s in Australia, questions began to be asked about what benefits had accrued from the higher levels of support. The federal Minister of Education established the Quality of Education Review Committee (1985) to examine the evidence, but it found little available. The authorities and agencies that had received the increased funds had tended to commit all their energies and resources to designing and implementing programmes with little serious attempt at evaluation. They did little to investigate the impact of particular initiatives and undertook no comparisons among systems to investigate the consequences of differences in policy and practice.

Although there were differences in resource levels committed per student in the different states, in the few national studies that were undertaken the possibility of inter-state comparisons was usually denied. This meant that nothing could be said about whether inter-state differences existed, let alone about whether any that did might have been related to different resource levels. Some of the states conducted periodic surveys of student achievement in the 1980s, and all of them have begun to do so annually by the mid-1990s. The earlier ones, documented by Spearritt (1987), and the more recent ones documented by the House of Representatives Standing Committee on Employment, Education and Training (1993) show, almost without exception, that standards of student performance have not declined but have rather been maintained at existing levels. The evidence is thin, however, because of the narrowness of the learning tested and the infrequency of the surveys. What the critics who first claimed that standards were falling now demand, in the face of evidence that they have not fallen, is that standards should be rising as a consequence of increased funding and in response to increasing social and economic demands on education.

The absence of any substantial evidence of improvement is soon enough interpreted as the presence of evidence of no improvement. The onus of proof is placed firmly on the education providers by the critics. Clare and Johnston (1993), for example, claim that there is a serious problem with literacy levels in schools. They do not so much seek to prove that there is a problem as to establish that no one has proved that there is not one. They support what now appears to be the conventional public wisdom, that there were no benefits of this period of increased expenditure, a view reinforced by a long-established tendency of each generation to conclude that the next is doing less well in schooling, and in most other ways, than it and its predecessors did. Cost reductions for many activities in the private sector in recent years also strengthen the view that the increases granted for schooling were unjustifiable and are now unsustainable.

From the claim that the increased resources of the 1970s and 1980s produced no benefits, the conclusion is then reached that resource levels could now be reduced without detriment. The broader conclusion then is that observable differences in resource levels between schools or school systems produce no differences in outcomes. There is some research evidence which is taken to support this contention (e.g. Hanushek, 1989) but that interpretation of the research evidence has been challenged in a re-analysis of the data on which it is based in a systematic meta-analysis by Hedges *et al.* (1994), in which they conclude that the 'analyses are persuasive in showing that, with the possible exception of facilities, there is evidence of statistically reliable relations between educational resources inputs and school outcomes' (p. 11).

It might appear surprising that strong policy formulations for resource reductions are based on such little evidence that there will be no negative effects. The explanation appears to be that what are offered as justifications for the public policy of cost reduction are not the reasons for the policy but rationalisations. In any case, the private behaviour of many who commend a public policy of expenditure reduction does not reflect a strong belief in the arguments which provide the basis for the public policy. This mismatch is evident in the last published data on per-student expenditure in government and non-government secondary schools in Australia, shown in Fig.1.1 with the non-government sector separated into the Catholic and 'other non-government' schools.

Expenditure levels in the different sectors are not precisely comparable, for a number of reasons, so it is difficult to make completely fair comparisons. The government school expenditure rates in Fig. 1.1 do not include employer contributions to superannuation or costs of servicing of borrowings, both of which are included in costs for non-government schools. On the other hand, government schools have to provide for all students wishing to enrol, including some with disabilities for whom provision is relatively expensive. Government schools also have to be provided in expensive,

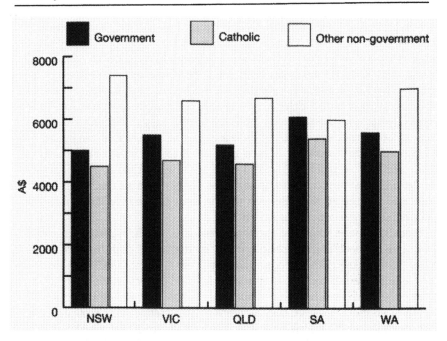

Figure 1.1 Annual expenditure per secondary student in mainland
            Australian states

remote locations where enrolments are likely to be small. Comparisons are
also made difficult by the fact that government expenditure is reported for
financial years running from July to June (in this case 1991–2) while non-
government school expenditure is reported for calendar years (in this case
1992). More recent comparisons cannot be made since the data on non-
government school expenditure are no longer published.

Expenditure levels in non-government schools in Australia are not independent of government policies. The federal government provides financial
support which is higher for schools with a lesser capacity to fund themselves. Low-fee schools attract higher government support. Catholic schools,
in general, have kept their fees low in order to maintain their general acces-
sibility for potential students and, as a consequence, obtain maximum
federal government support. The net effect is a level of per-student expenditure lower than that in government schools in all five mainland states.

In the 'other non-government' sector there is a wide range of schools. In
recent years, many low-fee schools have been established to enhance accessi-
bility of this sector. Like many Catholic schools, they operate with
considerable federal government financial support. The other non-government school sector also includes long-established, and now high-fee,
independent schools.

Figure 1.1 shows that, in all but South Australia, the per-student expenditure rate for non-Catholic, non-government schools is well above that for government schools. It is interesting to note that, in New South Wales, where the expenditure on government secondary school students is the lowest in the nation, the expenditure rate on students in non-Catholic, non-government schools is the highest in the nation. Many of those who argue most strongly for cuts in government expenditure on government schools, on the grounds that resource levels are essentially unimportant, enrol their own children in these most expensive non-government schools.

In seeking to judge the legitimacy of the current demands for expenditure cuts in public education to improve efficiency, we need to judge not only the claims themselves but also the inconsistency of the private behaviour and the public policy recommendations of many of those who commend the cuts in public expenditure.

Loss of commitment to the common good

Although those who commend reduced public expenditure on education do appeal to the lack of evidence of benefit from increased expenditure and to research evidence of no relationship between levels of input and output (e.g. Hanushek, 1989), the weakness of the evidence and the inconsistency of private behaviour and public policy proposals suggest that there are other reasons for the policy proposals. Galbraith (1992) suggests that the key underlying reason is a loss of commitment to the common good.

Galbraith argues that, whereas in the past 'the economically and socially fortunate were . . . a small minority – characteristically a dominant and ruling handful' (p. 15), now they are a majority, at least of those who vote. They are a contented majority, not without continuing personal aspiration to do better, but living and working in a system that advantages them while disadvantaging a significant minority underclass. The contented majority, according to Galbraith, takes a highly selective view of the role of government. 'The state is seen as a burden. . . . The need to lighten or remove this burden and therewith, agreeably, the supporting taxes is an article of high faith for the comfortable or contented majority' (pp. 22–3). While government in general is a burden, there are 'significant and costly exceptions from this broad condemnation . . . social security, medical care at higher income levels, farm income supports and financial guarantees to depositors in ill-fated banks and savings and loan enterprises' (p. 23).

Although the contented class clearly approves expenditure from the public purse for actions and programmes of which it is a beneficiary, the general view that taxation should be reduced and government cut back derives from a perceived asymmetry in the taxation system. In general, taxes are seen to come from the contented and benefits to go to others (Galbraith, 1992: 44). In further justification of the reduction in taxation and government activity, there is built the argument that anything government does it does badly. Private provision thus becomes, not a refuge for those with a capacity to look after themselves, but a desirable goal for all, for there lies efficiency. Even the word 'bureaucracy', which can as well describe the operations of large private corporations as large government agencies, tends to be preserved as a description of government, and a pejorative one at that.

In the education sector, moves to private provision are evident in the expansion of the private school sector in some countries, such as Australia, and in calls for voucher systems. In systems where public provision was the means by which equity was pursued, cost cutting in the public sector and a withdrawal by those who can afford it to privately funded, and state supported, private provision introduces real risks of inequity.

Market theory and public provision

Current restructuring of the public sector does not reflect only the current prevailing tendency to reduce the size of public sector expenditure. It is also driven by a desire to enhance the quality of schooling and thus to achieve improved outcomes. Making those gains in conjunction with cost cutting would be to achieve substantial efficiency gains.

It is frequently assumed that the best means of pursuing these efficiency gains is by exposing schools to the discipline of market forces. The faith in markets (or quasi-markets in many cases, as far as the public sector is concerned) is based on the expectations that diversity of provision will increase as providers respond to clients; and clients will be able to make informed choices among providers. In fact, the market theory most relevant to the provision of educational services may be that which accounts for the provision of professional services in circumstances where there is unequal distribution of information between provider and client, in favour of the provider. This market theory predicts that there will be differentiation of the market of providers with the result that those providers able to position themselves in superior market niches will choose their clients. Clients will not be able to choose their provider.

Evidence from UK reforms tends to confirm the validity of this prediction. Edwards and Whitty (1994) show that schools exercising a newly-granted right to pursue their own clients were more likely to display their distinctiveness than to respond to the market. They point out that 'schools are very unequally placed to be chosen [and] parents are very unequally placed to have their child accepted by a school which is over-chosen' (p. 31).

EDUCATIONAL CONTEXT

The presumptions made about school improvement in this economic context are that, at worst, school improvement is cost neutral, i.e. that schools can become more effective by better use of existing resources and that no additional resources will be required; or that, at best, school improvement can be achieved at the same time as cost reductions are achieved through increased efficiency.

Those presumptions should not remain unchallenged but, at the same time as they are put to the test in appropriate research, issues of effectiveness and improvement should also be addressed. In this work, scope becomes an important matter. One key question is where the locus of control lies in an education system, because leverage will depend on the reform effort being directed at the major points of control. In centralised systems, and for some issues in decentralised ones, the locus of control will be with central authorities. In decentralised systems, the locus of control will be at the local level, either the district or school. It is also important to focus on the smaller units through which programmes are delivered, because the variability among such units makes clear that the surrounding system does not entirely constrain choice. In this context, 'local' can mean the individual classroom, subject department or faculty within a school, and not only a whole school.

It is important, too, to look beyond system and even national boundaries. The cultural context of a nation or system has powerful shaping effects, of course, but both those effects and the relationships central to interpretations of the influences on school effectiveness can be better understood through comparative analyses that span cultures.

Locus of control

Decentralisation is a clear trend in many centralised education systems, but one for which the rationale is not always clear. If the context is to be properly understood, and any evaluation well focused, the reasons for decentralisation need to be clarified. They can range from an accommodation of cultural or geographic variation within a country or region, to establishment of local responsibility, or to winning a greater sense of local ownership of and commitment to the schools and their programmes. It also needs to be made clear just what aspects of the system are being decentralised so that false expectations are not set up on either side. If responsibilities are devolved in a context of resource reduction, there is a risk that obligations will be shifted without the capacity to fulfil them. The policy may then appear to be no more than an attempt to shift responsibility for the consequences of the resource reductions away from central to local authorities.

In some systems that have traditionally been highly decentralised, there is explicit centralisation under way. The introduction of a national curriculum and a national testing programme in England and Wales is one example.

Another is the move towards a more national perspective in the US, with the adoption of broad national educational goals and the definition of standards in a variety of curriculum areas. In these contexts, local initiatives for school improvement must take some account of the national goals in the establishment of local goals.

This pattern of central prescription can also be part of the context in formerly centralised systems which are currently decentralising. In some of these, there are explicit moves to retain or reintroduce central prescription of elements of programmes, through things such as curriculum frameworks and specifications of expected student learning, and to prescribe forms of behaviour through accountability requirements or review and audit mechanisms.

School improvement processes

The initial research interest in school effectiveness was aimed at illuminating differences in a range of characteristics between more and less effective schools, in the expectation that this would provide clues about how to improve the less effective ones. Subsequently, processes of school improvement have become a research focus in their own right as it was recognised that insights about differences between more and less effective schools did not yield immediate strategies for school improvement. Continuing research on both fronts remains a priority.

In work that does focus on school effectiveness and improvement, there is a need to extend the focus to the interfaces between institutions operating at different levels (e.g. primary and secondary; junior and senior secondary) to ensure that the quality of the transitions for students moving between institutions is part of the consideration in judging the effectiveness of an institution.

Much of the research and policy development concerned with school effectiveness and improvement has focused on organisational issues at the school and system level. There has been a surprising lack of attention to issues of curriculum and teaching. There is, of course, a substantial body of research on curriculum and teaching, though that work also does not forge clear links with the work on school effectiveness and improvement. The third edition of the *Handbook of research on teaching* (Wittrock, 1986), for example, has only a chapter dealing with classroom management and organisation, and nothing dealing with school or system issues. It will be interesting to see if this is true of the forthcoming fourth edition. It would be good for strong links to be forged between work on school effectiveness and improvement and work on curriculum and teaching.

School and instructional processes

Recent research, such as that of Hill *et al.* (1993), makes clear that differences in levels of effectiveness among classrooms are often more substantial than differences among schools. This suggests the need for research and policy development that focuses more on teachers and classrooms than on schools. That being the case, research on improvement should also focus on classrooms and not only schools as units. This will require that attention be given to teaching and learning processes. From the perspective of teachers, as managers of classrooms professionally responsible for students' learning, the task of managing teaching is a key concern that ought to be a focus of work on school and classroom effectiveness.

Attention to classroom effectiveness, however, should not be at the expense of attention to school effectiveness. The questions to be addressed in relation to school effectiveness, however, should include consideration of the ways in which actions taken at the whole-school level could facilitate the development and maintenance of effective classrooms.

Organisation and management

Many factors impinge on professional practice in educational institutions. Some are features of the institution, some of the system of which it is part. In professional practice, policy development and research, it is important to take account of this range of factors.

The implications for professional development of those in leadership roles in schools need particular attention in view of the ways in which their formal roles are altering. Increased devolution of responsibility to schools and requirements of more extensive engagement with the school community are two of the factors leading to changes in role. The changes in role may provide significant opportunities for school administrators to develop new skills, but they can equally result in dilution of the educational role in a way that amounts to deprofessionalisation. The question of how to balance the demands of management with educational leadership looms large in circumstances where a broader range of management tasks is incorporated within the principal's responsibilities.

CULTURAL CONTEXT

Educational context is embedded in cultural context, and issues of educational restructuring will need to be addressed in terms of that cultural context. For many educational systems, a key question is how to deal with national and local identity.

The issue of national identity raises questions about the proper role of education in helping to forge commonality and community of interest, often in multicultural settings. It also raises questions about how to counterbalance notions of national identity with the need to develop more global views. The issue of local identity raises questions about how to sustain regional provisions that cede appropriate local control and permit appropriate local variations, while taking account of the need to develop and sustain national identity and to honour national commitments, such as to multiculturalism.

Across national boundaries, however, there are many common interests and concerns which suggest that much can be learned from experiences in other national and cultural contexts than one's own. With appropriate attention to the subtleties of cultural differences, useful international light could be shed on key issues in school effectiveness and improvement. What is needed is a willingness to be open about within-country experiences to a sufficient extent for the lessons to be discerned and shared.

Policy development occurs in a political context and inevitably, and properly, reflects the ideology of the responsible authorities. Professionals developing and implementing policy, however, need to understand both this general relationship and the particular characteristics of the ideological position that defines their context. Furthermore, the profession as a whole needs to provide a critique of the ideology itself as well as of the policies and programmes that emerge. All of this points to the need for multiple perspectives on issues of school effectiveness and school improvement, for researchers, as well as for policy makers and practitioners.

EQUITY

Much of the work on school effectiveness and improvement uses average student improvement as the criterion with which to estimate the value that the school or the classroom adds. This approach assumes a uniformity of effect or, at least, does not explore the possibility of markedly different effects occurring for different groups of students.

Researchers, policy-makers and practitioners must always remain open to the possibility that what works well for some might not work well for others. This is all the more urgent in an economic context of constraint or cost reductions where the burdens might not be shared equally.

Questions of gender and ethnicity, for example, must be seen as being of continuing importance. Concern for equity might be forgotten in the current preoccupation with large organisational questions about issues such as devolution and local control. Worse, concern for equity can be rationalised away with assertions that attention to general concepts like the provision for each individual to pursue their full potential will automatically ensure that equity questions are addressed. A stronger, and more justifiable, position would be to hold that addressing the equity questions will put to a harder test the assertion that individuals are achieving their full potential, because it will enforce investigation of whether there are differences among subgroups that ought not to be there.

Quality must be sought in a way that is informed by concern about equity. The effectiveness of programmes and institutions must be judged in terms that genuinely evaluate the fairness of the distribution of the benefits of any improvement in quality.

REFERENCES

Aitken, M., Bennett, N. and Hesketh, J. (1981) 'Teaching styles and pupil progress: A re-analysis', *British Journal of Educational Psychology*, 51, 170–86.

Bennett, N. (1976) *Teaching styles and pupil progress*, London: Open Books.

Bowles, S. and Gintis, H. (1976) *Schooling in capitalist America*, London: Routledge and Kegan Paul.

Central Advisory Council for Education (England) (1967) *Children and their primary schools*, London: Her Majesty's Stationery Office.

Clare, R. and Johnston, K. (1993) *Education and training in the 1990s*, Background Paper No.É31, Economic Planning and Advisory Council, Canberra: Australian Government Publishing Service.

Coleman, J. S. *et al.* (1966) *Equality of educational opportunity*, Washington, DC: US Government Printing Office.

Connell, R. W. (1977) *Ruling class, ruling culture: Studies of conflict, power and legitimacy in Australian life*, Cambridge: Cambridge University Press.

Connell, R. W. *et al.* (1982) *Making the difference: Schools, families and social division*, Sydney: George Allen and Unwin.

Edwards, T. and Whitty, G. (1994) 'Parental choice and school autonomy: The English experience', *Unicorn: Journal of the Australian College of Education*, 20(1), 25–34.

Galbraith, J. K. (1992) *The culture of contentment*, Boston: Houghton Mifflin.

Halsey, A. H. (1972) *Educational priority: Vol. 1: E.P.A. problems and policies*, London: Her Majesty's Stationery Office.

Hanushek, E. A. (1989) 'The impact of differential performance on school performance', *Educational Researcher*, 18(4), 45–65.

Hedges, L. V., Laine, R. D. and Greenwald, R. (1994) 'Does money matter? A meta-analysis of the effects of differential school inputs on student outcomes', *Educational Researcher*, 23(3), 5–14.

Hill, P. W., Holmes-Smith, P. and Rowe, K. J. (1993) 'School and teacher effectiveness in Victoria: Key findings from Phase 1 of the Victorian Quality Schools Project', Melbourne: Centre for Applied Educational Research, University of Melbourne.

House of Representatives Standing Committee on Employment, Education and Training (1993) *The literacy challenge: Strategies for early intervention for literacy and learning for Australian children*, Canberra: Australian Government Publishing Service.

Jencks, C. *et al.* (1972) *Inequality: A reassessment of the effect of family and schooling in America*, New York: Basic Books.

Mortimore, P. *et al.* (1988) *School matters: The junior years*, Somerset: Open Books.

Quality of Education Review Committee (1985) *Quality of education in Australia* (Chair: Professor P. H. Karmel), Canberra: Australian Government Publishing Service.

Spearritt, D. (1987) 'Educational achievement', in J. P. Keeves (ed.) *Australian education: Review of recent research*, Sydney: Allen and Unwin: pp. 117–46.

Wittrock, M. C. (ed.) (1986) *Handbook of research on teaching* (3rd edn), New York: Macmillan.

Chapter 2

Connecting school effectiveness and school improvement
What have we learnt in the last ten years?

Louise Stoll and David Reynolds

INTRODUCTION: TWO DIFFERENT PARADIGMS

Over the years differing orientations have existed between the two bodies of knowledge, 'school effectiveness' and 'school improvement'. These two disciplines have come from very different places intellectually, methodologically and theoretically. Taking school improvement first, in the past thirty years approaches have been characterised by two different sets of assumptions. In the 1960s and 1970s, school improvement internationally displayed a technological view of change, in which curriculum innovations were mainly introduced 'top-down' to schools from outside. The focus was on the school's formal organisation and curriculum, outcomes were taken as given, and the innovation was targeted at the school rather than individual teachers. Improvement was evaluated through a positivistic, quantitative evaluation of effects. The worldwide failure of this model to generate more than partial take-up by schools of the innovations was explained within the educational discourse of the 1970s as due to a lack of teacher 'ownership'.

Out of recognition of this failure came a new improvement paradigm of the early 1980s, still reflected in much of the current writing on school improvement. This new orientation took a 'bottom-up' approach to school improvement, in which improvement attempts were 'owned' by those within schools, although outside consultants or experts could offer knowledge for possible use. This approach tended to celebrate practical practitioner knowledge rather than that gathered from research, and focused upon changes to educational processes rather than to school management, or to organisational features which were regarded as reified constructs. The outcomes or goals of school improvement programmes were opened up for debate and discussion, rather than merely accepted as given. Those working within school improvement also chose qualitative and naturalistically oriented evaluations of the enterprise rather than quantitative measurements, and improvement attempts were 'whole-school' oriented and school based, rather than outside-school or course based.

This new school improvement paradigm, outlined above, was limited in terms of generating school improvement, as some of its proponents began to realise. The process oriented 'journey' of school improvement was still stressed, but by the late 1980s the journey was also undertaken to enable schools to evaluate their processes and outcomes. This attitude was exemplified in the work of the OECD-sponsored International School Improvement Project (ISIP) (van Velzen *et al.*, 1985).

The school effectiveness research paradigm, with a very different intellectual history, has exhibited a very different set of core beliefs. It has been strongly committed to the use of quantitative methods, since many researchers were concerned to refute the 'schools make no difference' hypothesis advanced by Coleman *et al.*, (1966) and Jencks *et al.*, (1971) by utilising the same conventional methods of empirical research as these perceived opponents had used.

School effectiveness researchers have also been primarily concerned with student outcomes. Processes within schools are only important to them to the extent that they affect outcomes – indeed, one 'back maps' from outcomes to processes – and school effectiveness researchers have often talked of a 'good' or 'excellent' school as if that were unproblematic. The school effectiveness paradigm is also organisationally based, rather than process based, in terms of its analytic and descriptive orientation, preferring to restrict itself to the more easily quantifiable or measurable. The focus within the school improvement paradigm on the attitudinal, and on the culture of schools, is replaced within school effectiveness research by a focus on the more easily measured behaviour of persons.

School effectiveness research has also customarily celebrated the importance of a very limited range of outcomes, mostly academic and mostly concerned with the acquisition of basic skills. School improvement research, by contrast, has often conceptualised outcomes more broadly. Often, in the British tradition, the aim of the improvement attempt or project was to debate the 'possible' goals of education, as against the limited 'official' goals, as part of the process of securing professional development and school improvement.

Lastly, school effectiveness has differed from school improvement in that it has been concerned to celebrate the 'end state' of describing what effective schools are actually 'like', whereas school improvement has been more concerned to discover what it is that has been done to bring schools to that state. The orientation of school effectiveness has been a 'static' one, concerned with the 'steady state' of effectiveness; the orientation of school improvement has been a 'dynamic' one, focusing upon 'change over time'.

THE CALL FOR LINKS

An increasing number of scholars has begun to call for the synthesis of both bodies of knowledge in the interests of improving pupil performance and school quality. Mortimore (1991: 223) has argued for transferring 'the energy, knowledge and skills of school effectiveness research to the study of school improvement'. Stoll and Fink (1992: 104) maintain that 'it is only when school effectiveness research is merged with what is known about school improvement, planned change and staff development, that schools and teachers can be empowered and supported in their growth towards effectiveness'. Murphy (1992), a researcher who in his own empirical work previously existed within the effectiveness paradigm, now moves in directions that celebrate the potential not just of conventional school improvement programmes, but of a more radical 'restructuring' of the educational system, its power relations, and the teaching/learning process in schools. The mission statement of the journal *School Effectiveness and School Improvement* (Creemers and Reynolds, 1990) has also argued for the still, small voice of empirical rationality being used jointly to assess the validity both of existing models of school improvement and of existing, simplistic, factor based theories of school effectiveness. The work of Bruce Joyce and his colleagues (see Joyce *et al.*, 1983, 1988, 1992) has also for some time transcended both paradigms. Although located within the school improvement tradition, Joyce argues strongly for the raising of student achievement through the use of specific models of teaching and staff development designs.

THE NEED FOR MERGER

The potential benefits of a merged or integrated approach to improving school quality become even clearer if one considers how central the two disciplines or 'paradigms' are to each other. To take the practice of school improvement first, it is clear that knowledge is needed concerning the factors within schools and classrooms that should be changed to enhance processes and outcomes. Effectiveness research can provide that knowledge. Likewise, school improvement and its consequent changes to school and classroom factors can provide a testing ground for school effectiveness theories that relate processes and outcomes, and can therefore show if there are causal links involved.

Within the last ten years, a variety of projects have been set up in different countries that have attempted to bring the two paradigms closer together. Some draw more heavily on school effectiveness research, others more on the rationale underpinning school improvement. None the less, all have been influenced by the key ideas of both fields, and they represent no less than a new wave of thinking about how we improve school quality.

An analysis of these projects leads us to a set of principles that we believe are fundamental to any successful merger. In the rest of the chapter, we will describe these principles, illustrating them with examples from various projects.

A focus on teaching, on learning and the classroom level

It is of vital importance that any blended effectiveness and improvement initiative, to have a meaningful impact, must focus very closely on the learning level or on matters concerned with the instruction of students. Teachers' focal concerns are much more related to what occurs in their classrooms – teaching, pedagogy and curriculum – than they are related to school-level activities, like management and organisation. Indeed, in some schools a majority of staff define the role of the teachers as being completely related to curriculum and instruction, rather than being more broadly related to school-level management and organisational factors.

Any neglect of the classroom level and celebration of the school level may cost valuable teacher commitment. Furthermore, we know that the greatest variation is within, rather than between, schools: that there are significant teacher and departmental variations within individual schools. Indeed, the classroom learning level has maybe two or three times the influence on student achievement than does the school level (Creemers, 1994).

This focus on teaching and learning permeates several of the projects.

The Barclay–Calvert Project

In this project, the curricular and instructional package of Calvert School, a private elementary school in Baltimore (USA), is being implemented in an inner city public elementary school (Barclay) in the same city (Stringfield *et al.*, 1995). The population served at Barclay school is 94 per cent minority. Nearly 80 per cent of the school's students receive free or reduced-price lunch. In the late 1980s Barclay could be seen as having the typical problems of an inner-city American school, including poor achievement scores, attendance rates and levels of student discipline.

The Calvert school serves a predominantly highly affluent clientele. The curriculum itself is not revolutionary but reflects decades of high and academically traditional demands, blended with an emphasis on the importance of classwork and homework and an intensive writing programme. All work undertaken by students reflects the characteristics of effective teaching linked together with a high achievement level of the intakes. Results on norm-referenced achievement tests are very good. Virtually every grade of the select population of Calvert students score above the 90th percentile when compared to public, elite suburban and private school norms.

Barclay's principal became interested in Calvert's programme and the two schools developed a proposal to implement the entire Calvert programme at Barclay school. Implementation began in autumn 1990 in kindergarten and first grade. Each year one additional grade has been added. For two weeks each summer the Barclay–Calvert facilitator trains the next grade's Barclay teachers in the Calvert philosophy, curriculum and methods. The facilitator spends the school year working with each succeeding group of teachers in an effort to maximise the chance of full programme implementation.

The curriculum involves five processes:

1 Students read a lot (increasing opportunity to learn)
2 All students produce a lot of work
3 Teachers check students' work and also correct all their own work
4 Student folders are read and monitored by Barclay's project coordinator, the principal, or the Calvert principal every month
5 Student folders are sent home every month, increasing parental involvement in what students do and in checking homework.

Almost all teachers have made significant changes in their teaching. In classroom observation students' 'on-task' rates in the Calvert–Barclay classes were shown to be high, and teachers reported that, given high quality instruction and instructional support, the Barclay students responded well to the raised demands.

The Dutch National School Improvement Project

The National School Improvement Project (NSIP) in the Netherlands ran from 1991 to 1994. A major goal of the project was to prevent and reduce educational disadvantage, especially in reading (Houtveen and Osinga, 1995). The background of the study was that there are clear differences between schools in effectiveness, especially with respect to student performance in the basic skills of language and reading. The project made use of the knowledge base of school effectiveness research, especially the insights given by school effectiveness research into the factors that correlate with student performance. Special attention was also given to classroom instruction and management factors.

At the classroom level the following objectives were set:

1 Improving teachers' skills in direct instruction
2 Improving teachers' skills in group management, leading to more efficient use of pupil time
3 Promoting teachers' expertise around rigorous and methodical working
4 Using effective principles of instruction, including using the 'phonics' method for reading.

Lewisham School Improvement Project

The Lewisham School Improvement Project commenced in the spring of 1993 and arose out of a partnership between Lewisham schools, Lewisham Local Education Authority (LEA) and the Institute of Education, University of London. It aims to enhance pupil progress, achievement and development; to develop the internal capacity of schools for managing change and evaluating its impact at whole-school, classroom and student levels; to develop the LEA's capacity to provide useful data to schools; and to integrate the above with the system's ongoing in-service and support services to form a coherent approach to professional development (Stoll and Thomson, 1996).

The project's dimensions include a series of voluntary workshops with school senior managers; more intensive work with a group of schools (primary, secondary and special schools are represented), who have identified a teaching and learning focus for improvement; identification and development of system indicators of achievement and development for special needs pupils; development of school governors; project evaluation; and dissemination.

A primary school involved in the project has concentrated on students' writing, the curriculum focus from the school's development plan. The strategies have included: analysis of the school's own statistics on achievement; using relevant research findings to inform practice; paired classroom observations; staff development sessions; yearly targets for individual teachers related to the aims of the project; and the development of a commonly known and agreed monitoring scheme used by the headteacher and language teacher when they visit classrooms and give teachers feedback.

Some projects follow more traditional approaches to teaching. As understanding of how children learn increases, however, with contributions from cognitive and social psychology, different teaching methods may be explored that are compatible with a range of student learning styles and intelligences, see, for example, (Gardner, 1983).

Use of data for decision-making

It is increasingly clear that an audit of existing classroom and school processes and outcomes, and comparison with desired end states, is a vital part of improvement for effectiveness. Collecting data on students' current achievement, progress and social development can give a school indications of areas that need improvement. Furthermore, schools can have differential effects upon their pupils (Nuttall et al., 1989), and the fact that schools effective for some groups of pupils may actually be less effective for others has wide ranging implications for school improvement. Improvement attempts need to move away from the much vaunted 'whole-school, one-size-fits-all' strategies towards more finely targeted programmes that vary within the school in terms of content, focus and target groups. Schools need to disaggregate assessment data, whether academic results, attendance patterns, attitudes or other measures of students' progress and development, including their educational experiences, to look for variations between different subsets of pupils. By taking these differences into account, and focusing improvement at the levels of boys to girls, high ability to low ability pupils, and pupils from ethnic minorities to pupils from 'host' cultures, more appropriate school change strategies can be generated.

Similarly, the same pupils may experience inconsistency of teaching quality from subject to subject, as has been demonstrated in a study of differential effectiveness between secondary school departments (Sammons *et al.*, 1996). Without examining student data and experience from a subject perspective, it would be difficult to determine whether teaching strategies and organisational arrangements suitable for one subject are appropriate to another subject discipline.

The following examples show data being used to improve decision-making.

Halton's Effective Schools Project

The Effective Schools Project in the Halton Board of Education in Ontario and its 83 schools started, in 1986, as an attempt to bring the results of school effectiveness research into schooling practices, but it became clear that difficulties involved in the project's implementation could only be resolved by the adoption at school and system level of organisational and planning arrangements from school improvement literature (Stoll and Fink, 1992). Initially, a task force produced a model of the characteristics of effectiveness and a school growth planning process was developed, similar to the school development plan which is now a feature in many countries.

Within the assessment phase of growth planning, student, teacher and parental attitude questionnaires based on Halton's characteristics model were used to focus on where respondents thought the school was, in relation to a set of indicators, and how important each indicator was to create a more effective school. Through analysing the gap between where the school was and where it should be, schools could identify areas of need; schools also examined current curricula and instructional practices, school board and Ontario Ministry of Education initiatives, and a variety of information related to students' progress and development. They were also encouraged to disaggregate student data, to look for differences in achievement, progress or development between subsets of students.

The High Reliability School Project

This recent project was born from Stringfield's (1995) suggestion that educational systems had much to learn from the organisational processes of those firms and utilities that are not permitted to fail. These are known in the jargon of the trade as HROs or High Reliability Organisations. They are usually taken to be air traffic controllers, nuclear power plant operatives, electricity supply operatives and all those other organisations and their employees who have to generate one hundred per cent reliable functioning.

With eight secondary schools, a programme has been developed to model schools on these highly reliable organisations from other fields outside education.

All schools in the project have joined a performance indicator system that generates very high quality data upon student achievement, the ALIS (A-level Information System) and YELLIS (Year Eleven Information System) schemes pioneered by Fitz-Gibbon and colleagues at the University of Newcastle upon Tyne (Fitz-Gibbon, 1992). This data feeds back to schools their relative performance on their different public examination subjects, and relates directly to the effectiveness of their departments.

The schools are also testing their new pupils as they arrive from junior school. The testing will be repeated at the beginning of each school year, for both these pupils and for the new intake of pupils. Ultimately all pupils will be tested annually. These data will reveal pupils who have unrealised potential, and will also provide a 'gain score' for each year that will act as a baseline.

Thus, schools develop 'data-rich' environments that will give fine-grained analyses of where individual pupils and individual departments are. The departments can then be organised around quality issues, as schools begin to develop mechanisms to eradicate ineffectiveness. As the project progresses, more data, on more years of pupils, will become available.

The Dutch National School Improvement Project

A key aim of this project is to generate a 'results-oriented' school management in which concrete targets concerning basic skills at school and group levels are determined in advance. To achieve this aim, an analysis of the teaching activities and the organisational characteristics of the school is made with the help of a school diagnosis instrument, and regular and reliable evaluation of individual pupils' achievements is carried out using a pupil 'tracking' system. All pupils are regularly tested. In this way a database on groups of students, and individual students in the classroom, is available on which decisions with respective to the entire group, or to individual students, can be made.

A focus upon student outcomes

Historically, the impact of changes in improvement programmes has not been measured in relation to pupil outcomes. This may be due to reluctance of many within the school improvement paradigm to be explicit about what the nature of school outcomes, or the educational goals of their programmes, really are. However, the absence of data on the effects of improvement programmes restricts further understanding of the possible causal relationships between school processes and school outcomes. More recently, however, some projects have used 'hard', quantitative measures of outcomes as an essential component, both to build commitment and confidence among those taking part and to measure the success or failure of the project initiatives. Some have also developed new or more 'authentic' assessments of outcomes when these were appropriate.

Increasingly, however, outcomes appropriate for measurement in the 1980s, such as academic achievement or examination attainment, may not be the only outcomes appropriate to the 1990s, where new goals, concerning knowledge of 'how to learn' or ability in mastering information technology, may be necessary. This challenge has yet to be properly addressed.

The following projects show a clear focus upon student outcomes.

The Barclay–Calvert Project

In the evaluation of this project, student testing was included. The data from norm-referenced achievement testing programmes indicates that students in the programme are achieving academically at a rate significantly above their pre-programme Barclay school peers. This finding is consistent across reading, writing and mathematics, and is particularly striking in writing. The Barclay students are also making progress, not only in specific areas of academic content, but also in the ability to integrate new material and absorb new knowledge. Additional data indicates that the Barclay–Calvert Project has reduced student absences, reduced student transfers from the school, greatly reduced the number of students requiring special education services, reduced referrals to and diagnosis of 'learning disability', eliminated disciplinary removals and increased the number of students found eligible for the Gifted and Talented Education (GATE) programme.

The Lewisham School Improvement Project

Monitoring and evaluating the outcomes of this project at school and system level are important features. Baseline data has been gathered by the LEA for the project schools, against which progress is being measured. Interviews have been carried out in the schools to elicit insights into the change process. The project also acknowledges the importance of setting success criteria at school level, gathering and evaluating evidence, and using the knowledge and information gained. Schools are given training and support in data collection, developing and measuring success criteria and the ongoing evaluation of their project, its process and progress.

The Dutch School Improvement Project

In an evaluation study, 29 schools were included, 16 belonging to the 'experimental' group and 13 to a 'control' group. There has been a considerable growth in the experimental group over a period of two-and-a-half years with respect to task-oriented learning and instruction time, direct instruction, methodical working and the teaching of reading according to effective methods. In the student achievement study, 319 students were involved in the experimental group and 137 in the control group. These groups were tested in March 1993 (some months before the school year 1993/4), and in June 1994. There was a correction for intake for individual pupil characteristics such as intelligence, socio-economic background and attitudes towards reading. After correcting for the pre-test and student characteristics, there is a significant effect in favour of the experimental group against the control group upon student achievement in reading.

The High Reliability School Project

Schools are generating between two and four final targets for the goals to be attained by the end of school year 1999/2000, with intermediate goals and targets for school year 1997/8. These are ambitious goals, but they take account of what schools' differing 'start points' may be. Schools then forward (from their intake) and backward (from exam results) map the path necessary for a student to obtain 5+ A–C grades. Progress along these maps will be closely monitored, and the maps themselves revised annually as schools gather actual testing and process data.

In the middle year of the project there will be a focus upon improving departmental effectiveness. Once during the first year and twice a year thereafter, each department will examine the academic products of all students for a brief (two-week) period. The purpose will be to determine the extent to which all students are progressing. To the extent to which significant numbers of students are not making adequate progress, the department and administration will make suggestions for changes in those students' academic programmes, while maintaining a relationship with the National Curriculum objectives in each subject.

Addressing schools' internal conditions

School improvement needs to attend to the fine-grained reality of school and classroom processes. These school processes can be defined in terms of attitudes, values, relationships and climate, and are central to the process of improvement and development. Certain conditions have been identified as being more likely to facilitate improvement (Hopkins *et al.*, 1994; Stoll and Fink, 1996). These vary slightly according to the particular project, but broadly encompass climate setting, vision building, involvement and empowerment, joint planning and coordination, staff development, problem seeking and solving, and monitoring and evaluation.

School improvement has often adopted a 'rational technical' or 'rational empirical' approach which may be inappropriate to a real school community. There are more and more hints within the literature that some schools may be 'non-rational', in that they harbour delusions and associated cultures that may be an understandable reaction to their problems (Reynolds, 1996). As West and Hopkins (1995) point out, the majority of schools may not have the structures, the experience or the strategies to move the school, because of the existence of the 'ghosts' of past practice, or the 'shadows' of present tensions.

The following examples are of projects that are paying special attention to the internal conditions of improvement.

Improving the Quality of Education for All (IQEA)

The overall aim of IQEA is 'to produce and evaluate a model of school development, and a programme of support, that strengthens a school's ability to provide quality education for all its pupils by building upon existing good practice' (Hopkins and Ainscow, 1993). In the project, approaches and methods from the improvement and effectiveness paradigms are blended; in particular, these include use of and work on improvement and change processes with input on school and classroom effectiveness and measurement of outcomes.

The project, which began in 1991, currently involves schools in several areas of Britain. All staff of a school have to agree that the school will participate, and at least 40 per cent receive release time to engage in specific project-related activities in their own and each other's classrooms, although all staff participate in certain IQEA-focused staff development events. Two staff members are designated as coordinators and attend ten days of training and support meetings offered by the Cambridge Institute. The school selects its own priorities for development and its own methods to achieve these priorities. It also participates in the evaluation of the project and has to commit itself to share findings with other participants in the project.

The original conceptualisation of the project was based on the experience that effective change strategies focus not only on the implementation of centralised policies or chosen initiatives, but also on creating the conditions within schools that can sustain the teaching–learning process. From the IQEA project, a series of conditions that underpinned the work of successful schools were identified (Hopkins et al., 1994). Broadly stated, these conditions are: staff development; involvement; leadership; coordination; enquiry and reflection; and collaborative planning.

Lewisham School Improvement Project

It was agreed that each pilot school's project focus would be manageable and linked to the school's development plan, a recognition that school development and classroom development go hand-in-hand. A cross-role team of teachers coordinates project work in each school, to emphasise the importance of shared leadership and teacher ownership. While these teams are agents of change, they are not responsible for change in their school. They need, however, to facilitate that change, and therefore must understand the change process and its impact on people.

The Barclay–Calvert Project

A major impact of the implementation of the Calvert programme in Barclay school was that teacher attitudes changed at Barclay. They were convinced that the Calvert programme was helping them to teach more, teach better, and to help more children perform at higher levels. These are not, of course, unrealistic expectations; the teachers had good grounds for their optimistic beliefs, since they received meaningful, ongoing support.

Support was viewed as important in anticipating and solving problems. Barclay's principal visited classes, attended meetings and was active in involving parents. The Calvert coordinator at Barclay was supportive, bringing high levels of knowledge, competence and enthusiasm. Calvert's headteacher also assisted; he visited Barclay classrooms and repeatedly made himself available for consultations. Finally, the Barclay parents were actively involved at every stage.

Halton's Effective Schools Project

In schools with more successful growth planning, attention was paid early on to development of clear decision-making structures and organisational processes. In these schools a climate was built within which a more dynamic and ongoing planning process could occur. Time was spent building a collaborative culture in which teachers continued to learn and feel valued, and risk-taking was encouraged. Finally, teachers were encouraged to articulate their values and beliefs such that a shared vision for their school's future could be developed.

Enhanced consistency

It is clear that 'merged' school effectiveness and school improvement programmes have not always been necessarily organisationally tight. Because most programmes have been voluntary, there may have been a differential within schools in the extent to which programmes have been taken up.

Reading between the lines, it seems likely that many programmes have often impacted most on the competent 'leading edge' of teachers, while it is also clear that a more or less significant 'trailing edge' may not have participated in the programmes, or at least may not have participated very fully. It is highly likely that, within the schools participating in some programmes, therefore, there is a substantial variation in the extent to which they have permeated the schools and in the extent to which organisational innovations have moved through to implementation from the initiation phase, and ultimately moved to the institutionalisation phase. Given increasing evidence within school effectiveness of the importance of organisational cohesion, consistency and constancy, a situation in which there is greater variation between members of staff in a school because of differential take-up of improvement activities may have existed in certain circumstances and is likely to have adversely affected the quality of student outcomes.

It is important, therefore, that school improvement programmes address 'reliability' issues as well as validity ones by ensuring that innovations are reliably spread throughout project schools, to ensure cohesion of implementation.

The following examples of projects show this concern with reliability.

The Barclay–Calvert Project

The Barclay–Calvert project was very methodical and aimed at uniform, high-quality instruction. Barclay did not attempt to implement the whole Calvert curriculum and instructional programme all at once, but gradually, grade level by grade level. In this way it was possible to prepare teachers for the next grade level utilising a cascade model.

The High Reliability School Project

This project explicitly aims at ensuring that all teachers and departments in schools deliver the optimal instructional strategies that maximise learning. This is to be obtained by the 'benchmarking' of less effective persons and departments against those which are more effective, and by the bringing to schools of the knowledge bases of school effectiveness and teacher effectiveness in ways designed to ensure maximal 'take-up'.

Pulling the levers to affect all levels

While the school needs to be the centre of all improvement, the importance and potential impact of other educational institutions, arrangements and layers above the level of the school should not be forgotten (Coleman and LaRocque, 1991; Fullan, 1993; Stoll and Fink, 1996). As Hopkins (1990: 188) notes when discussing school improvement conducted within the ISIP, 'much thought . . . was given to the way in which improvement policies are established at various levels . . . to the structured factors related to support, e.g. . . . external support'. School improvement needs to be informed by knowledge as to what conditions outside the level of the school are necessary to generate process and outcome improvement.

It is also clear that there has been a limited pulling of levers in the sense that, while the 'school' lever to generate change has been pulled frequently, the manipulation of levers in a multiple fashion in the classroom (through teacher professional training programmes), and at the school level (through improvement programmes), the local authority/district level and the national level, has been rarely attempted.

The following projects have all been concerned to 'pull all relevant levers' by operating with outside and several inside levels simultaneously.

The Dutch National School Improvement Project

The main focus of the project was on the improvement of education at classroom level to increase effective instruction. But effective classroom instruction depends on classroom management and on different factors and characteristics at school and above school levels. So, a concern of the project was ensuring that policies at the classroom, school and board or governor levels (including parents) were achievement-oriented. The support strategy consisted of a combination of multiple elements, like informing the school board, consultation with the principal, guidance for the whole staff, and coaching of individual teachers in the classroom.

'Schools Make a Difference'

In their improvement project with all of their eight secondary schools (Myers, 1996), Hammersmith and Fulham LEA appointed a project manager to work with schools and LEA personnel. Within her role she regularly visited the schools and took their senior management teams to visit schools of interest around the country. She also organised in-service training for the coordinators, headteachers, senior management teams and various other staff members.

Halton's Effective Schools Project

The school district played an important role in the project. Its strategic plan emphasised three key directions. One of these was the growth planning process itself. The second was a focus on instruction, to highlight the central role in the determination of school outcomes of what actually goes on in the classroom, the teaching and learning process. The third direction supported the other two, and was an emphasis on staff development. Thus the system provided a framework within which growth planning could occur, and offered support for the process. Voluntary workshops were offered for school teams on growth planning, instructional strategies and assessment, and for entire schools' staffs on their chosen instructional goals. Regional consultants also worked with individual teachers or whole staffs to support classroom and whole-school practice. Thus the school was not seen as an isolated unit of change but as the centre of change, connected to a wider system. This system continued to grow and, in 1993, through a collaborative process involving representatives from the entire system and the local community, the three original directions were re-endorsed and a new one added, focusing on the district–community relationship.

Improving the Quality of Education for All

School-level conditions were the focus of early work with the IQEA schools. Subsequently, the project began to focus some of its research energies on to a parallel set of conditions which related to the notion of capacity at the classroom level. These conditions were connected to teacher development, in much the same way as the original set of conditions were to school development. As such they were supposed to be transferable across classrooms and between teachers, and related to a variety of teaching/learning initiatives designed to enhance the achievement of students. The list of classroom conditions which emerged from external project consultants' deliberations with schools included:

- Authentic Relationships – quality, openness and congruence of classroom relationships
- Rules and Boundaries – expectations set by the teacher and school of student performance and classroom behaviour
- Teacher's Repertoire – the range of teaching styles and models used by a teacher and amended according to student, context, curriculum and desired outcome
- Reflection on Teaching – the teacher's capacity to reflect on her/his own practice and test out ideas from other sources
- Resources and Preparation – teachers' access to a range of relevant teaching materials and the ability to plan and differentiate these materials
- Pedagogic Partnerships – teachers' ability to form professional relationships within classrooms that focus on studying and improving their practice.

IQEA now focuses upon the school and the classroom levels.

THE CONTINUING CHALLENGE

It should not be thought that all challenges in merging effectiveness and improvement have been overcome. Differences between schools in terms of their context remain a challenge for those working in school effectiveness and improvement. First, the variation in 'what works' by contexts has been a focus only of a limited amount of North American work (Hallinger and Murphy, 1986; Teddlie and Stringfield, 1993). For school improvement to occur, more is required than the notion of what works across context in the average school, or data on the relationships between school processes and outcomes for all schools. What is needed is knowledge of specific factors that will generate improvement in particular schools in particular socio-economic and cultural contexts. Since only a small amount of our school effectiveness database is analysed by context, the delineation of the precise variables that school improvement needs to target to affect outcomes is currently impossible.

A second contextual variable is that concerning different subsets of pupils within any individual school. The disaggregation of samples of schools to permit the analysis of contextual variation needs to focus on the precise organisational and process variables that may be responsible for differential effectiveness of schools with different groups of pupils within them.

A third related challenge is that many schools also vary in what they need to improve by their effectiveness levels. For example, many people wishing to improve schools often find themselves working in ineffective educational settings, yet the school effectiveness knowledge base may not be easily applicable to those settings. It is probable that these ineffective schools may possess interpersonal problems, projections, defences and the like which do not exist in the effective school. The knowledge required by improvers of ineffective schools is simply not found in school effectiveness research, where the good practice of effective schools is simply 'back mapped' on to ineffective schools, and then assumed to be sufficient to make them improve.

We need, therefore, to develop more 'contextually specific' school improvement strategies in which we tailor the precise nature of the programmes offered according to the level of effectiveness, 'presenting culture' and context of individual schools.

It should also be borne in mind that it is highly unlikely that there will ever be a knowledge base produced outside schools that will be absolutely appropriate for each individual school. If what is necessary for effectiveness varies considerably by context, it is highly unlikely that effectiveness research can provide, from outside the school, knowledge appropriate according to the school's nation, socio-economic context, phase of internal development, urban/rural status, age phase, cultural conditions, and educational personalities involved. Schools themselves must therefore play an integral part in the generation of their own knowledge.

CONCLUSIONS

We have noted in this chapter that two groups of persons have been involved in attempting to improve the quality of education. School effectiveness researchers have examined schooling in order to find out why some schools are more effective than others in promoting positive outcomes and what characteristics are most commonly found in schools that are effective for their pupils (Reynolds, 1992; Sammons *et al.*, 1996). School improvement researchers have focused their studies on the processes that schools go through to become more successful and sustain this improvement (e.g. van Velzen, 1987).

In the latter years of the 1980s and the early years of the 1990s, however, there have emerged in a number of countries intervention projects which are *neither* effectiveness based *nor* school improvement oriented, as defined by the limits of the old disciplines conceptualised and outlined here. Much of this 'convergence' or 'synergy' between the two paradigms has in fact resulted from practitioners and local authority/district policy-makers borrowing from both traditions because they do not share the ideological commitment to one or the other ways of working of researchers in the field, while some has arisen through the effects of the International Congress for School Effectiveness and Improvement in breaking down disciplinary as well as geographical boundaries.

Sometimes the adoption of ideas from research has been somewhat uncritical – for example, the numerous attempts to apply findings from one specific context to another entirely different context when research has increasingly demonstrated significant contextual differences (Hallinger and Murphy, 1986; Stringfield and Teddlie, 1990). Sometimes it is clear that projects are partial in their adoption of material from both paradigms – some projects reflect an understanding of what makes schools effective but the absence of an 'action plan' about how to get to the destination, while others have celebrated the 'core' school improvement ideas of ownership, collegiality and laterality without much acknowledgement of the key areas of school process and organisation on which to focus their attention.

Nevertheless, there are a number of projects that we have seen in action that represent no less than a 'new wave' of thinking about how we improve school quality, a new wave that is characterised by:

- a focus upon student outcomes as 'success criteria'
- use of high-quality data to generate high-quality decisions
- a focus upon the classroom and instructional level as well as upon the school level
- the pulling of all 'levers of change' that might affect students
- a willingness to focus on key conditions of school improvement and also use the effectiveness knowledge base in the interests of improving school quality

- a concern not just with the validity of the programmes but with their reliability also, in terms of ensuring that there is universal take-up of the improvement innovations to maintain school/classroom cohesion, consistency and constancy.

It should be obvious that there is still much more work to be done to deliver the promise of the new synergistic alliance of effectiveness and improvement persons, in such areas as 'context specific school improvement' that we noted earlier. It should also be obvious that the efforts to enhance the quality of schools now have considerably greater chances of ultimate success because of the evident willingness of persons in the field to suspend historical disciplinary rivalries and to concentrate upon the needs of children and of their teachers. We would hope that further 'waves' of new thinking will follow on from what we have described here.

REFERENCES
Coleman, J. *et al.* (1966) *Equality of Educational Opportunity*, Washington, DC: US Govt. Printing Office.

Coleman, P. and LaRocque, L. (1991) *Struggling to be Good Enough*, Lewes: Falmer Press.

Creemers, B. P. M. (1994) *The Effective Classroom*, London: Cassell.

Creemers, B. and Reynolds, D. (1990) 'School Effectiveness and School Improvement – A Mission Statement', in *School Effectiveness and School Improvement*, 1(1), 1–3.

Edmonds, R. R. (1979) 'Effective schools for the urban poor', in *Educational Leadership*, 37(15–18), 20–4.

Fitz-Gibbon, C. T. (1992) 'School effects at A-level – genesis of an information system', in D. Reynolds and P. Cuttance (eds) *School Effectiveness: Research, Policy and Practice*, London: Cassell.

Fullan, M. (1993) *Change Forces: Probing the Depths of Educational Reform*, New York: Falmer Press.

Gardner, H. (1983) *Frames of Mind: the Theory of Multiple Intelligences*, New York: Basic Books.

Hallinger, P. and Murphy, J. (1986) 'The social context of effective schools', in *American Journal of Education*, 94, 328–55.

Hopkins, D. (1990) 'The International School Improvement Project (ISIP) and Effective Schooling: Towards a Synthesis', *School Organization*, 10(3), 129–44.

Hopkins, D. and Ainscow, M. (1993) 'Making Sense of School Improvement: an Interim Account of the IQEA Project'. Paper presented to the ESRC Seminar Series on School Effectiveness and School Improvement, Sheffield, England.

Hopkins, D., Ainscow, M. and West, M. (1994) *School Improvement in an Era of Change*, London: Cassell.

Houtveen, A. A. M. and Osinga, N. (1995) 'A Case of School Effectiveness: Organisation, Programme, Procedure and Evaluation Results of the Dutch National School Improvement Project'. Paper presented to the Eighth International Congress for School Effectiveness and Improvement, Leeuwarden, Netherlands, January.

Jencks, C. *et al.* (1971) *Inequality*, London: Allen Lane.

Joyce, B. and Showers, B. (1988) *Student Achievement Through Staff Development*, New York: Longman.

Joyce, B. *et al.* (1983) *The Structure of School Improvement*, New York: Longman.
—— (1992) *Models of Teaching* (4th edn), New Jersey: Prentice-Hall.
Mortimore, P. (1991) 'School effectiveness research: which way at the crossroads?', in *School Effectiveness and School Improvement*, 2(3), 213–29.
Murphy, J. (1992) 'School effectiveness and school restructuring: Contributions to educational improvement,' in *School Effectiveness and School Improvement*, 3(2), 90–109.
Myers, K. (1996) *School Improvement in Practice: the Schools Make a Difference Project*, London: Falmer Press.
Nuttall, D. *et al.* (1989) 'Differential school effectiveness', in *International Journal of Educational Research*, 13(7), 769–76.
Reynolds, D. (1992) 'School effectiveness and school improvement in the 1990s', in D. Reynolds and P. Cuttance (eds) *School Effectiveness: Research, Policy and Practice*, London: Cassell.
—— (1996) 'Turning around ineffective schools: some evidence and some speculations', in J. Gray *et al.* (eds) *Merging Traditions: The Future of Research on School Effectiveness and School Improvement*, London: Cassell.
Reynolds, D., Sullivan, M. and Murgatroyd, S. J. (1987) *The Comprehensive Experiment*, Lewes: Falmer Press.
Sammons, P., Thomas, S. and Mortimore, P. (1996) 'Promoting school and departmental effectiveness', *Management in Education*, 10(1), 22–4.
Stoll, L. and Fink, D. (1992) 'Effecting school change: the Halton Approach', in *School Effectiveness and School Improvement*, 3(1), 19–41.
—— (1996) *Changing Our Schools: Linking School Effectiveness and School Improvement*, Buckingham: Open University Press.
Stoll, L. and Thomson, M. (1996) 'Moving together: a partnership approach to improvement', in P. Earley, B. Fidler and J. Ouston (eds) *Improvement Through Inspection? Complementary Approaches to School Development*, London: David Fulton.
Stringfield, S. (1995) 'Attempting to enhance students' learning through innovative programs: the case for schools evolving into high reliability organisations', *School Effectiveness and School Improvement*, 6(1), 67–96.
Stringfield, S., Bedinger, S. and Herman, R. (1995) 'Implementing a Private School Program in an Inner City Public School: Processes, Effects and Implications from a Four Year Evaluation'. Paper presented to the Eighth International Congress for School Effectiveness and Improvement, Leeuwarden, Netherlands, January.
Stringfield, S. and Teddlie, C. (1990) 'School improvement effects: qualitative and quantitative data from four naturally occurring experiments in Phases 3 and 4 of the Louisiana School Effectiveness Study', *School Effectiveness and School Improvement*, 1(2), 139–61.
Teddlie, C. and Stringfield, S. (1993) *Schools Make a Difference: Lessons Learned from a 10-year study of School Effects*. New York: Teachers College Press.
van Velzen, W. (1987) 'The International School Improvement Project', in D. Hopkins (ed.), *Improving the Quality of Schooling*, Lewes: Falmer Press.
van Velzen, W. *et al.* (1985) *Making School Improvement Work*, Leuven, Belgium: ACCO.
West, M. and Hopkins, D. (1995) 'Reconceptualizing School Effectiveness and School Improvement'. Paper presented to the European Conference on Educational Research, University of Bath, England.

Chapter 3

Restructuring through school-based management
Insights for improving tomorrow's schools

Joseph Murphy

RESTRUCTURING UNPACKED[1]

During the mid-to-late 1980s, the educational reform movement that had commenced around 1980 began to change form and texture. Up to that time, reform initiatives were informed by the belief that schooling could be improved if standards were raised, more effective prescriptions and regulations written, and educators, from the boardroom to the classroom, asked to do more. As the prevailing assumptions underlying the excellence movement came under attack, a new belief system began to take root – one that would grow to support what has become known as the restructuring movement. Central to this perspective on school improvement are the following assumptions about reform: educational problems are attributable more to the failure of the system of schooling than to the shortcomings of individual educators; empowerment (of students, teachers, and parents) is a more effective tool than prescription; and bottom-up, school-based solution strategies will lead to more satisfying results than will top-down, mandated ones.

Although there appears to be no shortage of schools that have embraced restructuring in countries throughout the world, there is still a good deal of confusion about exactly what this construct means. A number of analysts have commented on the vagueness that surrounds the concept (Tyack, 1990; Newmann, 1991; Peterson and McCarthey, 1991) and how, in the absence of a clear definition and in the presence of competing value systems (J. Chapman, personal communication, May 1992), the same ideas (e.g. choice) often mean different things to different people.

While such conceptual fuzziness makes understanding restructuring problematic on one level, the reasons for this lack of definition are certainly understandable. Definition of terms at high levels of abstraction is a long-acknowledged method of building initial support and momentum for an idea. As Mitchell and Beach (1991: 1) put it, restructuring 'appears to require enough vagueness and uncertainty that it can attract a broad coalition of supporters whose underlying disagreements would keep them from supporting a more clearly defined program of action'. The actual meaning of such an ill-defined concept unfolds within the context of everyday activity. Given the grass-roots nature of restructuring, its uncertain definition may be less of a problem than is widely believed. As Goldman *et al.* (1991: 2) remind us, 'The definition of restructuring is [and should be] being created daily as educators translate it into myriad programs and behaviors'. Given the local character of restructuring, it is not difficult to mount a defence for Mitchell and Beach's (1991: 2) assumption that 'the term restructuring means just what it means to those who are wrestling with assessing it and implementing it in the schools'.

The very comprehensiveness of restructuring also makes definitional efforts somewhat problematic. Systemic change is at the heart of the restructuring movement (Smith and O'Day, 1990). This approach to improvement requires an overhaul of most, if not all, of the major aspects of the educational enterprise somewhat simultaneously (Honig, 1990). Under these conditions, two things often occur. On the one hand, with so much to consider, people tend to focus on only one piece of the larger picture (e.g. teacher professionalism) and are hard pressed to recognise components not within their vision (e.g. teaching for understanding). Or, on the other hand, restructuring takes on so much baggage that it begins to lose meaning (Barth, 1991). It becomes 'a catch-all, or garbage-can, into which many loosely-defined ideas about school reform can be tossed' (Elmore, 1991: 2). In both cases, people often lose touch with the core principles of restructuring and become preoccupied with disparate pieces of the puzzle.

Based upon effective practices from corporate and educational enterprises (see Murphy, 1991), considerable energy has begun to be invested in re-creating educational systems. In most Western countries, politicians and bureaucrats have raised 'restructuring to the top of the policy agenda' (Mitchell and Beach, 1991: 34). In the American academic community, national as well as more project-focused activities have sprung up to study and promulgate restructuring practices. University-based investigators are busy trying to understand the phenomenon and its effects on school communities. In schools and school systems, teachers, students, parents, administrators and community members are labouring to reframe their conceptions of learning and schooling and their own roles in these processes. And at the nexus of these groups is a number of highly visible restructuring efforts such as Accelerated Schools, Essential Schools, Re:Learning, and Success for All in the USA, the British Locally Managed and Grant Maintained Schools, the New Zealand 'Schools of Tomorrow' and the Victorian (Australia) 'Schools of the Future'.

As has been discussed elsewhere (Murphy *et al.*, 1991), there is a variety of ways of knowing about restructuring. One can look to the research that informs the central elements of this reform strategy. For example, the research on cognitive and constructivist approaches to learning is particularly helpful in grasping the evolving conception of the core technology in restructured schools (Bransford *et al.*, n.d.; Shuell, 1986; Marshall, 1992). Reports, legislation, regulations and frameworks from the policy world in various countries provide a second way of knowing about restructuring (DES, 1988; Lange, 1988; Council of Chief State School Officers, 1989; David *et al.*, 1990; DSE, 1994). A third method is to study what is actually happening in communities, districts, schools and classrooms that are engaged in rethinking the routines of schooling.[2] To date, much of our understanding of restructuring has come from the first two sources, little from the third. Or, as Mitchell and Beach (1991: 2) conclude, 'Restructuring is primarily discussed as a reform and improvement approach that needs to be implemented, rather than one that has been in place long enough to evaluate on the basis of evidence collected in schools and classrooms'. In short, 'there is a notable paucity of empirical studies and research' on school restructuring (Peterson and McCarthey, 1991; Prestine, 1991: 7; Tindal, 1991; White, 1992).

The move towards restructuring education

Tyack (1990: 174) tells us that 'reform periods in education are typically times when concerns about the state of the society or economy spill over into demands that schools set things straight'. The current restructuring movement is no exception. It embodies 'the boosterish belief that formal education can patch any gash in the social [and economic] fabric' (Cohen, 1988: 2). In the early-to-mid-1980s, news of deteriorating economic conditions in the United States (and other countries) was increasingly trumpeted in press stories and educational reports:

> Our nation is at risk. Our once unchallenged pre-eminence in commerce, industry, science, and technological innovation is being overtaken by competitors throughout the world.
>
> (National Commission on Excellence in Education, 1983: 5)

> America's ability to compete in world markets is eroding. The productivity growth of our competitors outdistances our own. The capacity of our economy to provide a high standard of living is increasingly in doubt.
>
> (Carnegie Forum on Education and the Economy, 1986: 2)

During this period, 'schooling was seen as part of the problem and part of the solution' (Guthrie and Kirst, 1988: 4). The maxim of 'economic salvation through educational excellence' (Mitchell, 1990: 28) was widely accepted, even though the accuracy of the equation (Kerr, 1991) and its moral underpinnings (Giroux, 1988) were called into question.

It is perhaps not surprising that the initial response to this perceived crisis was not a general restructuring of schooling but a patching and repairing of the existing educational enterprise in what is generally regarded as the standards-raising movement (Sedlak *et al.*, 1986) or Wave 1 reforms (Murphy, 1990a). It was only after these efforts were proposed and institutionalised, and their limits began to be scrutinised (Cuban, 1984; Elmore, 1987; Combs, 1988), that new ideas were called for by practitioners, academics and politicians. Special concern was expressed for developing strategies that were isomorphic with the emerging values of a post-industrial society (Banathy, 1988; Beare, 1989; Clark and Meloy, 1989). New reform strategies and assumptions were judged to fit the bill and a new school improvement movement – restructuring – took root (Murphy, 1992a), drawing considerable energy from the backlash against the more traditional responses of the early 1980s to the economic crisis confronting the nation (Murphy, 1991).[3]

Demands for restructuring are also supported by the desire to repair an ever-widening tear in the social fabric – a gash that threatens 'our national standard of living and democratic foundations' (Carnegie Council for Adolescent Development, 1989: 27) and promises to overwhelm schooling. The number of social ills confronting society appears to be expanding geometrically. Ever-increasing numbers of families are falling into poverty. As the gap between the rich and poor grows, many are sinking even deeper into poverty. Children are disproportionately represented among the ranks of the poor, and the number of children in poverty – currently one in five in the USA – continues to grow. Minority student enrolments in schools are increasing. There is rapid growth in the number of students whose primary language is other than English. More and more children come from single-parent homes or from families where both parents work. At the same time, we are bombarded with news of alarming increases in measures of dysfunctions and ill health among youth and their families: unemployment, unwanted pregnancies, alcohol and drug abuse, and violence (see Kirst *et al.*, 1989; Quality Education for Minorities Project, 1990; Wagstaff and Gallagher, 1990; Hodgkinson, 1991).

Restructuring is not a new phenomenon. On the one hand, its heritage is the larger historical reform movement that characterises education (Tyack, 1990; Warren, 1990). Restructuring is part of the larger fabric of reform, one woven from cyclical waves of improvement efforts that have washed over education approximately every decade for the past 100 years (Passow, 1984; Powell *et al.*, 1985). On the other hand, and of equal importance, many elements of restructuring – such as site-based management and decision-making, teacher professionalism, and enhanced parental voice – enjoy a heritage of their own. For example, in an especially insightful analysis of teaching practice, Cohen (1988) reveals how recent reform ideas such as educating for insight (Perkins, 1991) and teaching for meaningful understanding (Evertson and Murphy, 1992) 'resemble early manifestos in a long revolution' (Cohen; 1988: 14) that he labels 'adventurous pedagogy' (Cohen; 1988: 16). Murphy (1992b) and Beck and Murphy (1993) trace recent trends in educational leadership and democratic management to traditions extending back to the mid-1880s. Murphy (1992a) uncovers the debt owed by restructuring advocates to earlier work on school effectiveness. Guthrie (1990: 225), in turn, reveals how 'proposals for educational privatization have existed literally for centuries'. The point here is that restructuring is linked in a longer chain of history and grounded in ideological perspectives that themselves enjoy a deep heritage. What is unique about today's restructuring is the re-emergence of so many 'romantic' ideas about schooling at the same time and the fact that these views may be holding centre stage for the first time.

Of all the reform measures of this era, none has received as much attention as school-based management (SBM). Primarily a strategy to decentralise decision-making authority to the individual school site, when implemented effectively SBM also facilitates the empowerment of parents and the professionalisation of teachers.

WHAT IS SCHOOL-BASED MANAGEMENT?[4]

School-based management has been characterised in a number of different ways. One of the most comprehensive definitions has been provided by Malen et al., (1989):

> School-based management can be viewed conceptually as a formal alteration of governance structures, as a form of decentralisation that identifies the individual school as the primary unit of improvement and relies on the redistribution of decision making authority as the primary means through which improvements might be stimulated and sustained.
>
> (Malen et al., 1989: 1)

Devolution of authority is the fundamental concept in SBM. Under this system of governance, schools, in effect, become deregulated from the central office. The basic message is one of expanded local control and influence with schools being given greater responsibility for their own affairs. The strategy of improvement is bottom-up change. School-based management is thus primarily an alteration in organisational arrangements in school systems. Authority and influence pass from higher to lower levels of the organisation. Structural changes often accompany this devolution of authority.

Concomitantly, SBM usually includes an internal redistribution of the authority decentralised to the local school site from the state and/or the district office. Increased influence at the local school site is shared with teachers, parents and other community members and, sometimes, students. Thus shared decision-making among key stakeholders at the local level becomes a defining characteristic of SBM.

Domains of school-based management

Local control and shared decision-making take on meaning as they play out in the real world of five educational operations: goals, budget, personnel, curriculum and instruction, and organisational structures. The more control a school exercises over each of these areas and the more widely that control is dispersed, the more extensive the pattern of SBM.

Goals

Decentralisation of authority provides schools with more control over the direction that the organisation will pursue. Both the goals and the strategies for reaching them are primarily determined at the site level. Equally important is the fact that the individual school exercises considerable discretion over the values upon which collective action is to be taken. This control helps each school develop a unique culture that is consistent with the needs of the community.

Budget

Control over the budget is at the heart of efforts to decentralise authority. Without the ability to allocate resources as deemed most appropriate by local actors, the other dimensions of SBM lack force. Decentralised budgeting often means the allocation of funds to the school in a lump sum rather than for predetermined categories of expenditures (e.g. a certain amount for books, a certain amount for salaries). This allows the school, rather than the district, to determine how funds will be employed. The larger the ratio of lump sum funds to monies restricted by categories, the greater the amount of decentralisation. The ability to roll over unspent money is the final element of site-based control of funds. In conventional accounting practice, fund balances revert to the central office. When budget authority is decentralised, schools are able to carry over budget surpluses.

Personnel

Closely connected to budgetary discretion is control over the defining of roles and the hiring and development of staff. As in the fiscal area, there are various levels of local influence. In the least aggressive model of SBM, the allocation of teaching positions is determined at the central level. Within this constraint, and subject to state regulations, members of the local school community exercise nearly full control over who will fill these slots. That is, teachers are no longer sent to the school from the central office. Teachers and administrators interview candidates, make the final choice, and pass their selection back to the district. Under more nearly comprehensive models of local control, the allocation of professional positions is not predetermined. While schools are still free to select personnel, they also have the option of using funds budgeted for teachers for other purposes. For example, they can take money allocated in principle for a teacher and use it to purchase books and materials or to hire two or three paraprofessionals. In the most advanced cases of decentralisation, authority – either full or partial – for the employment of the principal is held by members of the local school community.

Curriculum and instruction

'Within a school-based management system, the school site has near total authority over curriculum matters. Within broad outlines defined by the board [and the state], the individual schools are free to teach in any manner they see fit' (Lindelow, 1981: 122). School-based curriculum means that each school staff decides what teaching materials are to be used, as well as the specific pedagogical techniques that are to be emphasised. It also means that the principal and teachers at the local level determine their own professional development needs and contract with whomever they wish to meet those needs.

Organisational structures

Structures within which the educational process unfolds represent a final area of control for teachers, administrators and parents under SBM. These groups are free to alter the basic delivery structure in schools, to develop alternatives to the model of the individual teacher working with groups of 25 to 35 students in 50-minute time blocks. At the elementary level, schools are creating educational programmes that dramatically change the practices of grouping children by age for classes and by ability for instruction. At the secondary level, a number of decentralised schools are experimenting with alternative programmes, core curricula, and outcome-based education.

The educational imperative

Over the last few years we have learned (and relearned) a number of things about the implementation of SBM. First, it is a difficult intervention to get under way. Sharp differences of opinion at the school level about new roles for teachers, parents and students under SBM often make the change process problematic (Gips and Wilkes, 1993; Smith, 1993). Most studies in this area underscore 'the recurring problem of drawing all team members into equal partnership in school-based management/shared decision-making' (Jewell and Rosen, 1993: 9). 'Power transformation through collaborative decision making requires more than will. It requires continuing negotiation, skill, and knowledge to make institutional change and . . . we are unschooled in ways to do this' (Sabatini, 1993: 8). What reviewers often find 'is that the traditional, rational bureaucratic organisation may still be well and active even though structural changes have taken place' (Sackney and Dibski, 1992).

Second, there is a downside to SBM. Specifically, a number of analysts have found that 'participatory governance creates additional administrative burdens for teachers' (Wong, 1993: 15) and administrators (Murphy, 1994a), often taking both groups further away from the central issue of schooling – learning and teaching.

Third, at the same time, SBM offers hope for improving certain dimensions of schooling. For example, in their review Sackney and Dibski (1992: 15) conclude that 'SBM facilitates local autonomy, diversity, and responsiveness to individual student and community needs'. Elmore (1993: 2), in turn, finds that 'new governing structures can improve social relations among low-income minority parents, teachers, and pupils by creating a climate of trust and understanding that fosters staff morale and student aspirations and enhances parental support for teacher's work'.[5]

Finally, and most importantly, as we have discussed in detail elsewhere (Murphy, 1991) it appears that SBM in and of itself does not lead to improvement in student learning.

> [T]here is little or no evidence that [site-based management] has any direct or predictable relationship to changes in instruction and students' learning. In fact, the evidence suggests that the implementation of site-based management reforms has a more or less random relationship to changes in curriculum, teaching, and students' learning.
>
> (Elmore, 1993: 40)

Given this fundamental problem and the difficulties noted above, a number of thoughtful analysts have asked whether '[p]erhaps there are more productive ways to spend the 'reform energy' that is loose in the land' (Weiss et al., 1992: 365). We share this concern. However, our own reading of the reform literature leads us to conclude that what is needed is a marriage between SBM and our most powerful conceptions of learning and teaching. Specifically, 'revisions in organisational and governance structures should be more tightly linked to revisions in curriculum and instruction. Reforms should '"backward map" from the student' (Murphy, 1991: 74). Stated alternatively, SBM should '"wrap around" the core technology' (Murphy and Hallinger, 1993: 255).

IMPLICATIONS FOR STAKEHOLDER ROLES[6]

State policymakers

Under SBM, analysts discern a shift away from the state's historical role as monitor of educational process. In its stead, a new tripartite set of responsibilities is emerging. First, state actors tend to assume the lead role in working with all stakeholders in the educational process to establish a new vision of education and to translate that vision into desired student outcomes. Second, they try to support – through as wide an array of methods as possible – efforts at the district, school and classroom levels to empower parents and professional educators and to nurture the evolution of new forms of governance and organisation. Third, they hold schools and school systems accountable for what they accomplish. Operating in this fashion, state policy actors are less involved in the micro-level management of the educational enterprise. Instead, they will play a key role in charting the course and in assessing the results rather than in monitoring processes or effort. Parents, professional educators and students in each school in turn become freer to direct their own destinies.

What is particularly important here is that state policymakers send fewer, clearer, and more consistent messages to schools engaged in SBM. For example, schools are often confused when, in the midst of implementing SBM, the state mandates a new curriculum or statewide assessment system. It is also important that state policymakers model expectations for teachers, principals and parents at the level of the local school. Because, by definition, SBM promotes variety, actors at the state (and district) level must be prepared to accept the fact that schools will look different from each other. Finally, policymakers need to ensure that systems that support LEAs – for example, teacher and administrative training – are brought into alignment with the underlying principles of SBM.

In a 1990 article in *Education Week*, Jane Armstrong of the Education Commission of the States (ECS) summarised the comments of more than 300 participants from two workshops sponsored by the ECS and the National Governors' Association. She listed thirteen steps that policymakers can take to facilitate school restructuring initiatives such as SBM. These constitute an excellent framework for state policymakers:

1 Develop a vision of desired student outcomes and a vision of a restructured education system.
2 Build a coalition of business, community, education and political leaders.
3 Gain public and political support.
4 Provide flexibility, encourage experimentation, and decentralise decision-making.
5 Shift state and local education agency roles from enforcement to assistance.

6 Restructure teacher and administrator education.
7 Provide ongoing development opportunities for every teacher and administrator.
8 Hold the system accountable.
9 Give all students every chance to learn and contribute.
10 Use policies as catalysts to promote and support restructuring.
11 Identify pilot restructuring sites.
12 Reallocate existing resources for restructuring.
13 Use technology to support restructuring.

A similar set of 'state actions to launch restructuring' has been described by Jane David and her colleagues in the National Governors Association's 1990 report, *State Actions to Restructure Schools: First Steps*. In addition, unlike the reforms of the early 1980s, they remind us that, for each state, the beginning steps of restructuring are exploratory. This is uncharted territory with no road maps. Inside schools, districts or local education authorities, and state agencies, leaders and educators are learning by experimenting (David *et al.*, 1990: 35).

District or LEA office

Efforts are under way in a variety of communities to overhaul district operations to support school-based reform efforts. Reports from these districts reveal shifts in the purpose, structure and nature of the work of central offices.

Purpose

The main purpose of the district office becomes one of serving and facilitating local school success. In meeting this new objective in restructuring districts, as Hirsh and Sparks (1991: 16) state, 'Central office departments are shifting from monitoring and regulating agencies to service centers for schools'.

Structure

Consistent with their newly-emerging mission, central offices in SBM districts are undergoing four types of structural change. In some cases, most often in large, heavily centralised districts, there has been a dismantling of the larger bureaucracy into regional units. For example, in the late 1980s the superintendent of Milwaukee decentralised the school system by dividing the bureaucracy into six service delivery areas. Parallel changes have been made in Dade County, Cincinnati and Dallas.

A reduction in size of central office staff is a second type of structural change sometimes found in SBM districts, often accompanied by the elimination of entire layers of the central hierarchy. For example, the first year of the Chicago Reform Act (1988/9) saw a 20 per cent reduction in central office staff. In Dallas, two layers of the bureaucracy were removed when one deputy superintendent replaced two associate superintendents and the assistant superintendents for elementary and secondary education.

Third, employees who previously occupied middle-management roles at the district office are sometimes reassigned to support activities in individual schools. In other cases, the money used to fund these positions is freed up to support new initiatives at the site level. In Chicago, the shift in central office staff generated $40 million, which was directed to the schools. The streamlining of staff in Cincinnati is expected to save $16 million over the 1992/3 and 1993/4 school years, all of which is targeted to flow directly to schools. In addition, many of the former Cincinnati central office administrators who do not retire will move to positions at the school level.

Finally, as this flattening of the hierarchical structure occurs, responsibilities and tasks historically housed at the district office level are often transferred to schools, and responsibilities that are currently centralised are distributed over a larger number of people. Consistent with the shifting purpose discussed earlier, the job of middle-level managers becomes centred on providing services directly to schools.

Nature of the work

Consistent with the redefined purpose of district activity discussed earlier, some central office departments are becoming service centres for schools. In helping support school-based reform, the function of central office personnel changes from attempting to ensure uniformity across schools to 'orchestrat[ing] diversity to ensure that the common educational goals of the system are met, even if in many different ways' (E. J. Schneider, cited in Clinchy, 1989) – a change that one superintendent we worked with describes as moving from managing a school system to developing a system of schools. Central office personnel in districts engaged in restructuring spend less time initiating projects. They are serving as liaisons between the school community and district office, performing as brokers of central office services.

The principal

Largely because new legislation and other externally generated expectations have altered the context of education, principals in most SBM environments believe that their roles have been altered in fundamental ways. These changes can be grouped under the following three headings: leading from the centre, enabling and supporting teacher success, and extending the school community.

Leading from the centre

There is considerable evidence that principals who are taking the SBM agenda seriously are struggling – often against long odds, and often with only mixed success – to redefine their leadership role. For example, in their study Earley *et al.* (1990: 9) report that '[a]pproximately two thirds of the cohort believed they had become more consultative, more open and more democratic. Heads spoke of becoming increasingly aware of the need for more participative management and for staff ownership of change'. Nearly all the work in this area concludes that the attempt to reshape power relationships – to redistribute authority to teachers, parents, and occasionally students – is at the very core of this redefinition. Two tasks form the foundation of these redesigned power relationships – delegating authority and developing collaborative decision-making processes.

Initial studies convey both the importance and the difficulty of sharing power. First, they affirm that empowering others represents the biggest change and poses the most significant problems for principals. Second, they impart a sense of how hard it can be for the organisation and the community to permit the principal to let go. Third, these studies underscore the centrality of a trusting relationship between the principal and the teachers in making genuine delegation a possibility. Fourth, they reveal that only by learning to delegate can principals in SBM reform efforts be successful. Finally, work on the evolving role of school leaders under decentralisation indicates that, even given the great difficulties involved, principals do have an array of available skills and tools that are effective in moving away from hierarchical control and in empowering teachers to lead.

Principals in decentralised schools spend considerable energy creating alternatives to traditional decision-making structures and forging a role for themselves consistent with the recast authority relationships that define these structures. Certainly the most prevalent change here is the principal's role in the development of a variety of formal models of site-based decision making. In addition, to foster the development of professional school cultures, principals in some of these schools are taking a stronger role supporting the development of powerful informal networks.

Enabling and supporting teacher success

Foundation

Enabling and supporting teacher success encompasses a variety of functions. Building on the analysis above about leading from the centre, what appears to be as critical as the tasks themselves are the bases for the activities and the ways in which they are performed. To the extent that there is an emerging empirical picture of principal leadership in decentralised schools, it seems to be one that is grounded not so much on line authority as it is 'based on mutual respect and equality of contribution and commitment' (Prestine, 1991: 27). It reflects a style of management that is democratic, participative and consultative. Group-centred leadership behaviours are often crucial. The ability to orchestrate from the background is often paramount.

Functions

This foundation, in turn, provides the context for the set of five functions often performed by principals in schools emphasising shared decision making:

- helping to formulate a shared vision
- cultivating a network of relationships
- allocating resources consistent with the vision
- providing information to staff
- promoting teacher development.

Bounding all of these functions are efforts of principals to support and affirm teachers' leadership and to create the framework for teachers to enhance their own growth and expand their own roles.

Extending the school community

Reports from nearly all sectors of the decentralisation movement confirm that:

- the boundaries between schools and their communities are becoming more permeable
- environmental leadership is becoming more important
- principals are spending more time with parents and other members of the school than they have in the past.

Perhaps the most dramatic shift for principals in schools engaged in SBM reform efforts has been their need to expand the public relations activities with external constituents. In this new context, the entrepreneurial role of the principal is being enhanced. In nearly all SBM sites, there is a renewed interest in the importance of client perceptions of schools and a new emphasis on obtaining and retaining students. In short, because the public image of schools becomes a much more salient issue under SBM, more and more time of principals in decentralised schools is being directed towards public relations and the promotion of the school's image and to selling and marketing the school and its programmes to the community.

Teachers

Analysts concerned with the role of teachers envision significant changes in the work they perform in decentralised schools. These alterations cluster into two categories: structural changes and conceptual changes.

Structural redesign

At one level, teachers under SBM are taking on new responsibilities. They are assuming control over decisions that were historically the province of others, especially administrators. Changes in this area are of two types – 'those that increase teachers' right to participate in formal decision making [and] those that give teachers greater access to influence by making school structures more flexible' (Moore-Johnson, 1989: 2). Numerous examples of expanded teacher responsibilities are available from school districts that are engaged in SBM efforts.

Team approaches to school management and governance are particularly good collective examples of expanded responsibilities for teachers. For example, in the Cincinnati school system, an equal number of teachers and administrators now comprise the committee that determines the allocation of teachers to individual schools. The formalisation of teacher participation in decision-making forums from which they were previously excluded (e.g. principal and teacher selection committees and facility planning groups) has been accomplished in Dade County. Through expanded participation in collective decision-making models and professional support groups, teachers in schools emphasising shared decision making have also begun to exercise considerable influence over the type of evaluation procedures employed. Individual teachers sometimes assume greater responsibility for the mentoring and supervision of their peers – especially beginning teachers – evaluating the work of principals, providing professional development to their colleagues, and developing curricula for the school. In short, both individually and collectively, teachers in decentralised schools are accumulating new responsibilities that extend their role beyond the confines of their own classrooms.

Some teachers in SBM schools are not only adding new responsibilities to their current jobs but are also beginning to fill new professional roles – work redesign activities that may significantly alter the basic role itself. For example a master teacher may continue to work three or four days a week in his or her own classroom but may also spend one or two days working with colleagues in their classrooms or with peers developing student assessment materials. A teacher-facilitator or coordinator may actually leave the classroom for a semester or a year to create professional development activities or curriculum materials for peers.

Conceptual redesign

In trying to understand the conceptual core of restructured teacher work in decentralised schools, the classification system developed by McCarthey and Peterson (1989) is especially helpful. According to these analysts, the categories of teacher as colleague, teacher as decision maker, teacher as leader, and teacher as learner capture the essence of the new roles for teachers in decentralised schools. In addition, a number of analysts have emphasised the idea of teacher as generalist in developing their conceptual picture of redesigned teacher work. Each of these conceptual dimensions represents a significant shift in conventional ways of thinking about teachers. In conventional practice, teachers are entrepreneurs of their own classrooms. They orchestrate their own operations almost totally independently of their peers and engage in few leadership or decision-making activities outside their own cubicles. They are viewed as pedagogical specialists whose function it is to deliver educational services to their young charges. Little time and energy are available for or devoted to self-renewal and professional growth.

Analysts sketch a very different portrait of the teaching function under SBM. According to them, teachers are professionals who engage in regular, and important, exchanges with their colleagues. Teachers participate in decisions affecting the entire school and frequently perform leadership tasks. They understand that to perform in this fashion they need to be more collegial, to develop more interdependence with peers, and to share their knowledge with others in a variety of settings. They realise that, by engaging in learning themselves, they 'are more likely to facilitate in their students the kind of learning that will be needed in the next decade' (McCarthey and Peterson, 1989: 11).

CONDITIONS TO FACILITATE SBM[7]

A first set of enabling conditions is designed to foster the development of an organisational culture that will support SBM. Readiness is an important antecedent to the successful implementation of SBM. Not everyone will be comfortable with SBM. Some, in fact, will be quite sceptical of what they are likely to perceive as another round of lofty pronouncements, flurries of activity, and marginal improvements. The likelihood of personal loss, especially for those who currently control school systems, will be quickly noted by others. And the potential of SBM to aggravate existing tensions in the system will not be lost on many. It is therefore not surprising that a number of students of SBM have concluded that trust is a bedrock condition for change. One major strategy for nurturing this sense of trust is to focus first on the interpersonal dimensions – rather than the technical aspects – of change. Other guidelines extracted from current decentralisation efforts include:

- helping people clearly see the advantages of change
- recognising and accepting resistance
- allaying concerns and fears about the unknown
- developing strong working relationships among groups.

The lesson for schools engaged in shared decision making is that the development of trust must be addressed directly, frequently and regularly, especially in forums that strengthen personal relationships among staff members.

Readiness also includes a sense of direction, or purpose, that is widely communicated and internalised by all stakeholders in the change process. It appears especially necessary to create a belief that something different is possible along with some conception about what those potentialities are. The idea of what a school is is so well grounded in the minds of educators and parents that, when provided with meaningful opportunities for change, they are often at a loss about what to do. Likewise, a good deal of organisational sediment reinforces the *status quo*, making it difficult to see different ways of organising and acting. Also, schools have operated within such a confining web of externally imposed rules and regulations for so long that, even when they are removed, it is hard to imagine how things might be different. For all of these reasons, a sense of direction must be forged on the anvil of dreams and possibilities of what schooling might become. Systematic efforts – through readings, discussions and visits to other schools – to expand people's view of what can be done will facilitate the development of a sense of direction for restructuring schools.

Finally, readiness entails a commitment to take risks and the right to fail, conditions not normally a part of the culture of schools. Willingness to take risks in turn is composed of at least three ingredients – the sense of the possibilities noted above, incentives to change, and strong organisational support.

Analysts regularly emphasise the importance of time in implementing SBM (Wallace and Wildy, 1993: 15). Four aspects of this implementation issue receive a good deal of scrutiny.

Start-up time   Time is needed to get SBM initiatives under way. SBM measures should be phased in slowly. Pilot projects and volunteer schools often begin before extending shared decision making efforts more generally.

Adding/reconfiguring time   A second time-related theme is that the pool of available time needs to be expanded. Because time is needed for learning new roles, personalising schooling, working with new constituents and so forth, schools involved in SBM endeavours will need additional time to do reform work. Time may be expanded by adding to the total time pool available (e.g. providing time before the school year begins) and/or by reconfiguring the school day or teacher tasks to reduce the load on staff.

Cooperative work time   A third dimension of time illustrated in reviews of SBM schools is cooperative work time. 'Teachers must have time that is expressly allocated to the development of a common agenda for the school and in which the development of professional culture and trusting personal relationships can occur' (Louis and King, 1993: 244). Specific examples include: common planning times for same-grade-level or team-based teachers; work sessions and retreats for teachers, administrators and parents to assess school operations; regularly scheduled, cooperatively oriented professional development activities.

Time for results   Finally, there is the issue of an appropriate amount of time required for results, the need to develop a time frame that is sufficient to ensure that complex changes can unfold and begin to produce desired outcomes. Districts that have been successful in empowering professionals and in decentralising operations have often taken between five and ten years to do so.

Undertaking new roles and working in schools that are organised and managed in different ways represent immense new challenges to educators and community members. It is not surprising, therefore, that nearly every analyst identifies professional development as a key variable in the formula for successful implementation of SBM initiatives. Particular efforts will need to be made to ensure that professional development activities are integrated with the local reform agenda rather than remaining a freestanding set of activities, as is often the case in today's schools. Reviewers also demonstrate that professional development will be effective to the extent that it centres on opportunities for staff members to work collaboratively on an ongoing basis. Recent work helps extend the definition of professional development appropriate for SBM – from that of a passive consumer activity to active participation in school-based research and substantive dialogue, from a receptive event to a constructive activity, and from an individual event to a collaborative endeavour.

In general, case studies of SBM paint a picture of school communities that are unprepared to engage in the active, collaborative task of shared decision making and that are unfamiliar and uneasy with the new roles that this work entails. They direct attention to the importance of capacity-building across an array of interrelated process areas. To begin with, because SBM increases uncertainty, helping school staffs learn to deal with stress becomes important. Also, because increased cooperation enhances the potential for conflict, skills in conflict management are in great demand in schools engaged in shared decision making.

Under SBM, a premium is placed on communication. Yet, many educators do not demonstrate good communication skills. Analysts reveal that schools involved in complex reform projects such as SBM would do well to attend to this issue. Other collaborative skills – group process, planning, and decision-making skills – are also of critical importance in SBM. Again, however, reviewers report that staff members are often ill-prepared for inter-active work with other adults. For example, Louis and King found that teachers in their study 'were consumed with the immediate crises of lurching from day to day' (Louis and King; 1993: 228) and that their group process skills were poor, 'resulting in a great deal of wasted time in staff meetings' (Louis and King; 1993: 229). In addition, work in the area of SBM demonstrates that most teachers have not received training in leader-ship and are therefore poorly prepared to exercise such responsibility outside of their own classrooms. Training in all these skill areas is needed if SBM efforts are to be given a chance.

Finally, dexterity in collaborative inquiry – a combination of personal reflection and organisational analysis – is conspicuous by its absence in the skill arsenals of many teachers and administrators. The tools needed to operate as a learning organisation will not magically appear at schools engaged in SBM activities. The potential for confusion and mistrust is large. Without training in the types of process skills discussed above, there is little reason to assume that SBM initiatives will bear fruit.

Resources required for change take a variety of forms. One that has received considerable scrutiny in the school improvement literature over the years has been that of material resources. In the area of SBM, the primary message is that such assistance is most valuable when it is focused on two other important support areas – time allocation, and professional develop-ment. A second lesson concerning material resources is that while additional funding can be of real assistance, it is not imperative. The question of how much money – usually expressed in terms of additional funding – is desir-able is still open and is likely never to be answered outside the context of specific reform initiatives.

These investigations also reveal that there usually are times in the life-cycle of SBM initiatives when infusions of additional material resources can exert a significant influence. For example, start-up funds, even small amounts, are often of critical importance. Other influential lifecycle periods are more contextualised, such as the securing of a grant to facilitate the development of conflict resolution skills at one school and problem-framing skills at another. Analyses also demonstrate that the amount of total support is less significant than the ability of the school to map resources on to the school vision and plan.

The general message in this area is twofold. Policymakers at the state and district levels need to be attentive to issues of funding under SBM. Given that the real costs of staff development and time are decoupled from discus-sions of additional funding, these stakeholders should be wary of claims that restructuring education is largely a budget-neutral proposition. At the same time, studies show that even small amounts of additional resources that are well integrated with a school's vision can have dramatic effects on the structure and process of schooling.

If attempts to implement SBM are to be successful, we will need a good deal of patience, wisdom and trust; more than a little luck; and considerable support and direction from all educational stakeholders, especially formal school leaders. It would appear that not only is strong advocacy by the superintendent needed but also a similar level of commitment by the building principal (Lindquist and Muriel, 1989: 412). Students of SBM are reaffirming a lesson learned in earlier studies of school improvement. Those in leadership positions within education systems, such as superintendents or school inspectors, are often the sustaining force in change efforts. Even in decentralised systems, they act as gatekeepers for change at the district and school levels. Without their endorsement and support, their willingness to commit valuable tangible and intangible organisational resources, the seeds of decentralisation are likely to fall on barren ground. On the other hand, in systems where shared decision making is occurring, there is invariably a senior educator who endorses the concept.

As Hallinger and Hausman (1993: 139) remind us, 'If important decisions about educational programs [are] to be decentralised to the school level, there needs to be a structure and process in place . . . to ensure that these decisions [are] made in a participatory manner' and, we would add, to ensure that the complex work of shared decision making is conscientiously addressed. Well-developed working structures represent an important support mechanism in all cases where SBM is progressing favourably. The sub themes in this area are as follows:

- there is no universally appropriate working structure; what is required or useful at one site may be unnecessary at another
- it is desirable to have extensive overlap of personnel on the structures used for planning and for implementing SBM
- some type of schoolwide steering committee (e.g. a School Leadership Council) helps bring coherence to the overall SBM agenda
- the use of a coordinator or facilitator can significantly sharpen the focus of SBM activities while reducing reliance on formal administrative channels
- maintaining the stability of these working structures can greatly enhance their effectiveness.

A final form of support often enjoyed by SBM schools is regular acknowledgement for the work they are doing, a legitimisation of their labours. In most cases, a reasonable level of external affirmation bolsters locally-based reform initiatives. Types of legitimisation vary across sites. The most important are those that recognise staff expertise and those that help educators have access to and become intelligent consumers of research.

Four general categories of external acknowledgement are discernible in studies on SBM:

1 recognition and visibility from the media
2 participation in forums where teachers share what they are learning with others in formal presentations
3 opportunities to work with colleagues from other schools
4 acting as a learning laboratory for educators from other schools.

Internally, legitimisation comes to individuals when site-based peers begin to look to them for expertise and when managing the SBM process taps hidden strengths and talents.

EPILOGUE AND PROLOGUE

The restructuring movement is currently at centre stage in our efforts to improve schooling and education throughout the world. Yet, as popular and appealing as restructuring is, information about the effects of these approaches to improvement remains largely conspicuous by its absence. This is troublesome for four reasons. At the most basic level, attempts to turn the educational enterprise upside down in the absence of data about the best way to undertake its reconstruction seem premature. Second, the likelihood that certain components of the restructuring agenda (e.g. school-based management) will lead to enhanced outcomes for students is open to serious question (Murphy, 1991). There certainly is very little evidence that this will occur and at least some evidence that it will not (see, e.g., Elmore, 1988a; Cohen, 1989; Malen et al., 1989). Third, there is little evidence to suggest that restructuring elements such as choice and school-based management are the most powerful leverage to influence the mediating variables that are connected to student outcomes. That is, many elements of the restructuring agenda do not appear to be linked to student outcomes, either directly or indirectly. Finally, there is at least some reason to suspect that restructuring may result in some negative consequences for children and their families (Watt, 1989). For example, both self-managing schools and schools of choice have the potential to create 'serious problems of equity among schools' (Elmore, 1988b: 28).

On the other hand, there is a good deal of optimism afoot about the potential of the restructuring movement to improve education and schooling. It is important to remember that there is much to be said for providing voice to parents, students, and teachers, regardless of whether this leads to enhanced learning outcomes or not. And, while this stage production on transforming schools may not be quite as polished as many viewers suspect, there is still reason to believe that restructuring may actually have important effects on measures of student learning. This appears to be especially true for restructuring efforts that flow from the rich conceptions of learning embedded in our discussion of studenting. We therefore need a better understanding of what works in certain contexts – and why.

In short, the time has come to move beyond our preoccupation with conceptual discussions of restructuring to more grounded understandings – to learn what we can from ongoing efforts at transforming education.

NOTES

1 This section has been adapted from Murphy and Hallinger (1993).
2 For excellent discussions of the current and envisioned routines of schooling, see Cohen (1988), Elmore (1991), and Marshall (1992).
3 The fact that one of the most highly visible educational interventions of the past decade – the New American Schools Development Corporation – is privately funded by corporate America to create alternative models of schooling is worth noting at this point.
4 Also known in England as Grant Maintained Schools (Goodchild and Bragg, 1992).
5 For an illustrative array of choice options, see Elmore (1988a).
6 This section is adapted from Murphy (1990, 1991, 1994a, 1994b).
7 This section is adapted from Murphy (1991) and Murphy and Hallinger (1993).

REFERENCES

American Association of Educators in Private Practice (AAEPP) (1992) *Network News and Views*, 11 (3), iv.
Banathy, B. H. (1988) 'An outside-in approach to design inquiry in education', in Far West Laboratory for Educational Research and Development (ed.), *The redesign of education: A collection of papers concerned with comprehensive educational reform* (vol. 1, pp. 51–71). San Francisco: Far West Laboratory.
Barth, R. S. (1991) 'Restructuring schools: Some questions for teachers and principals', *Phi Delta Kappan*, 73(2), 123–8.
Beare, H. (1989) 'Educational administration in the 1990s'. Paper presented at the National Conference of the Australian Council for Educational Administration, Armidale, New South Wales, Australia, September.
Beck, L. G. and Murphy, J. (1993) *Understanding the principalship: Metaphorical themes from 1920–1990*, New York: Teachers College Press.
Boyd, W. L. and Kerchner, C. T. (eds) (1988) *The politics of excellence and choice in education*, New York: Falmer.
Boyd, W. L. and Walberg, H. J. (eds) (1990) *Choice in education: Potential and problems*, Berkeley, CA: McCutchan.
Bransford, J. D., Goldman, S. R. and Vye, N. J. (n.d.) *Making a difference in people's abilities to think: Reflections on a decade of work and some hopes for the future*, Nashville, TN: Vanderbilt University, Peabody College, Learning Technology Center.
Burke, C. (1992) 'Devolution of responsibility to Queensland schools: Clarifying the rhetoric, critiquing the reality', *Journal of Educational Administration*, 30(4), 33–52.
Carnegie Council for Adolescent Development (1989) *Turning points*, Washington, DC: Carnegie Council.
Carnegie Forum on Education and the Economy (1986) *A nation prepared: Teachers for the 21st century*, Washington, DC: Carnegie Forum.
Chubb, J. E. (1988) 'Why the current wave of school reform will fail', *The Public Interest*, 28–49.

Clark, D. L. and Meloy, J. M. (1989) 'Renouncing bureaucracy: A democratic structure for leadership in schools', in T. J. Sergiovanni and J. A. Moore (eds), *Schooling for tomorrow: Directing reform to issues that count* (pp. 272–94). Boston: Allyn and Bacon.

Clinchy, E. (1989) 'Public school choice: Absolutely necessary but not wholly sufficient', *Phi Delta Kappan*, 70(4), 289–94.

Clune, W. H. and White, P. A. (1988) *School-based management: Institutional variation, implementation, and issues for further research*, New Brunswick, NJ: Rutgers University, Eagleton Institute of Politics, Center for Policy Research in Education.

Cohen, D. K. (1988) *Teaching practice* (Issue Paper 88–3), East Lansing: Michigan State University, National Center for Research on Teacher Education.

—— (1989) 'Can decentralization or choice improve public education?', paper presented at the Conference on Choice and Control in American Education, University of Wisconsin – Madison, May.

Combs, A. W. (1988) 'New assumptions for educational reform', *Educational Leadership*, 45(5), 38–40.

Council of Chief State School Officers (1989) *Success for all in a new century*, Washington, DC: CCSSO.

Cuban, L. (1984) 'School reform by remote control: SB813 in California', *Phi Delta Kappan*, 66(3), 213–15.

David, J. L. *et al.* (1990) *State actions to restructure schools: First steps*, Washington, DC: National Governors' Association.

DES (1988) *Education Reform Act: Local Management of Schools*, Circular 7/88, London: Department of Education and Science.

DSE (1994) *Schools of the Future Information Kit*, Melbourne: Directorate of School Education.

Earley, P., Baker, L. and Weindling, D. (1990) *'Keeping the raft afloat': Secondary headship five years on*, London: National Foundation for Educational Research in England and Wales.

Elmore, R. F. (1987) 'Reform and the culture of authority in schools', *Educational Administration Quarterly*, 23(4), 60–78.

—— (1988a) 'Choice in public education', in W. L. Boyd and C. T. Kerchner (eds), *The politics of excellence and choice in education* (pp. 79–98), New York: Falmer.

—— (1988b) *Early experience in restructuring schools: Voices from the field*, Washington, DC: National Governors' Association.

—— (1991) 'Teaching, learning and organization: School restructuring and the recurring dilemmas of reform', paper presented at the annual meeting of the American Educational Research Association, Chicago, April.

—— (1993) 'School decentralization: Who gains? Who loses?', in J. Hannaway and M. Carnoy (eds), *Decentralization and school improvement* (pp. 33–54). San Francisco: Jossey-Bass.

Evertson, C. and Murphy, J. (1992) 'Beginning with classrooms: Implications for restructuring schools', in H. H. Marshall (ed.), *Supporting student learning: Roots of educational change*, Norwood, NJ: Ablex.

Gips, C. J. and Wilkes, M. (1993) 'Teacher concerns as they consider an organisational change to site-based decision making', paper presented at the annual meeting of the American Educational Research Association, Atlanta, April.

Giroux, H. A. (1988) *Teachers as intellectuals: Toward a critical pedagogy of learning*, Granby, MA: Bergin and Garvey.

Goldman P., Dunlap, D. M. and Conley, D. T. (1991) 'Administrative facilitation and site-based school reform projects', paper presented at the annual meeting of the American Educational Research Association, Chicago, April.

Goodchild, S. and Bragg, V. (1992) 'U.K. case study', paper presented at the International Congress for School Effectiveness and Improvement, Victoria, British Columbia, January.

Guthrie, J. W. (1990) 'The evolution of educational management: Eroding myths and emerging models', in B. Mitchell and L. L. Cunningham (eds), *Educational leadership and changing contexts of families, communities, and schools* (pp. 210–31), Chicago: University of Chicago Press.

—— (1992) 'The emerging golden era of educational leadership: And the golden opportunity for administrator training', the Walter D. Cocking Memorial Lecture presented at the National Conference of Professors of Educational Administration, Terre Haute, August.

Guthrie, J. W. and Kirst, M. W. (1988) *Conditions of education in California 1988: Policy analysis for California education* (Policy Paper No. 88–3–2). Berkeley, CA: Authors.

Hallinger, P. and Hausman, C. (1993) 'The changing role of the principal in a school of choice', in J. Murphy and P. Hallinger (eds), *Restructuring schooling: Learning from ongoing efforts* (pp. 114–42), Newbury Park: Crown.

Hirsh, S. and Sparks, D. (1991) 'A look at the new central-office administrators', *The School Administrator*, 48(7), 16–17, 19.

Hodgkinson, H. L. (1991) 'Educational reform versus reality', in American Association of School Administrators (AASA)/National School Boards Association (NSBA) (eds), *Beyond the schools: How schools and communities must collaborate to solve problems facing America's youth*, Washington, DC: AASA/NSBA.

Honig, B. (1990) ' "Comprehensive" strategy can improve schools', *Education Week*, 9(23), 36, 31.

Jewell, K. E. and Rosen, J. L. (1993) 'School-based management/shared decision-making: A study of school reform in New York City', paper presented at the annual meeting of the American Educational Research Association, Atlanta, April.

Kerr, C. (1991) 'Is education really all that guilty?', *Education Week*, 10(23), 30.

Kirst, M. W., McLaughlin, M. and Massell, D. (1989) *Rethinking children's policy: Implications for educational administration*, Stanford, CA: Stanford University, College of Education, Center for Educational Research.

Lange, D (1988) *Tomorrow's Schools: The Reform of Education Administration in New Zealand*, Wellington: Government Printer.

Lindelow, J. (1981) 'School-based management', in S. C. Smith, J. A. Mazzarella and P. K. Piele (eds), *School leadership: Handbook for survival* (pp. 94–129), Eugene: ERIC Clearing House on Educational Management, University of Oregon.

Lindquist, K.M. and Muriel, J. J. (1989) 'School-based management: Doomed to failure?', *Education and Urban Society*, 21(4), 403–16.

Louis, K. S. and King, J. A. (1993) 'Professional cultures and reforming schools: Does the myth of Sisyphus apply?', in J. Murphy and P. Hallinger (eds), *Restructuring schooling: Learning from ongoing efforts* (pp. 216–50), Newbury Park, CA: Corwin Press.

McCarthey, S. J. and Peterson, P. L. (1989) 'Teacher roles: Weaving new patterns in classroom practice and school organization', paper presented at the annual meeting of the American Educational Research Association, San Francisco, March.

McNeil, L. M. (1988) 'Contradictions of control, part 1: Administrators and teachers', *Phi Delta Kappan*, 69(5), 333–9.

Malen, B., Ogawa, R. T. and Kranz, J. (1989) 'What do we know about school based management? A case study of the literature – a call for research', paper presented at the Conference on Choice and Control in American Education, Madison: University of Wisconsin – Madison, May.

Marshall, H. H. (ed.) (1992) *Supporting student learning: Roots of educational change*, Norwood, NJ: Ablex.

Mitchell, B. (1990) 'Children, youth, and educational leadership', in B. Mitchell and L. L. Cunningham (eds), *Educational leadership and changing contexts of families, communities, and schools* (Eighty-Ninth NSSE Yearbook, Part II, pp. 19–68), Chicago: University of Chicago Press.

Mitchell, D. E. and Beach, S. A. (1991) 'School restructuring: The superintendent's view', paper presented at the annual meeting of the American Educational Research Association, Chicago, March.

Mojkowski, C. and Bamberger, R. (1991) *Developing leaders for restructuring schools: New habits of minds and hearts*, Washington, DC: United States Department of Education, Office of Educational Research and Improvement.

Moore-Johnson, S. (1989) 'Teachers. power, and school change', paper presented at the Conference on Choice and Control in American Education, Madison: University of Wisconsin – Madison, May.

Murphy, J. (1990a) 'The educational reform movement of the 1980s: A comprehensive analysis', in J. Murphy (ed.), *The reform of American public education in the 1980s: Perspectives and cases* (pp. 3–55), Berkeley, CA: McCutchan.

—— (1990b) *Restructuring America's schools*, Charleston: Appalachia Educational Laboratory.

—— (1991) *Restructuring schools: Capturing and assessing the phenomena*, New York: Teachers College Press.

—— (1992a) 'School effectiveness and school restructuring: Contributions to educational improvement', *School Effectiveness and School Improvement*, 3(2), 1–20.

—— (1992b) *The landscape of leadership preparation: Reframing the education of school administrators*, Newbury Park, CA: Corwin.

—— (1994a) 'Transformational change and the evolving role of the principal', in J. Murphy and K. S. Louis (eds), *Reshaping the principalship: Insights from transformational reform efforts*, Newbury Park, CA: Corwin.

—— (1994b) 'The changing role of the superintendency in restructuring districts in Kentucky', paper presented at the annual meeting of the American Educational Research Association, New Orleans.

Murphy, J., Evertson, C. and Radnofsky, M. (1991) 'Restructuring schools: Fourteen elementary and secondary teachers' proposals for reform', *Elementary School Journal*, 92(2), 135–48.

Murphy, J. and Hallinger, P. (1993) 'Restructuring schooling: Learning from ongoing efforts', in J. Murphy and P. Hallinger (eds), *Restructuring schooling: Learning from ongoing efforts* (pp. 251–71), Newbury Park, CA: Corwin.

National Commission on Excellence in Education (1983) *A nation at risk: The imperative of educational reform*, Washington, DC: Government Printing Office.

National Governors' Association (1986) *The governors' 1991 report on education*, Washington, DC: NGA.

Newmann, F. M. (1991) 'Linking restructuring to authentic student achievement', *Phi Delta Kappan*, 72(6), 458–63.

Passow, A. H. (1984) *Reforming schools in the 1980s: A critical review of the national reports*, New York: Columbia University, Teachers College, Institute for Urban and Minority Education.

Perkins, D. N. (1991) 'Educating for insight', *Educational Leadership*, 49(2), 4–8.

Peterson, P. L. and McCarthey, S. J. (1991) *School restructuring and classroom practice: Are the connections inevitable?* Manuscript submitted for publication.

Powell, A. G., Farrar, E. and Cohen, D. K. (1985) *The shopping mall high school: Winners and losers in the educational marketplace*, Boston: Houghton Mifflin.

Prestine, N. A. (1991) 'Completing the essential schools metaphor: Principal as enabler', paper presented at the annual meeting for the American Educational Research Association, Chicago, April.

Quality Education for Minorities Project (1990) *Education that Works: An action plan for the education of minorities*, Cambridge: Massachusetts Institute of Technology.

Sabatini, A. (1993) 'Observing the tortoise: Collaborative decision making among stakeholders at one comprehensive high school in New York City', paper presented at the annual meeting of the American Educational Research Association, Atlanta, April.

Sackney, L. E. and Dibski, D. J. (1992) 'School-based Management: A critical perspective', paper presented at the Seventh Regional Conference of the Commonwealth Council for Educational Administration, Hong Kong, August.

Schmidt, P. (1992) 'For-profit firm hired to manage schools in Duluth', *Education Week*, 11(26), 1, 18.

Sedlak, M. W. *et al.* (1986) *Selling students short: Classroom bargains and academic reform in the American high school*, New York: Teachers College Press.

Shuell, T. J. (1986) 'Cognitive conceptions of learning', *Review of Educational Research*, 56(4), 411–36.

Sizer, T. R. (1984) *Horace's compromise: The dilemma of the American high school*, Boston: Houghton Mifflin.

Smith, M. S. and O'Day, J. (1990) 'Systemic school reform', in S. H. Fuhrman and B. Malen (eds), *The politics of curriculum and testing* (pp. 233–67), London: Falmer.

Smith, W. E. (1993) 'Teachers' perceptions of role chance through shared decision making: A two-year case study', paper presented at the annual meeting of the American Educational Research Association, Atlanta, April.

Tindal, G. (1991) 'Operationalizing learning portfolios: A good idea in search of a method', *Diagnostique*26(2–3), 127–33.

Tyack, D. (1990) ' "Restructuring" in historical perspective: Tinkering toward utopia', *Teachers College Record*, 92(2), 170–91.

Wagstaff, L. H. and Gallagher, K. S. (1990) 'Schools, families, and communities: Idealized images and new realities', in B. Mitchell and L. L. Cunningham (eds), *Educational leadership and changing contexts of families, communities and schools* (Eighty-Ninth NSSE Yearbook, Part II, pp. 91–117), Chicago: University of Chicago Press.

Wallace, J. and Wildy, H. (1993) 'Pioneering school change: Lessons from a case study of school site restructuring', paper presented at the annual meeting of the American Educational Research Association, Atlanta, April.

Walsh, M. (1992) 'Whittle unveils team to design new schools', *Education Week*, 11(24), 1, 13.

Warren, D. (1990) 'Passage of rites: On the history of educational reform in the United States', in J. Murphy (ed.), *The educational reform movement of the 1980s: Perspectives and cases* (pp. 57–81), Berkeley, CA: McCutchan.

Watt, J. (1989) 'The devolution of power: The ideological meaning', *Journal of Educational Administration*, 27(1), 19–28.

Weiss, C. H., Cambone, J. and Wyeth, A. (1992) 'Trouble in paradise: Teacher conflicts in shared decision making', *Educational Administration Quarterly*, 28(3), 350–67.

White, P. A. (1992) 'Teacher empowerment under "ideal" school-site autonomy', *Educational Evaluation and Policy Analysis*, 14(1), 69–82.

Wong, K. K. (1993) 'Linking governance reform to schooling opportunities for the disadvantaged', paper presented at the annual meeting of the American Educational Research Association, Atlanta, April.

Chapter 4

Autonomy and mutuality
Quality education and self-managing schools[1]

Judith Chapman and David Aspin

The phrase 'Tomorrow's Schools' in the title of this book carries with it a number of positive notes. Implicit in the phrase is the assumption that schools in coming times will be better than those with which we are familiar from the past and the present day. That notion of 'improvement', however, means different things to different people: schools that produce students who are happy, well-adjusted and socially aware; students who can achieve high scores on a range of public examinations; students who will be well-fitted for a productive life in a competitive economic environment; students who will be able to operate effectively in the institutions of a modern partic-ipative democracy. For all of these constituencies 'Tomorrow's Schools' bears both an aspiration and a challenge.

It will be widely agreed that there is much about modern schools and school systems that inhibits or even militates against the achievement of such desirable outcomes. What no-one will disagree about is that the schools of tomorrow must, as well as being efficient and effective, be of high excel-lence: they must, in comparison with the schools of yesterday or today, show that they are institutions planned, organised and directed to offer educa-tional experiences, activities and outcomes that are marked by a concern that those experiences, activities and outcomes shall all be of the highest quality. It is with the problem of saying what that quality might be, and how it might be brought about in our educational institutions, that educators have now begun to grapple.

'Quality' is certainly one of the key terms in current educational debates: 'quality schooling', 'quality management', 'quality teaching and learning' and 'quality assurance' are all themes that have exercised the attention and drawn the criticism of policy-makers, administrators and practitioners widely across the international arena. No-one is against 'quality': all the stakeholders agree that it is a key part of the work of educating institutions; everyone wants to be assured that they will obtain it. But what is it, and how would we know when we had found it or failed to find it? Once having identified it or secured some broad agreement on what it consists in, how are we then to conceptualise and construct it so that it can be assured and successfully delivered in our educational institutions? What measures need to be introduced to promote it – and in ways that do not threaten or compromise other good things in our schools and school systems? How are we to manage its provision at the school site? It is with the tentative answering of some of these questions that this chapter is concerned. The chapter addresses themes and issues developed more fully in the authors' recent book, *Quality Schooling* (Aspin and Chapman, 1994).

Although the major data source for our book involved a close analysis of Australian educational policy and school reform, our work addresses a theme of international theoretical and practical importance. The research was informed by international considerations of issues pertaining to quality education, the effectiveness of schooling and school-based management. In designing the research we drew upon work which we had undertaken on behalf of the OECD for its Activity on The Effectiveness of Schooling and of Educational Resource Management (OECD, 1990) and devised a framework for the consideration of these issues in the Australian context. An interview schedule reflecting major areas of inquiry was developed and interview responses were analysed using the Ethnograph package.

Data were collected in each of the Australian states and territories. The perspectives available to the researchers came from principals, teachers, parents and students in schools; senior personnel (such as Directors General of Education and Chairpersons of national and state Commissions); middle-level management in educational systems (including directors of divisions, regional officers and inspectors); Presidents and officers of organisations such as Teacher Associations, Parent Associations, Principal Associations, Religious orders; support personnel (such as curriculum and professional development officers, teacher trainers and lecturers in Faculties of Education); and members of the wider community including representatives from business.

The theoretical perspective from which our work was undertaken is not one that has been widely used in past reflections on and analyses of school quality. We operate from a post-empiricist view of educational theory and research, in which we eschew positivist paradigms that hold fast to the tenability of theses resting upon alleged hard 'empirical' data, 'facts' which are regarded as free of value or theoretical prejudice, and 'findings' that are claimed to be neutral, impersonal and totally objective.

We reject such approaches and prefer to adopt one of a pragmatic kind, which draws upon the writings of such thinkers as Dewey (1938a, 1938b, 1966), Popper (1949, 1972), Quine (1953, 1974) and Lakatos (1976). On this basis we tackle what we believe to be the real problems, topics and difficulties constituting the staple of agenda devoted to the examination and elucidation of 'quality' issues. We concentrate upon the examination, comparison and criticism of various theoretical perspectives, taking our analysis to be one involving critical theory competition and correction, as part of a process of bringing to bear the various judgements we believe it is possible to make about the nature, values and goals of quality institutions, teaching and schooling.

We do this by taking a 'problem-based' approach in which we try to identify and isolate those problems that are amenable to treatment, and capable of resolution. We do not look for the arrival of any educational millennium and we are aware that our own conclusions may well turn out to be just one further set of hypotheses that stand as candidates for criticism and possible refutation. We are also aware, in our approach to the tentative conceptualisation and application of theories to real problems, that we do not come to such an enterprise free of 'prejudices' and theories of our own.

We seek to provide for our audience access to a range of problems, issues and trends that will enhance the understanding of policy-makers, administrators, teachers and parents as they address the theme of 'Quality Schooling' in the management of schools and school systems around the world.

OVERVIEW

This chapter is divided into three parts. First we discuss the concept of 'Quality Schooling'; next we concentrate on one aspect of our theory of 'Quality Schooling' arising from our research: that which has to do with the system-wide provision of quality education and the administration of quality schools, particularly as that pertains to decentralisation, devolution and school-based management. Finally, we conclude with a set of suggestions that we regard as constituting Agenda for Reform. In putting these forward we lay particular emphasis on new patterns of relationship for the management of schools based upon the values of autonomy and mutuality and the concept of education as a 'public good'.

THE CONCEPT OF QUALITY

Issues of 'quality' in education have been a matter of interest and concern for some time in different institutions, systems and countries. Saying something clear and comprehensive about that elusive concept has, however, proved far more difficult.

The reason for this is not far to seek. Like 'art', 'religion' and 'democracy', 'quality' is an example of what W. B. Gallie (1956, 1964) called an 'essentially contested concept'. To think that one can find an 'essential', 'basic' or incontestable definition of 'quality' is to embark upon a search for that mythical beast, the chimera. Instead of engaging in a futile search for the real meaning or definition of quality we believe that the best one can do is to follow Wittgenstein's advice (Wittgenstein, 1953, 1958) and 'look at its use' in discourse employing that term and centring on that topic and its

increasing importance in school and system-wide planning and administration. It was with these sorts of considerations in mind that we embarked
upon our national study of Quality Schooling.

At the end of our research endeavour, although, as we predicted, we could
not identify one particular version or 'meaning' for the concept of quality on
which all unambiguously agreed, our observation of 'talk' about quality
schooling indicates the operation, within broad parameters, of a lodestone in
such talk. In people's discussions and debates about quality we found that
what clearly matters, and what helps us to begin dimly to discern some sort
of 'truth', is the irregular flow and shifting interplay of a number of factors.
These include: the intellectual backgrounds and traditions, the individual
and collective intentions, the motivations and interests of participants in the
debate; the contexts in which such debates take place; the outcomes aimed
at and the purposes held in mind; the considerations that make certain
criteria important and certain moves decisive. These and other such locating
devices have given us far more of the flavour, direction and sense of the
particular ways in which quality has significance in such discussions than
any number of sophisticated definitions and conceptual analyses.

Notwithstanding the lack of agreement on the meaning of 'quality',
however, we found one outcome especially noteworthy. Our examination of
the use of the term 'quality' in the discourse of the educational community
appears to indicate a wide measure of agreement on certain 'core' values at
work in such talk. These core values are widely observed to subsist in, and
then to be looked for, as characteristic features of the 'quality', 'good' or
'effective' school, and, when found or agreed upon, are seen as ends to be
aimed at or values worth promoting in the activities and undertakings of
schools. These values help to structure and define the direction and aiming
points of educational policy and practice.

From our enquiry into quality schooling we discerned a number of values
that might be said to be typical of quality schools. Some of the core values of
quality schooling appear to be the following:

• schools should give their students access to, and the opportunity to
  acquire, practise and apply those bodies and kinds of knowledge, compe-
  tences, skills and attitudes that will prepare them for life in today's
  complex society
• schools should have a concern for and promote the value of excellence and
  high standards of individual and institutional aspiration, achievement
  and conduct in all aspects of its activities
• schools should be democratic, equitable and just
• schools should humanise our students and give them an introduction into
  and offer them opportunities for acquiring the values that will be crucial
  in their personal and social development
• schools should develop in students a sense of independence and of their

own worth as human beings, having some confidence in their ability to contribute to the society of which they are a part, in appropriate social, political and moral ways

- schools should prepare our future citizens to conduct their interpersonal relationships with each other in ways that shall not be inimical to the health and stability of society or the individuals that comprise it
- schools should prepare students to have a concern for the cultural as well as the economic enrichment of the community in which they will ultimately play a part, promoting the enjoyment of artistic and expressive experience in addition to the acquisition of knowledge and its employment
- schools should conjoin education for personal autonomy and education for community enmeshment and social contribution, enabling each student to enrich the society of which he/she is to become a part as a giver, an enlarger and an enhancer, as well as being an inheritor and recipient.

These are cited only as illustrations of some of the values of quality schooling; no doubt there are others. Nevertheless our research suggests that, whatever other functions a quality school might be said to perform, with the promotion of these values at least it is vitally concerned.

As an aside we might point out that this list constitutes a somewhat different set of characteristics and criteria for quality or effective schooling than that which emerges from studies using a strictly quantitative approach. Such an approach, that dominated American and some European models of school effectiveness, runs the risk of creating a situation in which the outcomes of education are so premised that the curriculum concentrates on and becomes narrowly prescriptive of instrumental and economic goals. Indeed such an approach can by definition concentrate on only those goals that are readily measurable in quantitative terms.

In contrast, the point that emerges strongly from our enquiry into quality schooling is that central to the concept of quality schooling is an emphasis upon values. Further, we believe that the chief of these incorporates a dual emphasis:

- one, upon the development of autonomous individuals, with their own powers of independent judgement and the capacity to be self-motivated and self-starting in action
- the other, that such autonomous agents must at the same time – and necessarily – be taken up into patterns and networks of mutual interrelation with other individuals and with the whole community, in all its economic, social and political aspects.

Such interrelationships form and structure the set of agreements and conventions about an inner core of values that then, in their totality and interdependence, function to provide us with the various kinds of capacities and strengths needed to deal with the difficulties, problems, tensions and controversies that beset us as we try to bring about quality schools.

The key questions in quality schooling, we argue, are ones that concern the form and content of our systems of values, codes of ethics and standards of conduct, that will be normative for both individual and society and become translated into policy and practice. In our debates about the future of education, these questions are clearly of central concern, and for that reason must precede any discussions about restructuring, concerning decentralised and devolved administrative arrangements. Our contention is that discussion and agreement on the form and content of the values and agenda that shall underpin our educational norms and conventions must necessarily come before any discussion of the ways and means of their institutional realisation and implementation. It is only, we maintain, when we have secured some form of agreement about substance, that we can then tackle the further problem of operationalisation and implementation.

THE OPERATIONALISATION AND IMPLEMENTATION OF QUALITY SCHOOLING: EDUCATION AS A PUBLIC GOOD

Proponents of quality schooling in countries such as Australia, Denmark, France and Norway have traditionally supported the principle that access to intellectual challenge and a high quality and empowering curriculum, in a caring and personally concerned environment, is among the most important features of education in and for a more just society – one in which social justice and equality of opportunity stand as achievable goals for education. In contrast, the conservative philosophy, adopted in countries such as England and Wales, is more minimalist as regards equity and social justice. In the form in which it is applied to education, it embodies the view that education as an agency can do little to redress the major inequalities existing in society; these are seen to be related more to individual talent and motivation. From such a perspective the administrative response to the promotion and provision of quality schooling leaves a far greater degree of responsibility to individual effort, management at the local school site, and the influences of the educational market place (cf. Ball, 1990; Chubb and Moe, 1990; Whitty and Edwards, 1992).

In this way we can see how differences in the political and ethical considerations between parties debating the best way to ensure quality in schooling relate to the commitments that people have to a set of beliefs regarding the nature of human beings, the most desirable form of society, and the ways in which they can best arrange and institutionalise their relationships for the various purposes they have in mind. Such differences of vision and perspective are fundamental to our conceptions of the idea of 'public service', the public provision and resourcing of goods and services, and our response to questions associated with restructuring education and the decentralisation and devolution of decision making to schools.

The market approach, for example, puts enormous stress upon the supposed freedom of the individual client – the parent and child; and on the freedom of the provider – the individual school. This has enabled conservatives to promote the superficially beguiling policies of parental choice, but at the same time it has also enabled them to locate blame for low-level performance and educational underachievement on the supposed inadequacies of individuals rather than on structural features of society or the obvious imperfections of institutions and public agencies.

The conservative emphasis upon the educational marketplace also enables them to restructure schools in such a way that major decision making is relocated to the school site and major responsibility for resource provision and resource management is located at the local level. For schools operating under such terms and conditions, 'success' is determined by their success in attracting – or choosing – the right class of customer, who can thereafter attract to the school the educational dollar to ensure the school's continuing survival; schools that 'fail' in the educational marketplace, in these terms, like bankrupt businesses, 'go to the wall' and are simply closed, thereby avoiding for government the potentially politically unpopular decisions of appearing to have discriminated against one section of society in favour of another. In this context we have the devolution both of problems and of blame to the local school site and its management: governments do not decide to close schools; it is simply 'market forces' that are alleged to do that.

If the market prevails, if education is seen as some kind of commodity to be offered for sale and 'bought' at a price, if additional enterprise is expected for schools to generate further funds on a local basis, then inequity and inequality within a system of education will almost certainly increase. The stark reality, as it appears at least in the UK, is that the much-sought-after schools are able to discriminate against certain types and classes of student; that the curriculum generally becomes more responsive to the demands of economic and societal elites; and that increasingly many people simply cannot afford to buy the educational goods and services that 'the best' institutions offer (cf. Bridges and McLaughlin, 1994).

In contrast to the notion of education as a commodity stands the notion of education as a public good, access to which is a prerequisite for informed and effective participation by all citizens in a democratic society (cf. Grace, 1994; Smethurst, 1995). The same may be said of such services as health, welfare and housing, all of which, with education, constitute the infrastructure upon which individuals may hope to construct, realise and work out their own versions of a life of quality. It is upon this notion of education as a public good that education for all children was made available in many countries. And in the modern world, in circumstances of so many and such complex demands and difficulties – economic, social and cultural – with which our future generations will have to cope, it is that principle which, from our research in Australia, we found that people are least willing to give up.

Certainly no-one would suggest for a moment that education, like other 'public goods' such as health and welfare services, requires no individual investment; they all have to be funded and supported financially and in a myriad other ways. But these services are vital and indispensable to the nature, quality and operation of the democratic society in which we all live and of which, as citizens, we have a share. Our point is that individuals can only develop as autonomous agents fit to participate in society if they are sufficiently informed, prepared and predisposed; if they are healthy and well-fed; and if they have the minimal domestic conditions for perpetuating existence. In our view, the whole of our society has a direct interest in securing, providing and safeguarding those conditions and services presupposed by and required in our participation in democratic life. These conditions are provided, at least in major part, by the contributions that all of us who shall benefit from them regard it as being in our mutual interest to make to the common wealth in a publicly-funded exchequer.

This is a point about the nature of our world. It is a complex conjunction of aggregations of individual human beings. As Aristotle maintained, 'Man is by nature an animal that lives in groups'; we do not live, indeed we could not start our existence or survive, if we lived on desert islands. The personal freedom and individual choice, that is so much prized by exponents of the market philosophy, is only possible as an outgrowth of the knowledge and values that other members of society have opened up to us. In this way they have given us some intimation of what choices are available to us and of what choosing, and the calculation of its consequences, might mean. For most of us this intimation is first made through our educational experiences, both formal and informal.

It is a paradox of our existence that our autonomy requires the work of other persons. It is given to us and increased by our education; and that requires the learning of language and the transmission of knowledge. Both of these are social activities and public enterprises in which at least two people must engage in an interaction predicated upon the assumption of the mutual tolerance and regard that is only embodied in the institutions of society. Without the one, there cannot be the other; and without that key institution called education, there can be neither. Autonomy is the flower that grows out of seeds planted and tended by heteronomous hands.

All this, at rock bottom, is what taxes are for – and those of us with different levels of resources contribute to the exchequer differentially as a result and in proportion. It is this contribution that grants us licence to access those good things that society wishes to be available for enjoyment by all of its members. The notion of that contribution brings out the mutual beneficence and interdependence of our economic arrangements for funding and running our society and providing appropriate levels and kinds of service for the benefit of all its constituents – including those who, because of history, handicap, weakness or sheer misfortune, may not able to contribute much to it at the moment but still need its support. And this makes society and its various institutions, especially the school, the very place and forum in which individuals can further develop their pattern of preferred life-options, and so increase their autonomy, and in which all sections of the community cooperate mutually for the benefit of the societal whole.

The concept of education as a 'public good' and the responsibility we all share for the mutual benefit of all members of society are fundamental to our theory of 'quality schooling'.

THE REDISTRIBUTION OF POWER AND ADMINISTRATIVE RESPONSIBILITIES: A RECONCEPTUALISATION OF RELATIONSHIPS IN SCHOOL MANAGEMENT

In the drive towards increasing the quality of schooling, education authorities in many countries have been undertaking reforms which have direct implications for the redistribution of power and administrative responsibility among the various levels within the education system, including the school itself (OECD, 1988).

Although many of these reforms have been undertaken under the overt agendum of decentralisation and devolution, the situation is far more complex than this. A closer examination of data and practices suggests that any attempt to elucidate the redistribution of power is likely to encounter and have to deal with a far more complex set of factors and variables than any account based on a one-dimensional conception of changed arrangements along the centralisation–decentralisation continuum would intimate (Chapman, 1990; Chapman and Dunstan, 1990).

In the state system of education in Western Australia, for instance, much of the rhetoric of school reform over the last decade has incorporated a good deal of talk and attention being paid to the idea and importance of the devolution of decision making to the local school site. Like uncertain teenagers, however, governments, policy-makers, administrators and school-based personnel are now beginning to ask 'how far should we go?' For, while current moves towards increased devolution are certainly giving schools increased responsibility in certain areas of decision making, many school-based personnel express concern regarding the loss of the sense of security, support and safety that was previously such a valued feature of the relationships subsisting between schools and the centre. 'Do we', they are asking, 'want or need all that freedom? Is it going to bring about a "better" education for children?' (cf. Vickery et al., 1993).

We are perhaps familiar with the idea of the dutiful servant of the Education Department, embedded in the bureaucratic mentality of nineteenth-century colonialism, and promulgated in schools and school systems in Australia. But in the appointment and promotion of such persons, it has not unfortunately been independence of thought and action, courage, initiative, mutual sharing, reciprocity, or disciplined disagreement that has been encouraged or valued. What was looked for instead was conformity, acceptance and unquestioning service. What was meant to be an escape from the nepotism and favouritism with which many institutions had been ruled and managed in England became in Australia the dry suffocating prison of bureaucracy in which mediocrity flourished and compliance was rewarded.

Over the last two decades policy-makers and administrators have been working steadily to get rid of these ways of thinking and doing. But it has required a considerable change of attitude to recognise that it is problems, and the need for policies to provide their solution, that are the real driving forces behind institutional change. It is now realised that neither ossifying bureaucracy nor the progression of favoured people for favoured places are good guides on the road towards the development of organisations and the fashioning of effective working relationships within them.

What we need now, therefore, is a reconceptualisation of policies relating to educational decision making and the administrative arrangements flowing from them. We need a notion of new sets and patterns of relationship and interactions based on new concepts and categories. Old ideas are no longer useful in describing and explaining the tortuous complexities that are now involved in and operate at the different layers, levels and loci of decision making. The former bureaucratic notions, based on hierarchical positional power within a single 'system', are now outmoded.

At the same time, however, it has become clear that other alternatives, developed in recent years, have proved similarly unhelpful. For example, the idea of a school or 'education centre' being located in, and available as, a 'community resource', with its simple presence and availability for access by voucher-users, so celebrated by Illich (1973) and his like, has been shown to embody some serious or even fatal errors. It fails to do justice to the necessity of continuity in the early years of schooling or to take account of the point that education requires the heteronomous activity of significant others who induct and initiate our young into the heterogenous sets of beliefs, norms and patterns of behaviour valued by society as a whole. Likewise, the corporate vision of education, based on the analogy of networks of business franchises making schools look like fast-food outlets, provides a wholly inappropriate model of the educational enterprise, if we are to accept the idea of education as a 'public good'.

We argue that education is a 'public good', in the sense and to the extent that access and entry into it is something we all have a vital and mutual interest in securing. For, without admittance to such a 'good', our young people will be much less likely to progress rapidly towards those minimal degrees of personal autonomy and civic responsibility by means of which citizens can ensure that the preconditions and mechanisms for community continuation, social justice or indeed any sort of advanced and sophisticated personal development are in place and available to all.

At this point we think it important to make the following observation. At the present time around the world, there is a great deal of talk about devolution, local management of schools, or self-managing schools; and there is much concentration in such discourse on independence, individuality, autonomy. To an extent this is good: autonomy is perhaps the key feature in any developed and self-conscious awareness of an individual's or institution's sense of identity and their own worth. But it would be a great mistake — indeed it would be a fallacy — to allow this debate on changed administrative structures and relationships in education to be suborned to the discourse of 'the market' and of economic rationalism, with its emphasis on the individual and complete freedom of choice, as if to imply that schools, and the individuals within them, were in some way self-contained and hermetically-sealed units, absolutely separate and free from all other-regarding considerations or obligations. Predilection for independence and autonomy does not entail the introduction of the 'market' approach in education.

We want to argue instead that the concept of education as a public good provides a decisive refutation of that concept of educational partition: we argue that, in a public system of education, there can be no such thing as a completely autonomous or independent self-governing school. To be sure, a certain amount of school autonomy may be readily countenanced and extended in certain areas of decision making. It is a paradox, however, that autonomy can only be rendered intelligible and made to work within the confines of a relationship with the system and the community based on a mutuality of benefit and regard.

Schools conceived thus enjoy a mutual relationship with the system and the community of which they are a part. The system ensures the basic protection of rights for all students; at the same time schools enjoy a mutual relationship with the community in which parents and other significant groups are able to have their voices heard in regard to matters of fundamental value and goals. There is also a mutual relationship within the school among school-based personnel, as decision making is shared, owned and supported. In return the school enjoys a greater degree of autonomy in the selection of community-related goals and the fitting of resources to meet those goals; it also enjoys a greater sense of its own standing and importance in providing community leadership, in promoting the value of education among all its stakeholders, and in this way promoting the idea of the learning community and the values of life-long education.

In sum, the model of relationships between school, system and community should mirror those of the strong, robust autonomous individual in mutual relationship with the society of which he/she is a part – our very goal in the provision of quality schooling.

AUTONOMY AND MUTUALITY: NEW PATTERNS OF RELATIONSHIP FOR SELF-MANAGING SCHOOLS

The concepts of autonomy and mutuality, and the epistemological and moral commitments presupposed and entailed by them, have emerged as key values in our research in and development of our theory of quality schooling. They have done so in two major respects: one, in respect of the character and dispositions of the human beings who emerge from their experiences in and of quality schools, and with their attainments gained in and from their life and work within them. The other concerns the nature of the institutions that we call schools, and their relationships with the systems and environments of which they are a part, including other educating institutions, such as universities and the whole tertiary education sector, and with the business and employment sectors of all kinds.

Arising from all the foregoing, we may now set out a set of final comments, suggestions and advice, that we believe will establish an Agenda for those whose main concern is the pursuit of the goals of quality schooling.

AGENDA FOR REFORM

Conceptions of management for quality schooling

First, we have come to certain conclusions about the ways and means by which quality schooling might be engendered and a set of agenda for its production set up. We wish to suggest that there is a new set of agenda for research and development in quality schooling, based upon a new conception of management. This view emanates from, and is a reflection of, our broad acceptance of the theory of knowledge acquisition proposed by the philosopher Karl Popper (1949, 1972), and this leads to the view we take of the functioning of schools as learning institutions composed of individuals in mutual interaction with each other. Policy and administration at the system level and leadership in management at the school level are, we believe, instances of Popperian evolutionary epistemology in action. They are manifestations of problem-solving as the gradual, piecemeal and provisional increase of knowledge and understanding in any large undertaking, the number, scale and complexities of the operations and procedures of which render them constantly liable to error. It is for this reason that those charged with the responsibility of managing and directing them must always regard them as open to inspection, evaluation, the detection of error, and correction.

Our conception of management stands, then, as a process of problem-solving. This is consistent with the view we take of schools as 'adaptive learning environments' (Evers, 1990) committed to the communication of knowledge and the exchange of views through the transmission of knowledge and the powers of rational argument. Inherent in this view of organisations and management is the value attached to the integration of substance and process, rather than to their separation or artificial holding apart (Zaleznek, 1989).

We contrast this view with that notion of educational management which holds to the notion of a necessary dichotomy between substance and process; this has given rise to the assumption of a distinction between academic work, teaching and learning on the one hand, and educational administration on the other, that has become hardened and coercive in the conception, construction and administration of educational institutions. We also contrast it with the view of management embedded in the notion of a hierarchical organisation exhibiting a structure of superordinate and subordinate authority relations. This is a model that, as Evers remarks (1990), is claimed to promote consistency and uniformity in the implementation and transmission of centrally-produced decisions, and in the communication and diffusion of directives, but which in fact frequently fails signally to do either.

We believe that this is so because there are two things wrong with this model. First, it requires unquestioning acceptance of the cognitive authority of centrally-made decisions, plans and directives. In contrast, we contend that the whole point of Popperian epistemology is to stress 'the fallibility and uncertainty of centrally dictated authority claims' (Evers, 1990). Second, such a notion also militates against the vital importance in public institutions predicated upon the 'open society' of knowledge, of a sense of shared ownership of decision making and the necessity of bringing all our cognitive resources to bear in the drive towards error-elimination in our various hypotheses to deal with intellectual, academic and organisational problems (cf. Popper, 1945).

On these grounds we argue that Popper's notion of evolutionary epistemology and his critical and cautious approach to problem-solving provides the proper safeguard against the authoritarianism and hierarchism of what we maintain are inappropriate and unsound approaches to school and system administration. Given a significant degree of collegial agreement in schools and school systems about the ways in which such public goods as the acquisition of knowledge and the growth of understanding can be provided for, managed and evaluated, along with all the additional epistemological advantages of adaptive learning strategies employed in the transmission and checking of knowledge, we believe that school communities will make efficient and effective decisions through the democratic processes of open, accountable and participative decision making.

Consistent with this approach, our notion of the role of school principals and leaders generally is that they concentrate on giving academic leadership in a joint endeavour, doing so by a commitment to management as evolutionary problem-solving. But, to be successful, this approach must be employed in a process of collegial collaboration and mutual assistance in the identification of problems, the formulation of trial solutions to them, the joint involvement in the implementation of those solutions, and the commitment to the detection and correction of errors, in the interests of improving the quality of schooling. Only in this way, we believe, can we function effectively in the leadership and management of learning institutions, so as to improve our decision-making processes and the quality, utility and value of the decisions that we thereby reach.

The school principal and new patterns of relationship for self-managing schools

In respect to institutional management of a school or a department, we need to stress the role of a school administrator as a facilitator of interactions among a range of school partners and as a 'bridge' or as a conduit in a devolved structure. We need also to emphasise the dual accountability of that manager, both to the system and the School Council on the one hand, but also to the Heads of Department and the members of staff located within the school on the other. Furthermore, in an educational institution, there is a third, and triadic, kind of accountability:

- to the cognitive imperatives incumbent upon and accepted by any member of the community of knowledge and its subjects – to advance, transmit and sustain knowledge in all its forms and to do so in conformity with the impartial norms and conventions governing warranted assertion, intelligibility and cognitive growth within it
- to the teaching profession and the education service, and to serving their needs and interests
- to the community, and to securing and promoting its welfare.

It is this accountability to the cognitive requirements of a field of study, subject or discipline, and to the moral responsibilities arising from teachers' work in educational institutions devoted to the furtherance of young people's interests and to community welfare generally, that makes any attempt strictly to apply the approaches of business management to the management of a school inappropriate on both conceptual and moral grounds.

We take the view that the role of a school principal or leader will not be that of a chief executive officer in a business enterprise, but rather as one of a guide, reconciler, healer and framer of tentative hypotheses that can be tested to see how far they fulfil the requirements and promote the ends of an institution concerned with human welfare and betterment. For this reason we maintain that, among the main items on the agenda for the school principal or leader will be:

- to develop a culture of learning, principled action and commitment to moral principles based on the values of autonomy and mutuality
- to develop a commitment to excellence, rigour, and the growth of the life of the mind and of the whole human personality
- to encourage assent across the community to the proposition that among a nation's greatest powers and best gifts to the world are the powers of critical and creative imagination, conceived, brought to birth, fostered, extended, promoted and allowed full expression in our institutions of learning and education and more widely in the community
- to empower and encourage staff colleagues and students to pursue their own excellences, at the same time promoting equity, justice and democracy
- to fight vigorously on behalf of the school for funding in the broader arenas of the system and the community
- to negotiate the distribution of resources inside the school in an open, rational, fair and equitable manner
- to trust the abilities of Heads of Departments and others charged with responsibility to manage effectively their own units within the context of a shared commitment to and ownership of the strategic plan of the department and the larger mission of the school – though all this within the overall supervision, guidance and responsibility of the principal and the school council
- to work in partnership with a wide range of constituencies concerned with and for the provision of quality in education.

We are convinced that these are values that principals, schools and the whole learning community should hold dear and attempt to preserve, protect and defend. This is not to say that schools should simply accept and continue to adhere to past policies or practices. Such an approach can only end in stasis or ossification. We would argue, rather, that future growth has to stand on the shoulders of past achievements and this is where values can be dynamic and illuminate those avenues of advance that will prove to be positive, enlarging and upward-looking, rather than negative, diminishing and inward-looking.

It is for this reason that we believe in the advantages accruing to schools from working in partnership with their communities and adopting an evolutionary and gradualist approach to problem-solving and the management of change, based on the values of autonomy and mutuality and the notion of education as a public good.

NOTE

1 This chapter draws substantially on the book by D. N. Aspin and J. D. Chapman, with V. Wilkinson, *Quality Schooling: A Pragmatic Approach to Some Current Problems, Trends and Issues*, London: Cassell, 1994.

   Our thanks are due to Messrs Cassell for their kind permission to draw upon that publication.

REFERENCES

Aspin, D. N. and Chapman, J. D., with Wilkinson, V. R. (1994) *Quality Schooling: A Pragmatic Approach to some Problems, Trends and Issues*, London: Cassell.

Ball, S. J. (1990) *Markets, Morality and Equality in Education*, Hillcote Group Paper 5, London: Tufnell Press.

Bridges, D. and McLaughlin, T. H. (eds) (1994) *Education and the Market-Place*, London: Falmer Press.

Chapman, J. D. (ed.) (1990) *School-based Decision-Making and Management*, London: Falmer Press.

Chapman, J. D. and Dunstan, J. F. (eds) (1990) *Democracy and Bureaucracy: Tensions in Public Schooling*, London: Falmer Press.

Chubb, J. E. and Moe, T. (1990) *Politics, Markets and America's Schools*, Washington, DC: Brookings Institution.

Dewey, J. (1938a) *Logic: The Theory of Enquiry*, New York: Holt, Rinehart and Winston.

—— (1938b) *Experience and Education*, New York: Macmillan.

—— (1966) *Democracy and Education*, New York: Free Press.

Evers, C. W. (1990) 'Organisational Learning and Efficiency in the Growth of Knowledge', in J. D. Chapman (1990) *School-based Decision-Making and Management*, London: Falmer Press.

Evers, C. W. *et al.* (1992) 'Ethics and Ethical Theory in Educative Leadership: A Pragmatic and Holistic Approach', in P. A. Duignan and R. J. S. Macpherson (eds), *Educative Leadership*, London: Falmer Press.

Gallie, W. B. (1956) 'Essentially Contested Concepts', *Proceedings of the Aristotelian Society*, 56.

—— (1964) *Philosophy and the Historical Understanding*, London: Chatto and Windus. See Chapter 8.

Grace, G. R. (1994) 'Education is a Public Good: On the Need to Resist the Domination of Educational Science', in D. Bridges and T. H. McLaughlin (eds), *Education and the Market Place*, London: Falmer Press.

Illich, I. (1973) *Deschooling Society*, Harmondsworth: Penguin.

Lakatos, I. (1976) 'Falsification and the Methodology of Scientific Research Programs', in I. Lakatos and A. W. Musgrave (eds), *Criticism and the Growth of Knowledge*, Cambridge: Cambridge University Press.

OECD (1988) *Decentralisation and School Improvement*, Paris: OECD.

—— (1990) *The Effectiveness of Schooling and of Educational Resource Management*, Paris: OECD.

Popper, K. R. (1945) *The Open Society and its Enemies* (vol. 1: Plato; vol. 2: Hegel and Marx), London: Routledge and Kegan Paul.

—— (1949) *The Logic of Scientific Discovery*, London: Hutchinson.

—— (1972) *Objective Knowledge*, Oxford: Clarendon Press.

Quine, W. V. (1953) *From a Logical Point of View*, Cambridge, Mass.: Harvard University Press.

—— (1974) *The Roots of Reference*, LaSalle, Ill.: Open Court.

Smethurst, R. (1995) 'Education: a public or private good?', *RSA Journal*, CXLIII(5465), December, 33–45.

Vickery, R., Williams, I. and Stanley, G. (1993) *Review of Education and Training*, Perth, WA: West Australian Ministry of Education.

Whitty, G. and Edwards, T. (1992) 'School Choice Policies in Britain and the U.S.A.: Their Origins and Significance', paper presented at the *Annual Meeting of AERA*, San Francisco.

Wittgenstein, L. (1953) *Philosophical Investigations*, trans. G. E. M. Anscombe, Oxford: Blackwell.

—— (1958) *The Blue and Brown Books*, Oxford: Blackwell (p. 87; cf. pp.17, 20, 125).

Zaleznek, A. (1989) *The Managerial Mystique*, San Francisco: Harper and Row.

Part II

Assuring quality in schools and school systems

Chapter 5

Inspection and school improvement in England and Wales
National contexts and local realities

Kathryn Riley and David Rowles

INTRODUCTION: THE MOVE TO NATIONAL INSPECTION

Over recent years, the terms 'effectiveness' and 'standards' have entered the lexicon of education terms. Within England and Wales, external inspection has become one of the tools for ensuring that national standards of effectiveness are achieved. However, the users' education dictionary also includes 'success criteria', 'school review', 'self-evaluation' and 'the creation of a learning organisation', terms which draw on very different assumptions and strategies. The new education language (which has international currency) now embraces two traditions, each with different antecedents and modes of operation, yet each aiming to achieve school improvement. The context for this chapter is the uneasy tension between those two traditions: one based on inspection (and the use of external criteria to judge the effectiveness of a school); and the other rooted within the school itself (and focused on its capacity to engage in a process of self-reflection and review).

Over a period of years, central government in the UK has sought to prescribe quality through the introduction of the national curriculum, standard assessment tasks and the publication of league tables on examination performance. In the new framework set by central government, quality was to be judged against set standards with responsibility for performance placed directly at the gate of individual schools. Schools were now accountable to the market. Quality, standards and the measurement of performance became central elements of a national government strategy aimed at ensuring compliance to national goals (Kogan, 1993; Riley, 1993). For a complex range of political and historical reasons, the education legislation for England and Wales has been different from that for Scotland and Northern Ireland. This chapter concentrates on the impact of legislation upon England and Wales.

United Kingdom concerns about standards emerged in the mid-1970s and were first expressed by a Labour Prime Minister, James Callaghan, in 1976, in a now-famous speech made at Ruskin College. Callaghan argued that state education had failed to respond to technological change and that high investment in education had not yielded commensurate economic gains: a view shared by leaders of many other industrialised countries. But it was the election of a Conservative government in 1979, led by Margaret Thatcher, which heralded major social, economic and political changes. Education moved into the central political arena in the third Thatcher term of government, with the introduction of the 1988 Education Reform Act.

The 1988 Education Act was a watershed in legislation. It aimed to change the funding, organisation and administration of education. A national curriculum and national testing were introduced, and schools, colleges and local authorities were propelled into a major – and ongoing – programme of educational reform. The Act was part of a complex web of legislative changes designed to reduce public expenditure, introduce greater competition and choice, and challenge producer and professional interests.

Underpinning the Act was a market philosophy based on new forms of consumerism which emphasised individual rights. Local management of schools was introduced and schools were given responsibility for school budgets through their governing bodies. Parents were also given the oppor- tunity to vote to take their school out of local authority control and to acquire grant-maintained status (direct funding from central government and a larger degree of autonomy). The 'opt-out' debate became politically charged: fuelled by financial settlements which benefited grant-maintained schools at the expense of schools which had stayed beneath the local authority umbrella.

The 1988 Act aimed to increase parental choice, but the right to choose a school became, in reality, the right to state a preference and the right to appeal if that preference were not satisfied. It was a guarantee of process rather than of outcome and one which increasingly benefited those with the 'know-how' to choose 'wisely' in the new education market place (Riley, 1994a). Egalitarian notions about education which prevailed in the 1970s and early 1980s were firmly rejected in favour of greater individualism (Riley, 1994b). Speaking in the debate leading up to the introduction of the 1988 Education Act, Conservative Member of Parliament Norman Tebbit – an acolyte of Mrs Thatcher – argued this point in the following terms.

> The Bill extends choice and responsibility. Some will choose badly, or irresponsibly, but that cannot and must not be used as an excuse to deny choice and responsibility to the great majority.
>
> (Hansard, 1987)

Throughout the Thatcher years, local government (whose responsibilities included the administration of the local education system) became a political battleground. Government ministers viewed local government with suspi- cion: a rival elected power base which, in their view, was producer-dominated and which had failed to make the improvement of education quality a central concern. The locus of local education authorities

(LEAs) to allocate resources, determine quality standards, work with schools to assess performance, or support school improvement was challenged.

The issues of quality and accountability were reinforced by the Education Schools Act 1992 and the introduction of a new school inspection system. The Act created the Office for Standards in Education (OFSTED), which absorbed a drastically reduced Her Majesty's Inspectorate (HMI). A new semi-privatised inspection system, with a four-year cycle of school inspection, was introduced, in which registered inspectors tendered for inspection contracts.[1] A 'claw-back' by central government of 50 per cent of LEA spending on inspection and advice funded the new scheme, which began in September 1993. Schools which, as a result of OFSTED inspection, were 'considered to be at risk' would be given a period of time to take appropriate action but, if progress was not made, 'failing' schools would be taken over by an Education Association appointed by central government. The creation of the new inspection framework – alongside standard assessments tasks (SATs) linked to the national curriculum, and the publication of league tables of examination results – completed the new national evaluation system.

The impact on the ground

Not surprisingly, the impact of the OFSTED framework has been the focus of much inquiry. A study conducted in 1993 on the changing role of the LEA (within the context of OFSTED) broadly asked the question: 'Is quality still the business of the LEA?' (Riley, 1994c).[2] It sought to examine how far LEA approaches to quality were within a broad school self-improvement or development framework, or how far the new external inspection procedures had created alternative models. It also examined the nature of the changing relationship between schools and LEAs. The study drew on a wide range of source documentation, and on interviews with headteachers and local authority officers in seven LEAs (two county councils and five metropolitan authorities or boroughs), and with senior staff from OFSTED, from the Association of Metropolitan Authorities, the Department for Education and a range of new agencies which had emerged to carry out inspection.

In response to the question, 'Is quality still the business of the LEA?', the overwhelming weight of opinion (with the exception of one LEA) was that public authorities needed to be in the business of quality: 'Quality is what we're about. If we're not in the business of quality, we might as well pack up and go home.' There were two essential elements to this definition. Quality was about ensuring that public money was spent wisely, but it was also about ensuring that school improvement took place. Both schools and LEAs agreed that quality could not be left to schools alone, nor to distant government mandarins.

Government officials interviewed in the study suggested that whether

LEAs had a role was dependent on how the LEAs themselves reviewed their activities and whether they developed a partnership with schools and governors. 'Over the last two to three years LEAs have made experiential gains. The system is now responding to how the Government perceives quality. The schools as purchasers may change the LEA role.' They also suggested that LEAs were in a unique position to pursue quality, given the privilege they enjoyed of easy and direct access to classrooms and schools on a regular basis. Management training was a particular area in which LEAs had much to offer and schools much to learn. There were both opportunities and threats for the LEA: 'Ideally you need a local system to support schools, one that understands the local context, that will respond to local in-service needs and will ensure value for money. . . . [But] If the LEA doesn't take on that role, other systems will develop.'

From the LEA's perspective, the combination of the new OFSTED framework, reduced funding, local management of schools and the presence of the grant-maintained sector had created the impetus for major changes at the local level. LEAs were struggling to establish a relationship with schools based on partnership rather than paternalism. Headteachers were largely supportive of this new role, but argued that it could only be based on merit and not on right. LEAs could not lead without the consent of schools.

In the new power realignments, headteachers were beginning to exert their influence – in one authority to get the LEA to play a more proactive role than in the past; in another to provide educational leadership on the national curriculum; and in another to carry out small research studies. In the view of headteachers, remaining in the LEA had been a positive decision but one from which they expected to reap some rewards. Access to school improvement projects, for example, should be offered to schools who had chosen to stay beneath the LEA umbrella rather than to grant-maintained schools which had already taken more than their share of the local educational cake.

The research identified some differences between the perceptions of primary and secondary headteachers. Primary headteachers were more likely to see their peers in neighbouring schools as collaborators, whereas secondary heads frequently saw them as competitors. Primary headteachers looked to the LEA for support, particularly on management issues. Secondary heads valued inspection and targeted information about school and pupil performance, but were less keen on LEA advisory services and more likely to consider purchasing those services from a range of providers which included the LEA: 'To sustain quality you need external validation but you also need to go out and bring that back within the context of the school. LEAs can provide that validation but so can other organisations.'

Both headteachers and LEA officers in the study were united in their view that, for school improvement to take place, schools had to break away from the isolation to which the new competitive environment drove them. The

LEAs' role was to help reduce this isolation. 'No school should be left to monitor on its own, although ultimately they are responsible for improvement.'

Local authority approaches to quality

Findings from the study suggested that there were four approaches to quality (which broadly described the activities of the LEAs studied) and which could be categorised as a continuum ranging from interventionist, interactive and responsive, through to non-interventionist. LEAs within the study broadly fell under one of the four constructs:

- interventionist (the LEA as a major player in quality, intervening when requested and when it saw fit)
- interactive (a quality framework which derived through the interaction between the LEA and schools)
- responsive (the LEA was unsure about its new role but responded to new demands from schools)
- non-interventionist (the LEA concluded that it no longer had a role in quality).

The interventionist, interactive and responsive LEAs saw quality as their business: a business which they now shared with schools. For the non-interventionist LEA, quality was the business of central government and of schools. The four broadly different approaches (summarised in Fig. 5.1) reflected historical traditions and perspectives, the political administration, and were also the product of changing conditions and new power relationships.

The interventionist LEA

Local democratic accountability was a strong element of the purposes of the interventionist LEA. Whether it saw itself politically on the right or the left, its past activities had been characterised by a strong quality-control thrust (with checks to ensure that pupils had achieved expected quality standards). Quality control had given way to quality assurance (ways of assuring that the processes were in place to ensure that a quality learning experience was achieved). The interventionist LEA saw itself as the defender of children's rights in its locality.

> My job is to do what national government can't do, to seize the moment, to be the fly on the wall. . . . Only Government can be daft enough to think that a school can't go off the rails in between its flimsy four yearly inspection programme. It only takes six months for a school to go downhill.

INTERVENTIONIST	INTERACTIVE	RESPONSIVE	NON-INTERVENTIONIST
VALUE			
'The LEA is the last defender of children's rights in the locality.'	'It is the quality of our educational leadership that will provide our raison d'etre.'	'If schools want it we'll try and set a direction, if not a vision.'	'The Framework set by national politicians.'
EMPHASISE NEEDS OF			
Pupil	Teacher	Teacher/parent	Parent
ROLE OF SCHOOL			
Self developing, validated by external inspection	Self-developing	Semi-autonomous	Autonomous
NATURE OF PARTNERSHIP			
Priorities tested out with heads	Encourage schools to join the LEA club	Develop 'wise' customers	Market forces
ACTIVITIES			
Monitoring, evaluation, developmental	Developmental	By negotiation, but should provide overview. Activities largely organised in quasi-business units	Monitoring
Examples of activities			
Assigned inspection visits. Provision of new educational leadership e.g. curriculum	Support schools in what they have done. Joint projects on e.g. school effectiveness	Customer surveys	Quantitative indicators

Figure 5.1 LEA role in quality

School self-development was encouraged, but within a framework of a continued LEA inspection programme and systematic monitoring and evaluation. The LEA sought to develop 'the thinking school'. In the new relationship between schools and the LEA, the LEA constantly tested its approaches to quality with its headteachers but did not hesitate to intervene when it saw that a school was failing. One LEA inspection report (which went to an inspection panel which included elected members) described a failing primary school as: 'Inefficiently managed, with poor communication, delegation and organisational systems.' A primary head who took over that school described the strong leadership role of the LEA in the following terms:

> The local authority emphasises quality for children. They treat us as professionals and we negotiate what we want. . . . Quality is still the business of the LEA. Their job is to make sure that we don't get stuck in our schools, that we have a wider vision. . . . I took over a school that was failing. The head wouldn't admit that there were problems. He failed to recognise the weak teachers. The situation escalated and it was the strong intervention of the LEA which changed things. Since taking over they've given me every kind of support and they do not pull their punches.

The LEA offered a comprehensive range of inspection and advice activities and was critical of the continued assertion by central government that 'LEAs do not act in good faith. . . . The Government is still too caught up with what some LEAs have failed to do in the past, rather than what most of them are doing now.' It analysed and published local and national test information; set local and school targets for achievement; worked with schools to monitor whole-school development plans, looking at their relationship to local-authority-wide budgetary policies and budgetary processes. The interventionist LEA saw a critical element of its role as trying to counter the cynicism which existed in many schools about testing and evaluation and which got in the way of quality. A fundamental element of this strategy was the creation of a local vision about education – sustained by innovation – which would break down the isolation of schools.

The interactive LEA

The interactive LEA was determined to improve schools by enhancing and developing the capabilities of staff. It saw schools as being self-developing but not always able to evaluate what they had done on their own, or to know that they had achieved their objectives. A focus of the LEA's activities was helping schools to develop methods of measuring improvement. It was in this way that the LEA conceptualised its educational leadership. 'We are, above all, an education authority and it is the quality of our education leadership that will ultimately provide our *raison d'être*.'

The success of the LEA's strategy was dependent on fostering good relationships and providing a critical but supportive forum in which schools could evaluate their progress. The interactive LEA was strongly committed to encouraging all schools to 'belong to the (local authority) club', membership of which offered strong guarantees of quality assurance in schools.

Inspection remained part of the LEA's role but as part of a wider strategy to evaluate effectiveness. The LEA aimed to bring together the outcomes from inspection with realistic and situational specific information, and to feed this back to schools. School evaluation was carried out jointly by the LEA and schools, and drew on criteria which had been developed in partnership. The interactive relationship between the LEA and its schools was critical, and it was through this that a shared vision could be created. 'The point about the service we provide is that it is specific, local and valued. . . . The relationship between schools and the LEA is good, but it mustn't be cosy.'

The services provided by the interactive LEA were valued by its headteachers: 'We haven't the time to shop about but we have a broad measure of trust in our local services.' 'They provide local legitimacy and a local voice . . . but it's not just the product, it's the process.'

There was a close interaction between the LEA and its schools and, because of this, the LEA was able to reflect on the nature of the new relationship and to look at how this might be improved in the future.

> The quality of communication is still an issue. We're getting much better at the product, for example, how to deliver a large in-service programme, although we have still to work at the process. We have relied heavily on monitoring and evaluation in the past and not enough on research. We need to move in that direction in the future.

The responsive LEA

The responsive LEA had taken a more distant and uncertain role in quality in the past, through a combination of diminishing resources and the presence of a number of opted-out schools. According to both LEA and headteacher respondents:

> For the last few years we've experienced uncertainty and demoralisation, the LEA couldn't provide leadership and that was part of the trigger to schools to opt out. The situation is now changing, we're seriously considered and we're choosy about what we want.

However, the responsive LEA was also experiencing change, and headteachers were beginning to exert their influence and to demand a more proactive role on quality from the LEA. For example, a large group of primary heads in one local authority with a high number of opted-out schools expressed their collective views in a letter to the local newspaper, making a positive assertion about the role of the LEA and emphasising the importance of local education leadership linked to accountability:

> There is a strong sense of belonging which is an essential element in providing a high quality service. . . . Local accountability is an essential part of community education . . . The professionals we rely on have a strong sense of commitment to us which would go if the service was sold off. Heads, staff and governors should have access to locally coordinated induction, development and on-going support which has a local focus based on local and national initiatives.

The responsive LEA was struggling to provide a vision and to offer direction to schools – if that was what schools wanted – and was having to deal with the criticism from schools that it had been reactive rather than proactive in the past. In managing the tensions in the current situation, it was seeking (with varying degrees of certainty) to shape schools by challenging their isolation; offering a perspective on quality that reflected local purposes; and providing information to enable them to benchmark their progress. Research, analysis and customer surveys were frequently part of this strategy.

> In the past our approach has been driven by inspection and monitoring. We're now more focussed on quality improvement . . . it's a much more developmental role.

The authority was also grappling with the duality of its role as a regulator of services provided by schools (such as special needs provision) and as a provider of other services for sale to schools (such as inspection for pre-OFSTED purposes).

> The tension which characterises the LEA internally is the need to have a business relationship with schools – to sell services – and the fundamental responsibility that we have to secure proper provision.

The responsive LEA saw its quality role as 'monitoring the overall health of schools through a total quality assurance approach'. One LEA had established an inner quality team to report to the Director of Education on a regular basis about quality issues. It had abandoned inspection and had set up a quasi-business unit to provide advice, undertake surveys and contextualise information. Its activities were aimed at supporting teaching and learning, and effective school organisation and management. The LEA's role was to interpret the needs of schools; the impact of new legislation; and the findings from research. It aimed to provide an overview and facilitate networking and the exchange of information. Schools needed to be curriculum leaders, 'wise customers' in the new entrepreneurial environment but protected from the worst excesses of the market.

Headteachers wanted more, rather than less, services from the responsive LEA, but recognised with resigned regret that the LEA needed to sell its services across local authority borders to keep them viable. Heads did not want to spend their time bartering for services: 'I already spend too much of my time monitoring contracts. I want a local agency that I know and can trust providing me with the services that I need.' Schools saw a 'new partnership with the LEA emerging', but the elements of that new partnership were still in the melting pot.

> In the past we didn't know where the influence was, or how money was spent. The grip that members had on education was too tight. That's all changed. The system's more accountable, but it's also more vulnerable and that's a problem. In my view the Government has deliberately undermined the education changes . . . that's where we need the expertise of the LEA. As heads we have to take responsibility as active learners, ultimately we're responsible for the school, but the LEA can help us manage it. We need locally managed support agencies.
>
> There's a big river now between LEAs and schools, but the LEA needs to send things over by bridge.

The non-interventionist LEA

The non-interventionist LEA had put its services out into the marketplace some time ago. It had withdrawn its own inspection services, as elected members thought objectivity could only be provided by inspection which was external to the authority. It argued that the quality framework set by central government and the inspection arrangements through OFSTED would largely ensure that standards were maintained. Schools were seen as autonomous, responsible for their own successes and failures and, as the LEA had made the decision to maximise the devolution of resources to schools, quality became the direct responsibility of schools.

The role of the LEA in quality was limited to developing key indicators which could throw contextual light on specific areas of performance or expenditure. National indicators on standard assessment tasks, public examinations and truancy were to be used as the major indicators of school performance. This information would also be made available, as widely as possible, to parents. The LEA no longer retained a capacity to support development work in schools, or to support an action programme following an OFSTED inspection. This was seen as the responsibility of the autonomous schools themselves.

Critics were concerned that the creation of the non-interventionist LEA would leave schools vulnerable to future problems.

> The problem about the new system is that schools can easily go adrift without the support of a semi-detached visitor. . . . Schools know very little about guaranteeing quality, it's partly our fault that we haven't trained them to do this.

CHANGES SINCE 1993: MOVEMENT ALONG THE CONTINUUM

A follow-up study was conducted in 1995 to elicit changing trends within LEAs, variations between LEAs and to illustrate changes over time (Riley *et al.*, 1995). The study drew on interviews with headteachers, LEA officers, school governors and councillors in seven local authorities, and concluded that there had been considerable movement along the continuum described in the 1993 study. Those LEAs which had been in the strictly non-interventionist mode had moved towards a degree of involvement and there was a general trend towards greater proactivity on quality on the part of local authorities.

In the case of one local authority, movement had been from being a non-interventionist LEA to one which took an interactive role (in relation to LEA schools) and a responsive role (in relation to grant-maintained schools). Another LEA, which described itself in 1993 as having 'moved so far to non-intervention that [it] had fallen off the continuum', now saw itself as being firmly on the continuum and taking a proactive and planned role. 'The LEA now has a quality drive which is part of a five year agenda.' This dramatic change had come about through a combination of change of political leadership – although not party control – and the appointment of a new officer core. Those LEAs which had been strongly interventionist (in a way that headteachers and governors considered to be too heavy-handed) still remained largely interventionist but were keen to negotiate elements of their intervention.

The general movement along the continuum had largely been in the following direction:

Interventionist >Interactive < Responsive < non-interventionist <

The shift: general movement towards greater proactivity on quality with some negotiation about the nature and level of intervention.

Movement along the continuum towards greater proactivity does not represent an increase in levels of services but a change in attitude or approach and a targeting of limited resources towards specific activities. Many LEAs appear to have created clearer school-based goals for themselves and have gained some confidence in the contribution they can make to school improvement – developments welcomed by schools. There was also a growing awareness that different approaches have to be adopted to meet different circumstance and activities and that LEAs need, for example, to be 'responsive' to community development initiatives but 'interventionist' on special needs, or when dealing with a 'failing' school. Increasingly, governors and headteachers want the LEA to retain an interventionist role as a 'safety net', although the nature of that intervention remains unclear.

We are therefore faced with an interesting irony. On the one hand, central government has introduced a centralised inspection system and reduced the financial and organisational capacity for LEAs to be involved in school improvement. On the other hand, LEAs are – with the willing consent of schools – taking a more proactive role in quality. The interesting question is: how has this come about?

THE OFSTED INSPECTION MODEL[3]

Prior to OFSTED, inspections had been carried out locally by LEAs and nationally by HMIs (Her Majesty's Inspectorate). Locally, a wide range of patterns and procedures had existed. Nationally, schools could anticipate a full inspection every twenty-five years.

When the new model was introduced, OFSTED claimed that it would give 'priority to promoting inspection of the highest possible quality. Only in this way can schools be offered sound evaluation to use as a basis for improvement.' The *framework* for the inspection document and its accompanying handbook were widely welcomed by educational professionals as valuable and informative guidelines. There was general acceptance that the new model provided clear criteria and procedures; judgements made would be firmly based on evidence gathered and cited; the main thrust would be on classroom observation; the inspection would be fully comprehensive and include all aspects of a school's organisation and performance; inspectors would work to a clearly established code of practice; and the local community would be involved both in the gathering of information and the dissemination of the report.

However, the idea of a full and extensive review, involving (at secondary level) large teams of specialist inspectors considering in detail all aspects of the educational provision, in order to make judgements which would become public, elicited a range of responses. Given the complexities and the newness of the system, OFSTED was aware of the scrutiny to which its procedures would be exposed. During the first term, all inspection teams were closely monitored by HMI, and detailed feedback was obtained from a representative sample of headteachers whose schools had been inspected. A report published in the Spring of 1994 (by Coopers and Lybrand) testified to the 'efficiency and effectiveness' of the vast majority of inspections carried out in the Autumn term of 1993 but, as the inspection process became more widely experienced, views began to crystallise.

OFSTED's own view was that its findings and reports would establish a baseline for schools, and responsibility for moving forward would be fully in the hands of the governing body and senior management team. Headteachers responded in differing ways as these two quotes show (TES, 1994):

'The nature of inspection with its underlying purpose is not developmental. Judgements delivered with limited sensitivity and with no recourse to challenge can hurt and humiliate. The dangers are obvious.

The temptation to play it safe, to avoid drawing attention to weak points, to cover up local difficulties is great'.

'The new inspection system can be productive if approached in a constructive way. The framework is a useful and helpful statement of good practice and particularly strong on criteria for evaluation. At this school . . . we have modified our existing performance indicators in the light of the framework and have set out to review and evaluate every aspect of our performance. The result has been improvements of many aspects of the school. If preparation for inspection is incorporated into a schools development plan it provides both extra motivation and a clearer focus. The overall aim has to be to move the school forward and create a better school: a good inspection report is then just an extra bonus'.

These conflicting opinions were reflected elsewhere: 'The new inspection system is a great opportunity for schools' (Secondary Heads Association); and 'If the main aim is to improve schools, the government would do better to spread the money over four years for schools to employ registered consultants. . . . The imposition of such expensive procedures diverts energy and resources from imaginative approaches' (Registered Inspector).

The opinion of the vast majority of headteachers was that the OFSTED report and findings did not usually inform them on matters about which they were unaware but had given helpful precision and sharpness, adding a confirmatory element. From the headteacher's perspective, other benefits included the following:

- The framework and handbook had proved to be extremely useful documents to help schools undertake their own review and drive towards school improvement. The sections on the quality of learning and teaching had been particularly helpful.
- The rare chance to have a full and detailed external audit (or, as a head described it, 'an enforced consultancy') had been extremely informative and beneficial. The need to prepare for rigorous inspection procedures had promoted a similarly rigorous and systematic approach within schools.
- The professionalism and the focused judgements of the inspection teams and Registered Inspectors (who led the teams) were welcomed.
- An impending inspection provided schools with the impetus to 'spring clean' their policies and schemes of work and to explore the link between stated policy and current practice.
- The fact that the inspections involved such a thorough and structured review of classroom practice was also widely welcomed. Inspectors spent at least 60 per cent of their time in school observing lessons, and most secondary school teachers were seen two or three times.
- The governors' action plan (required by OFSTED as a follow-up to the main findings and key issues of the report) was based on a clear list of

identified priorities and provided a basis for the school development plan for the next three years or so. It was a particularly useful lever to operate in schools or departments reluctant to change.

However, an equal number of concerns were expressed by headteachers about the new model:

- The judgements made about schools were seen as being too broad and too tightly tied to rigid criteria, with little heed being paid to the individual school context, or the progress that the school had made in the past few years starting from a low baseline.
- The emphasis on evaluation without advice was often questioned and the lack of feedback to individual teachers was regretted. In many instances there had been no real professional dialogue and little chance to question interpretations. Heads claimed that change was less likely to happen if conclusions were not explained or tested out for accuracy.
- Several heads and senior managers stressed that the OFSTED model was over-reliant on two or three days of observation, and that this snapshot took relatively little note of previous work. The value of grading lessons was also challenged, involving – as it must – a strong subjective element. Moreover, critics asked how significant was an overall judgement such as '67 per cent of all lessons seen were found to be satisfactory'? Other heads felt that, by attempting to focus on the measurable outcomes, inspectors often ignored processes.
- Inspection reports were subjected to substantial criticism, usually for language which was thought to be bland or to contain too many references to the word 'satisfactory' without any clear indication of its import.
- There was a strong consensus that there had been an over-emphasis on the amount of documentation to be produced by schools and that this might have rendered the inspection something of a cosmetic exercise.

The diversity of views about OFSTED was reflected in the final judgements that heads made about the new inspection. For some, the inspection process (compared by one head to a typical white-knuckle ride – 'expensive, alarming, sometimes exhilarating') had been a welcome window of opportunity, for others, it was an exhausting experience which in some cases led to a feeling of anti-climax and loss of momentum. As one head put it: 'OFSTED has dominated everything in the school for a whole year and stifled all the developments.'

Inspection and school improvement: an assessment of the changes

What, therefore, has been the impact of the new OFSTED system, and how are the system and perspectives on school improvement likely to change in the future?

Our assessment to date indicates a system in transition, although not in turmoil, and the beginnings of a renaissance in thinking about school quality. The new quality framework set by the UK Government has undoubtedly forced schools to articulate their quality needs, and LEAs to be clearer about their quality role. Aspects of the new OFSTED inspection have been a useful lever in those schools which have been resistant to change. There is clear evidence that it has made a marked effect on the thinking, aspirations, apprehensions and planning of schools.

OFSTED did attempt to create a fair, consistent process by carefully monitoring the first year of inspections. A number of significant changes have been made to the original model, including two reviewed versions of the framework and handbook. Further recommendations have been made and additional changes and amendments have been planned, as the OFSTED inspection model – essentially secondary-based in concept – is applied to more primary and special schools. Amended models of the framework will in future permit a phase-related approach, and OFSTED claims to have heeded other criticisms in attempting to make a very burdensome exercise more manageable for inspection teams, and more worthwhile for schools, by concentrating on strategies for improvement and development.

Apart from the introduction of a phase-related approach, the main differences in the new approach will centre on the following:

1 An increased focus on the four main strands of inspection, i.e.:
    standards of achievement;
    quality of education;
    efficient use of resources;
    spiritual, moral, cultural and social development.

2 Evaluation criteria have been reformulated and there will be a greater focus on benchmarks and standards of good practice. In order to ensure that the essence of an individual school is captured, only 'significant' features, strengths and weaknesses will be reported.

3 The section on 'Standards of Achievement' has been overhauled and will be re-titled 'Attainment and Progress'. Judgements about attainment will be based on national standards and expectations of what children know, understand and can do, in relation to national curriculum requirements. An important inclusion will be a reference to pupil progress in relation to prior attainment.

4 There will be increased importance attached to pupil attainment in the core subjects of mathematics, science and English. Variations in the progress of different groups of pupils will be highlighted.

5 Increased attention will be paid to equal opportunities and special educational needs although, controversially, these will no longer be treated as discrete areas.

6 There will no longer be a separate section on the 'Quality of Learning',

but there will be a new emphasis on the quality and effectiveness of the teaching, children's response to it, their attainment and progress.

It is impossible, of course, to predict whether, in addition to these specific changes, there will also be alterations to the spirit and nature of the inspection process – perhaps the greatest area of criticism. The OFSTED experiment has a number of inherent tensions. A whole school audit is generally accepted as a useful starting point for school improvement (and the extremely thorough OFSTED procedures can potentially provide the best review the school has ever had). However, OFSTED is only one of several evaluative mechanisms – and perhaps one that has become unduly over-emphasised. Effective evaluation needs to be comprehensive, regular and ongoing, not just (at best) something that occurs every four years, and yet one of the effects of OFSTED has been to reduce the capacity of LEAs to provide this support[4]. There has also been considerable evidence to suggest that, in many instances, change and improvement have been the result of school or LEA reviews carried out in preparation for inspection, rather than the result of the OFSTED experience itself.

Nevertheless, the inspection reports – with their clear location in the public domain – have had a significant impact. In the new OFSTED climate, schools have been held responsible for the implementation of their post-inspection action plans. (OFSTED only intends to carry out a follow-up exercise with a sample of schools, except where schools are adjudged to have 'failed' the inspection process.) The impact of this decision may well be significant. Schools will need to establish their own procedures for monitoring, review and evaluation. In turn, this may well lead to an agreed and structured form of school self-review as a future alternative to the OFSTED model, which is seen by some as being in danger of crumbling under its own weight.

OFSTED has also had to revise the number of primary schools due for inspection because of the lack of enthusiasm from Registered Inspectors, many of whom have viewed the prospect of involvement in the primary phase as being even more arduous and less financially rewarding than secondary inspection. Moreover, in order to meet even this revised target, OFSTED has had to recruit and train 200 'assistant inspectors' in the form of seconded primary headteachers and deputies.

Some observers – gazing into the crystal ball – have suggested that OFSTED may in future need to restrict its inspection activities solely to the core subjects of the national curriculum; that inspection teams may visit groups of schools rather than concentrating so intensely on individual institutions; or that a second four-year cycle – if ever implemented – might apply only to those schools which were deemed to be unsatisfactory during the first cycle. The future of the OFSTED model is unclear, both for professional and practical reasons, not only because of the difficulty of finding inspection teams for the primary sector but because the spotlight is being increasingly focused on improvement, rather than measurement. Support is also needed for the implementation of the major review of the national curriculum, undertaken by Sir Ron Dearing (AMA, 1993).[5]

These factors combine to emphasise the importance of a local system which can interpret national objectives and provide both support and challenge to schools. LEAs can, and increasingly do, take that role through support for schools in preparing for OFSTED and in evaluation activities designed to ensure effective implementation of the post-inspection action plans. At one time, central government criticised local authorities for providing both inspection and advice, but there is now a growing acceptance that the two can be complementary and that the LEA can provide the bridge between them. Undoubtedly, too, the combination of external pressures and internal reappraisal has stimulated some radical rethinking within LEAs.

The growing diversity between LEAs will also have an impact on the future system for quality and school improvement. While some are still muddling along, waiting for the next bolt from on high, the findings presented in this chapter suggest that others are in the process of creating new and distinctive roles for themselves. New models have begun to emerge that reflect different value choices and priorities and that are based on effective partnerships between schools and LEAs. LEAs are becoming more proactive on quality, but there are still tensions for the future. For LEAs, the tension is between their emerging role as protector of children's rights and their task of supporting schools. From the LEAs' perspective, 'Schools want devolution and freedom but we also have a hard-edged role – to be the champion of parents. There has to be some reality behind the rhetoric.' From the schools' perspective, the challenge remains how to reconcile the freedom which their new autonomy gives them with a recognition that isolation can also stultify growth and development. For both, however, the opportunity exists to retain some of the clarity generated by the national inspection system and harness that to the energy, creativity and capacity for self-renewal which lies within our schools.

ACKNOWLEDGEMENTS

The authors wish to thank the Local Government Management Board, for sponsoring the research on the LEA's role in quality; the National Association of Headteachers, for their support for the seminars; and all those who contributed to the research or seminars, for their cooperation and enthusiasm.

NOTES

1 Despite original Government intentions, it was the LEAs who provided the bulk of the 'independent' OFSTED inspectorate, rather than any of the large private-sector consultants such as Coopers and Lybrand. This created an unusual dual role for local education authorities, particularly when – somewhat surprisingly – they were allowed to inspect schools in their own patch.

2 Specific questions explored in the study were:
 • Is it still feasible for the LEA to play a prominent part in sustaining quality, given its reduced financial capacity and the creation of the new national inspection system?
 • If so, what is that role?
 • How is that role perceived by schools and the LEA?
 • What are the different approaches to quality which have been developed by schools and LEAs?
 • How far is equality part of these approaches?
 • What organisational arrangements have been set up in response to the new framework for inspection?
 • What will be the impact of the new national inspection system?

3 The analysis presented in this section draws on seminars and workshops conducted with over 1,000 headteachers in some thirty locations throughout England during 1993/4. The seminars were part of a major development programme undertaken by the Centre for Educational Management, Roehampton Institute, in partnership with the National Association of Headteachers.

4 For example, the role of the 'attached' inspector for individual schools (prevalent in some shape or form in most LEAs) has now greatly diminished – or simply disappeared – in the new culture. Additionally, a combination of reduced grants from central government and increased devolution of training budgets to schools has reduced the capacity of LEAs to provide support to schools.

5 Throughout 1993/4, national government was unable to gain the cooperation of headteachers for the carrying-out of, and recording of, pupil performance on the standard assessment tasks. Teacher (and parent) opposition focused around the time-consuming nature of the tests, concern about how the results would be used, and overload in the national curriculum. A review body was set up under Sir Ron Dearing to review and reduce the content of the national curriculum and the standard assessment tasks.

REFERENCES

Association of Metropolitan Authorities (AMA) (1993), *The Role of LEAs in the National Curriculum and Assessment*, London: AMA.

Coopers and Lybrand (1994), *Focus on Quality*, Detroit: Coopers and Lybrand.

Hansard (1987) 'Order for the Second Reading of the Education Reform Bill', 1 December: House of Commons.

Kogan, M. (1993) *Models of Education Systems, Theme Paper, Education: A Major Local Authority Service?*, Luton: Local Government Management Board.

Riley, K. A. (1993) *Quality, Effectiveness and Evaluation, Theme Paper, Education: A Major Local Authority Service?*, Luton: Local Government Management Board.

—— (1994a) 'Managing Myths and Magic in Education', inaugural lecture, London: Roehampton Institute.

—— (1994b) *Quality and Equality: Promoting Opportunities in Schools*, London: Cassell.

—— (1994c) *Managing for Quality in an Uncertain Climate*, Luton: Local Government Management Board.

Riley, K. A., Johnson, H. and Rowles, D. (1995) *Managing for Quality in an Uncertain Climate, Report II*, Luton: Local Government Management Board.

Times Educational Supplement (TES) (1994) 15 July.

Chapter 6

Quality assurance for schools
Case study – New South Wales

Peter Cuttance

INTRODUCTION

This chapter discusses the range of approaches to quality improvement and quality assurance that are appropriate to school systems. The terms 'quality improvement' and 'quality assurance' are first discussed in the context of business, industry and government before the relevance of various approaches to quality improvement and quality assurance in school systems are considered.

RELATIONSHIP BETWEEN QUALITY IMPROVEMENT AND QUALITY ASSURANCE

Quality assurance and quality improvement are two different but complementary aspects of the framework for achieving quality outcomes in any organisation.

Quality improvement is part of the overall management function. Key elements in quality improvement include strategic planning, allocation of resources and other systemic activities for quality, such as quality planning, operations and evaluations. Quality assurance includes all the planned and systematic actions necessary to provide adequate confidence that a product or service will satisfy given requirements for quality. Within the quality assurance function there are two types of evaluation activities: these are quality audits and quality reviews.

Quality audits are carried out to verify the conformance and compliance of practice with the standards set out for the procedures and processes, and the evaluation of whether product and design standards are met by the finished product or service. Quality reviews, on the other hand, have a developmental function and involve the examination of a design, product, process or system for the specific purpose of optimising its effectiveness.

APPROACHES TO QUALITY IMPROVEMENT AND QUALITY ASSURANCE IN BUSINESS AND GOVERNMENT

Over the last two decades there has been a growing recognition that the attainment of quality outcomes in any organisation requires a systematic approach to building quality from the broadest parameters of management to the smallest operations involved in producing each individual product or service.

In the post-war period a range of techniques was developed in Japan and packaged by the management consultancy industry in the USA into a number of brands of quality improvement and quality assurance. Most of the derivative brands included a mix of quality improvement and quality assurance strategies.

Quality improvement

The brand name that we associate most readily with quality improvement today is Total Quality Management (TQM). Today the acronym is used to refer to a cluster of techniques and strategies for improving quality in organisations.

Although TQM incorporates mechanisms for 'continuous' or 'incremental' change, these are unlikely to lead to substantial or fundamental improvements or developments of the type that can only come from considering radically different ways of configuring the design of a product, or by re-engineering processes. Quality approaches, of the type described above, focused initially on the manufacturing sector. In recent years there has been a move to apply the concepts and fundamental understandings of these approaches to the service sector. One of the primary manifestations of this has been the development of 'customer service' approaches in large private-sector firms, such as those in the insurance, banking, hospitality and air travel industries.

A recent study by the American Quality Foundation[1] described 945 quality improvement practices in 580 organisations in 4 industries. There were a number of significant findings, the most important of which are that there appears to be very few universally effective quality improvement strategies; and that different strategies are effective at different stages of the performance development cycle of organisations.

The American Quality Foundation study was the first to systematically evaluate the effectiveness of a wide range of quality improvement strategies against bottom-line results: profitability, productivity and quality. It was also the first significant study to systematically question the received wisdom that there is a universally beneficial set of quality improvement strategies for organisations, regardless of the level of their performance.

Quality assurance

A wide range of practices in the private sector are congruent with the generic definition of quality assurance. The accreditation of an organisation's quality systems against standards known internationally as the ISO 9000 range is one strategy of quality assurance. Quality assurance does not require that this type of formal certification process be a part of the means of assuring quality; it is simply that accreditation is one of the practices that is in use as part of the process of assuring quality in some industries.

DIFFERENCES BETWEEN PUBLIC AND PRIVATE SECTOR IN THE FRAMEWORK FOR MANAGING QUALITY

In their highly influential book *Reinventing Government*, Osborne and Gaebler (1993) argue that there are ten principles which describe effective public-sector organisations. Such organisations:

- promote competition between service providers
- empower citizens by pushing control out of the bureaucracy and into the community
- focus on outcomes rather than inputs
- are driven by their goals – their missions – not by their rules and regulations
- redefine their clients as customers
- prevent problems before they emerge
- earn revenue as well as spend it
- decentralise authority
- prefer market to bureaucratic mechanisms
- catalyse public, private and voluntary sectors to solve community problems.

The characteristics identified by Osborne and Gaebler elucidate some of the factors that may restrain the impact in the public sector of quality improvement programmes conceived of simply as TQM.

The difference in the extent and type of competition in the public and private sectors masks a significant feature of the management of quality in the two sectors. Another major difference between the public and private sectors is the fact that unsuccessful organisations go bankrupt and disappear in the private sector, whereas they are subject to reform or rejuvenation in the public sector. This masks the fact that some private-sector organisations which have introduced TQM and other strategies for the management of quality have not been saved from extinction by the introduction of these reforms.

The lack of efficacy in specific quality improvement strategies will be more evident in the public sector, as such organisations are usually not allowed to disappear, because their mission is to serve fundamental public needs. For example, the provision of universally available schooling is likely to lead to the retention of schools, except in the case of significant demographic changes. If a public school is perceived to be ineffective it is likely to be subject to reform and rejuvenation but rarely to closure for this reason.

QUALITY IMPROVEMENT AND QUALITY ASSURANCE FOR SCHOOL SYSTEMS

Quality systems for schools

Some of the key dimensions of a system for managing quality improvement in schools are shown in Table 6.1. The quality system is defined as the organisational structure, responsibilities, procedures, processes and resources for implementing quality improvement.

Schools focus on their clients by looking to their needs in determining the direction and development of the school. Their direction and purpose is derived from effective leadership which, among other things, results in focused involvement and ownership of the school's development programme by its stakeholder groups. Decision-making for both day-to-day management and future development should be based on evidence and data which is systematically collected and analysed.

The dimension of learning is a key feature of organisations that learn from their experience. Such schools take a proactive approach to planning and constructing their future, rather than responding after the event to changes in their environment and situation.

Table 6.1 Dimensions and characteristics of a quality system for schools

Organisational dimension	Characteristic of the quality system
External	Client focus
Leadership	Direction and purpose
Ownership	Focused involvement
Decision-making	Quality evidence and data
Systems perspective	An emphasis on interrelated processes
Mission and objectives	An emphasis on student learning outcomes
Learning	Improvement based on experience
Future orientation	Strategic management and scenario planning
Monitoring and assurance	Tracking progress and assuring outcomes

The research literature on school effectiveness and school improvement has shown that certain strategies are particularly important to building and maintaining a quality system.[2]

- a clear and shared vision of what students are to learn
- a means for translating the vision into a mission supported by a strategic development plan for the school
- ownership of the vision for development by all stakeholders in the school community
- action plans as working documents for implementing the school development plan
- identification and provision of the professional skills and knowledge required by staff to implement the school's development programme
- structures and processes for monitoring the implementation and effectiveness of strategies for school development
- provision for interactive feedback from the monitoring process to the implementation process
- an annual review and evaluation of progress that takes stock of the needs for further development in the school.

A commitment to professional development and training is vital if the school is to ensure that all staff are capable of and do achieve the outcomes that are stated in school plans. Such professional development needs to be integrated into the school's everyday operation in a way that allows individual staff to learn from colleagues and provides access to external sources of knowledge and skills.

To achieve stakeholder ownership of the vision and to obtain continuous feedback on progress, planning and development processes within schools should involve active community participation. Strategic plans for development require following through with straightforward monitoring and more extensive progress reviews to ask whether or not the school is achieving its intended outcomes for students. The planning, development and review cycle provides the basis for interactive feedback in a continuous development cycle.[3]

Management of quality improvement in schools

Quality improvement practices in school systems are often collectively referred to as development, planning, improvement or review practices. The main quality improvement approaches are based around strategic planning and internal monitoring by schools of their progress against their management and development plans.

School development and strategic planning

All Australian state education systems have introduced strategic planning over the last few years. This coincides with the broader use of strategic approaches to management in both the public and private sectors. Strategic planning has been implemented at the state level as a means of moving towards an agreed vision and the medium-term objectives of policies.

The other area in which strategic planning has become widely used is at the school level. Strategic school development plans have been established in most state systems as the basis for the implementation of systemic and local school priorities. Action plans for the implementation of strategic school objectives, regular monitoring of students and an annual review of progress are essential elements of this approach to strategic management.

Internal school review

Effective schemes for internal school-based reviews:

- are based on a systematic review and evaluation process, and are not simply an exercise in reflection
- obtain information about a school's condition, purposes and outcomes
- lead to action on an aspect of the school's organisation or curriculum
- are a group activity that involves participants in a collegial process
- are based on processes which provide the school with ownership of the outcomes
- have school improvement as their primary objective.

This list of characteristics has benefited from hindsight gained through the evaluation of school-based evaluation schemes. In reality, few schemes conform to this idealised set of characteristics. A major problem has been their failure to undertake analytically critical reviews and evaluations of the process of schooling. Evaluations must be directed at processes central to learning and teaching. Finally, the development that should follow an internal review requires careful and skilled management if it is to result in the intended improvements.

Successful change in schools through a process of review, development and evaluation requires a high level of complex skills and management. It requires motivation and access to training in skills of evaluation and the management of change. The significant investment of time required for successful school development means that all the participants must have a strong commitment to the changes required and be prepared to divert time and energy from other activities into the various phases of the programme.

TQM as a strategy for managing quality in schools

Over the last decade there have been a number of attempts to apply TQM to the change and development process in schools. One of the best-known attempts has been at Mt Edgecumbe High School in Alaska. However, there have been few attempts to apply the core idea of statistical analysis of variation to education processes. Where such techniques have been utilised in educational settings they have most often been applied to the non-pedagogical aspects of the organisation, such as administrative and general management functions.

The education literature that discusses TQM draws on a plethora of techniques and perspectives for managing improvement. It is difficult to read this literature with a sense that there is a unified set of underlying principles or strategies to be applied in improving schools. The papers currently in print cover the full gamut, from those which interpret TQM in light of key aspects of current restructuring programs – The Coalition of Essential Schools, Comer School Program, Outcomes-Driven Development Model, Outcomes Based Education, Accelerated Schools, etc. – to some which hark back to Deming's fourteen principles.

Probably the most significant attempt to interpret and adapt the concepts and ideas of Deming to school settings is that of William Glasser in *The Quality School* (Glasser, 1992). The most accessible guides to its application in schooling are *Total Quality Management and the School* (Murgatroyd and Morgan, 1993) and *Creating the Total Quality Effective School* (Lezotte, 1992). The reader should be warned, however, that these two books present quite different, although complementary, approaches to TQM. The first provides a view based on the substantive issues in effective schooling while the second is a compendium of strategies that may be applied to particular aspects of the planning, review and implementation phases of the improvement process in schools.

In assessing the utility of TQM as a system for managing quality in schools it is necessary to decide which facets of the literature one is addressing. TQM is manifest in the literature in two forms, either as a philosophical orientation to the improvement process or as a set of strategies for managing the improvement process. The former is based on an extension of Deming's fourteen points into the arena of schooling, while the latter is based on the collection of techniques and strategies that draw from a wide range of approaches to quality improvement, mostly emanating from developments in Japanese industry and more recent adaptations and developments in US industry.

There is a need to understand the differences between TQM and alternative approaches to school development, which include school development planning, the effective schools approach and school improvement models. Reading the educational literature on TQM often leaves the impression that it could be describing parts of all these alternative approaches, but the description is usually provided at the level of a philosophy or approach so it is difficult to know how the application of TQM overlaps with any of these alternatives. Lawrence Lezotte warns, however, 'It is unlikely that schools will be able to manage the . . . principles of TQM if they are unable to meet the challenge of successfully installing the tenets of effective schools'

(Lezotte, 1992: 22). Lezotte provides three foundation beliefs for the application of TQM in the context of effective schools approaches:

1 The primary evidence of quality teaching is demonstrated student learning.
2 Instructional strategies should build on the knowledge base of effective teaching and the laws of learning.
3 Repeating practices that do not work cannot be justified.

The need to emphasise the core business of student learning is reinforced by David Langford, one of the pioneers of applying TQM in schools. He says that 'educators have put too much emphasis on using TQM to improve administrative processes' and that TQM needs to be perceived as a tool that is relevant to the classroom, otherwise 'you'll turn off huge groups of teachers' (Langford, in Willis, 1993: 5).

School development planning, effective schools and school improvement models are approaches that have grown out of the research base on educational change and development. It would be odd if we were to take up a strategy that has been developed outside of education if we cannot provide a clear argument as to why it is likely to be more relevant than the educationally-derived alternatives. I believe this is the reason why there has been only limited take up of TQM in education – there is a range of accepted strategies in use that educators have found to be effective and appropriate.

It is important that the strategies and the 'method' of TQM do not become the focus of the improvement process in schools. The objective is one of improving student learning outcomes and, although methods of analysis and strategies for implementing change must be efficient, empowering and effective, they must never be allowed to dominate the process if it is to achieve its overall objective. This is a danger with any set of techniques that has an existence independent of the process of educational improvement itself.

Quality assurance in school systems

Quality assurance processes are normally associated with various forms of review, inspection, accreditation and student testing. Review and inspection strategies are prevalent in UK and European systems and those that derive from them. The quality assurance functions in these systems integrate aspects of quality audit with quality review as a process which is essentially external to the school.

NSW QUALITY ASSURANCE REVIEWS OF SCHOOL
PERFORMANCE AND DEVELOPMENT

The New South Wales quality assurance school review programme has established a methodology for reviewing the development and performance of schools. The reviews aim principally to fulfil a quality assurance function by undertaking quality reviews focusing on improvement and audits of a school's quality system and its educational practice and functioning.

In today's framework of delegated management it is important that there be a significant element of stakeholder involvement in the school review process. It is also important that the quality review process strategically focus on the key issues for further development in each school. To effect this the reviews analyse data on student outcomes and obtain a self-audit against outcomes achievable from best practice in the system. When fully implemented, this audit process will provide information on the performance of key aspects of the practice and functioning of schools.

To date the school reviews have focused mostly on fulfilling the role of quality reviews. They have not yet established an equal focus on their quality audit function. Before the latter can be achieved, a shared understanding of the core elements of a quality system for schools needs to be established. This is one of the purposes for the statements of outcomes that can be achieved from best practice that are currently being developed in collaboration with schools. The core set of outcomes achievable from best practice will provide the basis for auditing and reviewing the effectiveness of a school's quality systems.

There is a challenge for the quality review component to adapt the methodology of reviews to the particular needs of schools, including the specific needs of schools that may be performing below the level of other schools serving similar communities and for those at the leading edge of performance where students are making most progress.

In the former case the fundamental aspects of the quality system and practices required for improvement in teaching and learning must be a focus of the review. The quality review and quality audit components need to converge to focus on the core quality system issues if the review is to provide the most effective support for the school.

Reviews in leading-edge schools need to be adapted to challenge such schools to restructure their organisation and develop pedagogical approaches beyond current best practice and to set more advanced benchmarks for quality teaching and learning. Such schools, which are drawn from the full spectrum of schools in the system, are the most likely sources of any significant breakthroughs that may be made in teaching and learning.

It is necessary to include the full range of schools in the quality assurance process if low performance is not to be institutionalised. Approaches to quality assurance that target only the schools considered to be performing below some pre-determined level simply establish a sub-system designed to detect and prop up failing schools. In this case, they fulfil the classical role of inspection – the post-production process of detecting products that fail to meet design standards. Inspection approaches of this type have little impact on the long term improvement of the system, because they do not focus on the improvement of the *processes* that produce the *outcomes* of interest.

THE SCHOOL REVIEW PROCESS

There are three clearly defined yet closely linked stages in the school review process developed in NSW.

Stage 1: pre-review

The first stage occurs up to six months prior to the visit by the review team and includes a meeting between the leader of the review team and key stake-holders in that school's community. The meeting has three major purposes. The leader of the review team provides information on the major steps and aspects of the school review process. The team leader also asks the school to check the accuracy of the statistical profile of the school that has been drawn from administrative records, and seeks additional detail in preparation for the review. The third and significant purpose of this meeting is to establish the basis on which to negotiate the focus areas to be addressed during the quality review.

The review methodology is being further developed to ensure that the negotiation of focus areas takes account of the school's analyses of student learning outcomes information and the school's self-audit against a set of statements of the outcomes achievable from best practice.

The review team leader negotiates the focus areas with the school community and establishes the basis of the timetable and means for gathering the data required for the review.

Stage 2: the review

The period of the visit by the review team varies between two and five days, depending on the number of students enrolled in the school. The team gathers information from a wide range of sources through interviews, observation and document analysis, and analyses the information to determine the major strengths and achievements, to be made and significant findings in relationship to improvement in the chosen focus areas with an indication of the recommendations for the school's future development.

The visit by the review team concludes with a presentation of a preliminary oral report from the team to the school.

Stage 3: post-review

The team leader writes the formal report, consulting with the principal who checks the report for accuracy. School reports are public documents. Following the release of the report the school principal is the individual with primary accountability for implementing the developments required to effect the improvements indicated by the recommendations.

The report is provided to the Minister and the Director-General, who have established monitoring systems to track progress towards the achievement of recommendations made in the review reports.

Review methodology

The school quality reviews draw on a range of methodologies that have been developed in the educational evaluation and social science literature. They follow a basic methodology which establishes the evaluation questions, collects data, processes information, interprets and gives meaning to the information and reports the findings. The findings give rise to suggested future directions and recommendations of outcomes to be achieved from further development for improving student learning.

Interviews are scheduled with random samples of each of the stakeholder groups. Students meet in groups of 2–5 with a member of the review team, while interviews with staff and parents are normally held as one-to-one discussions with a member of the review team. In addition, interviews are held with individuals who have specific responsibilities or have been central to the development of the areas which are the focus of the review. The review process is open to any member of any stakeholder group who wishes to meet with the review team. A typical review of a 400-student primary school normally holds discussions with about 80 persons in total.

The information collected from interviews, observations and analyses of documents is analysed to achieve the following objectives:

- to ensure that the contextual nature of the information is fully apprehended by the review team
- to point to the flaws or inconsistencies in the evidence provided from individual stakeholders and in the interpretations of individual review team members
- to clarify, extend and modify the interpretation of the evidence by the review team
- to establish a number of competing plausible inferences
- to assess the credibility of the evaluative judgements made.

In general, issues are analysed until a consistent interpretation is available from corroborating evidence. This may involve triangulation of evidence from a range of sources by a range of methods; however, the principle of corroboration overrides that of triangulation.

The reviews do not aim to estimate in any quantitative sense the actual incidence or severity of matters relating to each particular issue. Rather, they seek to determine whether the particular issue indicates an important aspect of the school's functioning and operation that would benefit substantially from improvement efforts.

The recommendations are targeted either at incremental improvement – the extension of a programme to other groups of students, for example – or at fundamental development. Fundamental development refers to changes that will require the school to effect structural or cultural changes to the way that it currently operates – the restructuring of the way in which student progress is reported to parents, for example, or the substantial raising of the expectations that staff, students and parents have for learning at the school.

The process is conducted with a significant degree of school community participation. The school's principal and a member of staff are present at all sessions during the review where the evidence is discussed. A member of the local community also joins the 3–5 external members of the team who have been trained in quality assurance review practices and procedures.

Stakeholder response to the process

School communities have found the reviews to be useful in validating their current achievements and providing direction for their future improvement and development.

> The review has provided the school with a validation of current achievements and a mandate to continue to pursue alternative strategies. At this stage our future directions will include organisational changes and amended teaching strategies to facilitate more effective learning, communicating the school's values to the community and the further development of a intercultural, holistic curriculum.
>
> (Primary school principal)

> [The review] has made students recognise that they are part of a significant period of change in the school and that this change will be ongoing. This is a good thing provided the implementation of the review recommendations is discussed and debated.
>
> (Secondary school student)

Reviews focus on quality systems, particularly those essential for the support of quality student learning. Review teams work with schools to identify factors enabling and hindering desired learning outcomes.

Recommendations will result in structural changes to the school, school organisation and curriculum scope and implementation. The end result will be a closer match between the ideal condition for effective learning and the reality of daily school life.

(Primary school principal)

By enabling students to become more actively involved in the process and structures of their own schooling, the most obvious outcome will be young people who value others, display tolerance, are able to set goals and plan well to achieve them.

(Secondary school student)

Self-determining and self-reviewing schools need to have their own internal review processes in addition to periodic external quality assurance reviews. One of the main reasons for the failure of school-based evaluation activities in the past was the lack of technical expertise in schools. The quality assurance review process models best practices in evaluation and is designed to influence school beliefs and practices in this area. There is some evidence that this is happening.

The School Council is considering adopting the process to review one aspect of the school's operation each year.

(Primary school principal)

The Quality Assurance review made the importance of evaluation more visible and has given us a greater understanding of some of the ways in which ongoing evaluation can be carried out, both on a small scale at the classroom level and for the school as a whole.

(Secondary school student)

As with most innovations in education, a range of views has been expressed about the merit and worth of the programme, although positive views significantly outweigh the negative. The majority of those providing feedback about quality assurance school reviews are very supportive.

The data collected by an independent group was perceived to provide a more accurate view of the current situation and therefore the recommendations carry more weight.

(Secondary school teacher)

For the parents, the review is seen as a key part of public accountability – a measure to ensure that their children are receiving quality education.

(Secondary school parent)

DISCUSSION

The roles of quality improvement and quality assurance are complementary, although separate. They are both vital aspects of the overall management of quality. Quality improvement focuses on the actions and structures necessary to manage quality on an ongoing basis. Quality assurance, on the other hand, is the process by which the quality improvement process itself is assured. Ideally quality assurance needs to go beyond this to assure the outcomes from the organisation, although classical quality assurance based on ISO 9000 standards does not.

Public education systems have had quality assurance systems in one guise or another since their inception over a century ago. In recent times these systems have undergone substantial restructuring and are now more closely aligned in intent with the quality assurance systems that have been developed in industries such as health. Education has always focused on the quality of outcomes to a significant degree and the quality assurance systems in place today also seek to assure the processes responsible for the quality of outcomes.

Only quality assurance systems that are independent of the operational system for schooling are capable of assuring the quality of school systems. Other systems that seek to combine quality assurance and quality improvement functions are not able to provide sufficient levels of assurance to be credible as quality assurance processes.

A range of systems for quality improvement in schools has been developed and is in use. Most systems have a heritage in long-standing educational research. Total Quality Management is a recent addition to the range of approaches in use. Thus far it appears to have a weakness in that it is not sufficiently focused on student learning – which is the core business of schools. The long-term utility of TQM as a basis for quality improvement in schools will depend on the success of future applications that show it to be effective in generating development and improvement in student learning outcomes. To achieve this, TQM will need also to show that it is capable of being the vehicle for cultural and structural development in schools, in addition to incremental changes through continuous improvement.

The NSW model is focused mainly on quality assurance – in both senses, as quality review and quality audit – and is not designed to provide a major input to the strategies for managing quality in individual schools. Through the audit of school quality systems and educational practices, however, quality assurance reviews provide the basis for schools to develop more effective practices to manage quality teaching and student learning outcomes.

Unlike quality assurance processes based on the international standard for quality assurance (ISO 9000), NSW quality reviews seek to develop ownership and the participation of the community in the process so that their recommendations for improvement are more likely to be implemented. The strengths of the approach include its potential to act as a catalyst to the further development of schools and the opportunity for all stakeholder groups in the school community to contribute to the further development of their school. The external members of the review teams provide both credibility and the opportunity to work through a disinterested party to tackle particular development issues that may be considerably more difficult, if not impossible, to address through an internal review initiated from within the school, thus simultaneously enhancing accountability and development.

School reviews are also a key element of the systemic review function of the quality assurance program. The collective information from individual schools provides formative evaluations of the development and performance of the systems that support schools and of the system as a whole.

NOTES

1 Reported in *The International Quality Study: Best Practices Report. An Analysis of Management Practices that Impact Performance* (1992), New York: American Quality Foundation.
2 See, for example, the recent reviews by Reynolds and Levine in Reynolds, D. and Cuttance, P. (eds) (1992), *School Effectiveness: Research, Policy and Practice*, London: Cassell. Sam Stringfield's paper, 'Underlying the chaos of factors explaining exemplary US elementary schools: the case for high reliability organisations', presented to the International Congress for School Effectiveness and Improvement, Melbourne, 3–6 January 1994, provides a different look at the development and performance of schools through the perspective of 'high reliability organisations'.
3 See Cuttance, P. (1995) 'Building high performance school systems', keynote address to the eighth International Congress for School Effectiveness and Improvement, Leeuwarden, The Netherlands, 3–6 January 1995; and Hargreaves, D. and Hopkins, D. (1991) *The empowered school: the management and practice of development planning*, London: Cassell.

REFERENCES

Glasser, W. (1992) *The Quality School*, New York: Harper Perennial.
Lezotte, L. (1992) *Creating the Total Quality Effective School*, Michigan: Effective Schools Products.
Murgatroyd, S. and Morgan, C. (1993) *Total Quality Management and the School*, Buckingham: Open University Press.
Osborne, D. and Gaebler, T. (1993) *Reinventing Government: How the Entrepreneurial Spirit is Transforming the Public Sector*, New York: Plume.
Willis, S. (1993), 'Creating "Total Quality" Schools', USCD Update, 35(2), 5.

Chapter 7

Ano te Hutinga o te Harakeke (The plucking still of the flaxbush)
New Zealand's self-managing schools and five impacts from the ongoing restructuring of educational administration

Ken Rae[1]

Hutia te rito o te harakeke
Kei hea te korimako e ko?
Ki mai ki i ahau
He aha te mea nui o te ao?
Maku e ki atu
He tangata, he tangata, he tangata hi![2]

(If you pluck the heart from the flaxbush, where will the bellbird sing?
If you ask me what is the greatest thing in the world,
I will give you this reply –
It is the spirit and the drive of humankind)

Traditional Maori Waiata

INTRODUCTION

The themes of devolution and self-managing schools might suggest a centrifugal redistribution of power. It is proposed in this chapter that, from a New Zealand perspective, the redistribution of power is ambiguous, and that the relationships between devolution, democracy, efficiency, effectiveness, quality and equity are problematic, particularly in an acknowledged pluralistic state. The chapter will demonstrate the problematic ambiguity for leaders of New Zealand schools, on the basis of five features of the New Zealand Education scene in 1993.

INTERNATIONAL AND NEW ZEALAND CONTEXTS OF EDUCATIONAL ADMINISTRATION

The new relationships between politicians and the bureaucracy and the schools of the reconstructed New Zealand State carefully distinguish the owner/funder, and the purchaser, and the regulator interests of the Crown. These relationships have been discussed fully by Boston *et al.* (1991) in terms of public choice theory, principal–agent theory, and managerialism.

The input of the Treasury as a significant 'control department' was discussed by Lauder *et al.* (1988) in terms of New Right philosophies and economics. The aim of the other major 'control department', the State Services Commission, has been described by Dale and Jesson (1993) as the 'mainstreaming' of education into the administrative model applying elsewhere in the state sector. A thorough analysis of the Picot reforms instituted on 1 October 1989 as redistribution of 'power' within the education structures to school level is that of Cusack (1992).

In the OECD context, Judith Chapman in a monograph on 'The Effectiveness of Schooling' (1991: 6) depicted the environment facing education managements across the developed world as follows:

> At present, there is an environment of more stable demographic change but continuous public financial stringency and competing social demands. Combined with recent concerns about the goals and outcomes of schooling, the quality of education, labour market adjustments and the relationship between education and international economic competitiveness, such pressures have forced education authorities to reassess educational needs, both qualitatively and quantitatively.
>
> In response to these demands, education authorities in some OECD countries have undertaken certain reforms which have direct implications for the redistribution of administrative power among the various levels within the education system, including the school itself. In an attempt to understand these changes, a recent OECD report suggests that the redistribution of power is in fact more complex than any account based on a conception of rearrangements along the centralisation–decentralisation continuum would suggest. . . . Thus, terms such as 'centralisation' or 'decentralisation' in this context become too limited to give a complete account of what are far more complex developments, problems and issues.

Thrusts to both devolution and centralisation are discernible within the New Zealand structures, and these can be located within competing theories.

Public choice theory   This posits that human behaviour is dominated by the self interest of 'rational economic man' (sic), which behaviour is held to be of benefit to a responsive economy but detrimental when it is mobilised by politicians and by interest groups close to politicians. Exponents of the theory are therefore concerned to reduce the discretion available to politicians, and the influence of pressure groups surrounding them, and to diminish the entrenched interests of the bureaucracy. From this theory fall concepts of 'provider capture', 'contestability', the extension of 'market disciplines', and a drive for the 'minimalist state'.

Layers of intervening bureaucracy in New Zealand, between the centre as funder and policy maker, and the school as site of service delivery, were demolished in 1989. The charter signed by a school board of trustees is an undertaking direct to the Minister, who, in the last resort, can replace a board with a commissioner. The negotiation of teachers' conditions of service, taken away from the Department of Education in 1988, has since been managed by the State Services Commission, a control department (O'Brien, 1990; Rae, 1991b). Moves in the direction of a reduced state have thus, by 'perverse effect', in New Zealand Education become a centripetal thrust, particularly in the significant field of industrial relations.

Principal-agent theory   This theory derives from concepts of 'bounded rationality' and 'opportunity costs' of decision-making and the 'moral hazard' of making appointments. These concepts are derived from theories of the micro-economics of organisations (Boston *et al.*, 1991). The theory is concerned for ensuring that the will of the principal shall prevail over the agent, and proposes the setting up of contract relationships wherever possible, and the close definition of goals, objectives and functions. In New Zealand this has resulted in charters as a quasi-contracts, contracts for principals of schools as agents of boards, and single-function agencies at the centre such as the Special Education Service, the New Zealand Qualifications Authority and, in particular, a separate Education Review Office. The power flows both ways within this concept, but it is the principal who has the final say. (For an analogous analysis of the structures in England and Wales, see Levacic, 1993.)

Managerialism   This provides for decentralisation, deregulation and delegation within clear guidelines, in the belief that managers should be encouraged to manage, the best decisions being made by those closest to the action, but with accountability procedures clearly spelt out. In New Zealand schools this has led to exploration of a governance/management split, promoted by the Lough Committee which, in 1990, was charged with a review of the implementation of the major structural changes (Education Implementation Team, 1990). Managerialism is certainly a centrifugal distribution of management power, but in the present structures of New Zealand education key controls remain at the centre in the setting of national goals for education, and in setting the total price that the Crown will pay. (See Figs 7.1 and 7.2.)

Some New Zealand commentators have perceived the New Zealand administrative restructuring in education as the implementing, at long last, of an emphasis on increased community input into curriculum and school management, one that had been recommended in a sequence of reports from at least the time of the Education Development Conference of the Labour

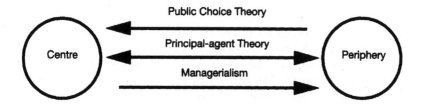

Public Choice Theory – Political will maintained over bureaucracy.
Boards sign Charters directly to Minister

Principal - Agent Theory – Relationships established by Contract
wherever possible. Single purpose agencies – MOE/ERO/NZQA

Managerialism – Devolution of management within clear guidelines.
Decentralisation, deregulation, delegation. In schools concept of
governance/management split (Lough)

Figure 7.1 Theorising the reconstructed New Zealand state balance of power
and control

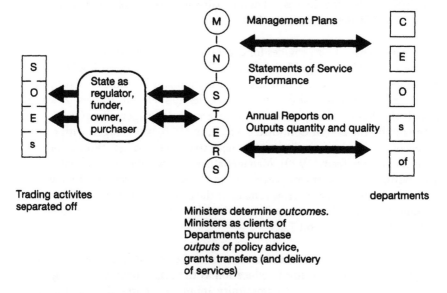

Figure 7.2 Reconstruction of the New Zealand state

administration of 1972–5 (Barrington, 1991; Philips, 1993). Others perceive the restructuring as a strategic withdrawal by the state facing a legitimation crisis arising from a crisis of capital accumulation in a developed capitalist economy. The restructuring is interpreted as the response of a state faced with fiscal crisis which is impacting on its ability to fulfil its role in social service delivery (Nash, 1989; Middleton et al., 1990; Smyth, 1993).

From Australia, Cuttance (1992: 20) distinguishes the changes in New Zealand as devolution in a 'political', as opposed to an 'organisational', form; Beare and Boyd (1993: 8) distinguish the reforms in New Zealand as focusing on school-level change as opposed to change at the level of district, province or state.

The title of this chapter suggests that the balance between school-level reform and community power, and central leverage to attain national objectives, was still being trimmed in 1993 in New Zealand. The initial stance of 1988–9 promoting local management within national guidelines continued in place, but was undergoing continuing adjustment, a process still happening.

The shift in power has been described by the Auditor-General as 'dramatic' (Cameron, 1992). He noted that, by 1991, 2,700 school boards controlled directly:

- expenditure of state grants of nearly $500 million
- employment of teachers at a cost of $1,500 million
- use of school land and buildings estimated to be worth $2,800 million.

The Chairman of the Task Force to Review Education Administration appointed in July 1987, Brian Picot, was a prominent businessman and a member of the Auckland University Council. Figure 7.3 schedules the principal changes proposed by the task force.

Brian Picot was invited to revisit his recommendations, five years on, by an Auckland conference of primary school principals. He commented (Picot, 1993):

We were asked to review a system that had served education well for a long time, but which had become under stress and was largely held together by the dedication of some good people.

We were called together at a time when most of the developed world was examining the rising cost of social services and the New Zealand education sector had received a funding increase of 20% in real terms in the previous three year period.

Our job therefore was to prepare a blueprint that would enable the human and material resources of the Education Sector to be freed up to provide the best possible educational outcomes for learners.

Brian Picot noted that, even in advance of the devising of block grants for teacher salaries, still not fully achieved in 1996, the per-pupil funding avail-

- the establishing throughout the land of single-school boards elected by parents, with powers of governance and the appointment of staff, a structure long known in secondary education but a bold initiative in the primary sector, the more so given the size of a majority of primary schools;

- the bulk funding of the boards, with responsibility on them to adopt a budget on the recommendation of the principal, who as a member of the board in the role of manager entered into a new relationship with the staff;

- the passing to the board of responsibility within nationally negotiated industrial awards for setting up a personnel policy which conformed to the 'good employer' and 'equal opportunity' criteria of state sector industrial relations legislation;

- the charging of each board with responsibility for maintenance and minor capital works;

- the complete removal therefore of property supervision, personnel, finance and professional guidance roles of education boards and regional offices of the Department and their removal from the scene;

- at the centre a fined-down Ministry, and clear separation of policy makers from deliverers of 'services';

- the knitting together of centre and periphery, to meet concerns for national comparability and equity for disadvantaged groups, by the device of the Charter, a schedule of agreed school objectives within National Guidelines – seen by the task force as a 'lynch pin';

- the achievement of quality assurance by an independent Review and Audit [sic] Agency, charged with measuring the educational and managerial achievements of schools against their Charter objectives by school visits every two years; and

- two safety nets to allow discussion and negotiation without fallout – at district level Community Education Forums able to make representations to the Ministry (later modified in 1991) and at national level a Parents Advocacy Council able to report to the Minister on the one hand or advise parents on issues such as home schooling on the other (which was later abolished in 1991).

Figure 7.3 Recommendations of the Picot report: Rae (1990)

able for use at local discretion moved in the first year of restructuring from a level of $50/pupil to $800/pupil.

A Ministry of Education publication (1993c: 9) has described the change as:

> an upheaval of reform that transformed the landscape of education administration. The bureaucratic maze of the Department of Education with its regional offices, and associated boards and advisory committees, was demolished.

Figures 7.4 and 7.5 contrast the structures of educational administration in New Zealand, pre-1989 and post-1989.

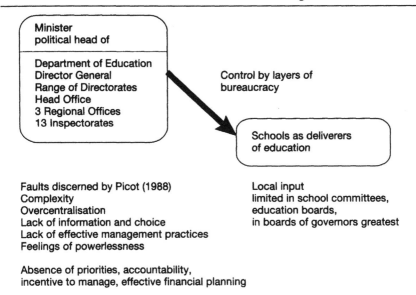

Faults discerned by Picot (1988)
Complexity
Overcentralisation
Lack of information and choice
Lack of effective management practices
Feelings of powerlessness

Absence of priorities, accountability,
incentive to manage, effective financial planning

Figure 7.4 The structures of education administration in New Zealand pre-1989

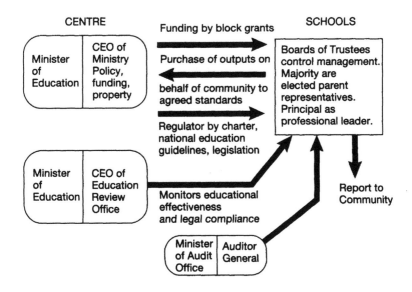

Figure 7.5 Education administration in New Zealand post-1989: State is funder/owner; purchaser of education services; regulator of standards

FIVE IMPACTS ON NEW ZEALAND SCHOOLS IN 1996

Prime Minister Lange in 1988 lauded the Picot reforms because they would empower the trustees of the 2,700 boards in a common search for equity. The rubric for his time in office, and for the term of his successor, the Hon. Phil Goff, was efficiency, effectiveness, economy – and equity. With a new government elected at the end of 1990 and the appointment of Dr Lockwood Smith as Minister, the watchwords have become achievement, choice, enterprise and national competitive advantage.

The transition has been discussed elsewhere (Rae, 1992). The next section of the chapter will instead focus comment on five initiatives from the centre in 1993 which continue to impact significantly on New Zealand schools.

The New Zealand Curriculum Framework

On 7 April the Minister of Education sponsored the release of the New Zealand Curriculum Framework, described as 'the first curriculum document in our history to provide a coherent framework for learning and assessment across the total school curriculum' (O'Rourke, 1993a).

In 1990 an 'Achievement Initiative' had been a major plank of the education component of the new government's election manifesto. It emphasised a reshaped curriculum, with new assessment procedures setting levels of student achievement to raise educational standards – particularly in the 'basic subjects' defined as English, Mathematics, Science, and Technology. The model was similar to, but not as prescriptive as, that introduced in England and Wales by the Education Reform Act of 1986.

The 1988–9 reforms had occurred by contrast during a hiatus in curriculum development, posing difficulties for those who believe key concerns for educational administration are to do with curricular issues, concerning the valued learning of an increasingly pluralist society, and the appropriate measurement and accreditation of its learners.

The Curriculum Framework was published in 1993 in English and Maori. Its nine principles and seven essential learning areas are intended to 'underpin all teaching and learning', and they provide a basis for curriculum development at national level, scheduled initially in the fields of mathematics (a syllabus up to form IV – year ten – reached the schools in 1992), science, technology, English, Maori language, and social studies. The curriculum statements, in all learning areas, were to be completed by 1997 (but timelines were suspended by a new Minister in 1996).

The document also provides a framework for curriculum development at school level. It specifies 'essential skills, attitudes, and values' to be developed by all learners, and it promotes principles of in-school and national assessment. The initial curriculum document in mathematics was supported by suggested activities to aid schools in the assessment of pupils against eight levels of achievement.

Some years after restructuring, evaluation of the effectiveness of schools as places of learning could at last have a theoretical base more securely framed in terms of learning outcomes. The 'curriculum statements' deemed in law to be part of every school charter will be reviewable by the Education Review Office.

Issues arising

At issue for school level administrators, i.e. for the principals, and for the boards responsible for 'control of the management of the school' (Section 75 of the Education Act, 1989), were the continued existence of syllabus statements not developed on the new model and so without levels, criteria or exemplars; the managing of the change; and, especially in senior secondary schools, the transition from established 'subjects' to new 'learning areas', and within a new qualification framework.

At issue initially for the Education Review Office is the situation that, pending a technical amendment to legislation, the Curriculum Framework has not been officially Gazetted, and, to allow for flexibility during the start-up phase, was not for two years. This will create difficulties for Assurance Audits which focus on matters of compliance. By late 1996, this technical amendment had not yet been passed into law.

National education guidelines

On 30 April, 1993 schools were advised by the Ministry of Education (O'Rourke, 1993b), by notice in the Education Gazette, of amendments to the compulsory 'national guidelines' section of their charters, amendments that in 1989 had been 'hardwired' in, and in 1990 promulgated by Gazette notice.

Those initial guidelines were subject to controversy when first issued, with cries of undue focus on goals seen as 'social engineering'. As a result a revised 1989 version inserted, as a paramount goal for every school, 'the enhancement of children's learning'. Guiding principles in the 1989–90 preamble related to 'Curriculum', 'Equity', 'Equal Educational Opportunity', and 'Treaty of Waitangi'. Families of goals and objectives dealt in turn with curriculum, community partnership, equity, Treaty of Waitangi, personnel policy, staff development, financial management, and property management.

By late 1989 there was further controversy when the concept of the Picot Report and of the subsequent White Paper, 'Tomorrow's Schools' – of the 'charter as contract' – became 'charter as undertaking', and in one direction only – from the board to the Minister. At issue was the sovereignty of

Parliament, and its power annually to vote supply – which could not be constrained by any prior agreement with a lesser entity. The word 'paramount' also disappeared from charter guidelines at that time, on the basis that the legislation did not provide for a hierarchy of goals.

The 1993 announcement had the significant potential to reduce seventeen goals, and forty-six objectives, to ten National Education Goals and six Administrative Guidelines. These guidelines covered fields of curriculum, personnel practice, financial and property management, health and safety legislation, legal requirements on pupil attendance, and the length of the school day and the school year. There are no nationally specified objectives and the number to be pursued in any school is therefore left to the decision of the individual boards.

The Education Review Office will be able to assess each board of trustees on its management in terms of two new requirements of the 1993 notice – that the board documents how the National Education Guidelines are being implemented, and that it maintains an ongoing process of self-review.

Issues arising

At issue for boards of trustees is the extent to which they wish to go through required procedures of consultation prior to forwarding to the Minister an amended charter, in order to take hold of benefits of the more broadly expressed new framework of goals and guidelines, and to specify a more limited set of priority objectives.

At issue for the Education Review Office are the manner in which it can measure compliance against two alternative National Education Guideline Statements, the one written into all school charters from 1989, the second now Gazetted as its replacement and deemed part of every charter; whether one framework or two should be applied across schools; and how to establish standards of compliance on the taking of 'all reasonable steps' to meet guidelines.

A legislative base for the Education Review Office

A major portion of the Education Amendment Act 1993, passed in late June, inserted a new 'Part XXVIII – Review of Educational Services' into the 1989 Act. The section amended and consolidated earlier provisions for actions by the Office that were scattered through the principal Act, and made possible a clearer distinction between the power and function of the Chief Review Officer, and the regulatory and operational functions of the Secretary of Education and of the range of agencies in the Education sector.

The legislation spells out the power of the Chief Review Officer to carry out reviews, either as directed by the Minister, or on her own initiative, reviews of a wide range of educational services that will be general or particular; to have reports prepared for the Minister on the basis of those reviews; and to 'give the Minister such other assistance and advice on the performance of applicable [i.e. educational] organisations as the Minister from time to time requires'.

In 1988 the report of the Task Force to Review Education Administration proposed (Task Force, 1988: 60) a Review and Audit Agency to make judgements on both local and national concerns, to be responsible for:

- the review and audit of every institution's performance in terms of its charter
- the provision of independent comment on the quality of policy advice, and how well policies are implemented at national level.

Reviews of schools undertaken by an interdisciplinary team, assisted by a co-opted principal and by a community representative, would have as their purposes:

- helping the institution assess its own progress towards achieving its objectives (a catalyst role)
- providing a public audit of performance in the public interest (an audit role).

Reviews would be 'a cooperative attempt to improve the quality of education being provided . . . an impartial and informal assessment able to be absorbed in the institution's staff development programme'. (1988: 60–1) After the initial visit a draft report would be left in the school to allow comment and/or changes in school practice, and after a return visit one term later a final report would be made public and forwarded to the Minister.

The 1993 legislation reflects the negotiation in early 1992, between the Minister and a new Chief Review Officer appointed in that year, of reshaped outputs for the office. The four classes of output were advised to school boards and principals by ministerial announcement in the Education Gazette of 2 June 1992 as:

- Assurance Audits – measures of compliance with legislative or regulatory or contract requirements, including the quality of service delivery (discretionary audits could 'follow up regular audits which had disclosed poor performance – or in cases of community concern')
- Effectiveness Reviews – evaluation of the contribution made to student achievement in terms of both standards and progress from the quality of the teaching services, management systems and practices of the institution
- Evaluation Services – national impact evaluation of effects of curriculum policy or of management structures – and overview reports provided by analyses of assurance audits and effectiveness reviews
- Ministerial Services – briefings, correspondence, speech notes, parliamen-

tary questions – including advice on policy developed by other agencies, and policy development services.

In late 1992 the Office launched its Assurance Audits, after extensive staff training, and the production after extensive research of a Compliance Manual of all the legal and other requirements on boards. Quarterly assurance survey overview reports were released – to a measure of media comment. The Office has also affirmed that accountability and openness are served if, after a period of twenty working days for the board to comment on a report, and a further twenty working days to advise amendments to policy or practice, the media are advised of the availability of the individual school audits.

In early 1993, the Office launched a three-month trial of its Effectiveness Reviews. After a pause to review its own practice, with a view to refining procedures and to meeting any staff training needs, it has resumed and maintained the programme. An important initial stage in the notified Effectiveness Review process is the preparation by a board of its own 'Achievement Statement' – 'a clear description of the learning priorities set for the students in that school.'

In a presentation to the Canterbury Branch of the New Zealand Education Administration Society (NZEAS) in July 1993, a representative of the Office set out a framework for Effectiveness Reviews based on three key questions:

1 What counts as success for you? This builds on the school's Achievement Statement.
2 What difference have you made? This will allow the school to use entry and later data to demonstrate progress.
3 What has made the difference? This allows analysis of in-school factors and study of the school's view of external factors.

In a speech to primary principals the Chief Review Officer suggested in October 1993 that the Office was resisting pressure to define standards of best practice, preferring instead, as external reviewer, to 'discover not invent; expose not impose; and evaluate not regulate.' She went on, however, to propose that the Education Review Office has two expectations:

that principals and boards will enter knowingly into an informed contractual relationship with the Crown to provide school-based education at the local level;
that the Crown will enter knowingly into an informed contractual relationship with each local board for the provision of school-based education which not only meets local needs but satisfies national requirements, and the larger goals of the society.

Issues arising

There is room in this new review process for initiatives on the part of the school and its board, particularly in their drawing up of a statement of student achievement considered appropriate to their school. Of interest to the schools is the production of consolidated 'quality data' required by the Office in advance of nationally developed assessment initiatives sponsored from the centre, and in advance of the development of the full range of National Curriculum Statements and their levels exemplars.

Of concern to the Ministry is the need to establish a feedback loop into policy development, and the suggestion that the Office will set in place its own policy development services. Of keen interest to schools is the Office's stance on release of reviews to the media.

Of special interest to professional leaders in the schools is the stance of the office that the board is the legal entity, charged with control of the management of the school, and their statement in the Third Quarter Summary 1992–3 that '88% of boards had not taken all steps necessary to fulfil their obligation to administer [sic] the curriculum'. Ownership of the curriculum is a focal point of board–principal relations, particularly if an atmosphere of mutual trust does not prevail. The Education Act, 1979, in fact separates 'control' and 'management' in Section 75, as it gives to boards 'complete discretion subject to any enactment of the law of the land' to 'control the management of the school'. Section 76 gives the principal, subject to the board's general policy directions, discretion on 'the day to day management of the school's administration'. These perspectives need to be applied to the formula used by the Education Review Office, which was repeated in its quarterly summaries to September 1993.

It is of interest to schools that the inspectorates pre-1989, in writing reports, incorporated both 'commendations' and 'recommendations'. The quarterly summaries being issued had, by the end of 1993, yet to include the equivalent of the former, even though the September statement incorporated new experimental Effectiveness Reviews. Such supportive comment could only serve to reinforce any perceived effectiveness in school management.

New Zealand Qualifications Authority (NZQA) accreditation procedures

On 23 July 1993, NZQA wrote to all secondary school principals to update them on procedures of accreditation and moderation, which would permit incorporation of the programmes of each of their schools into the National Qualification Framework and so into the awarding of the National Certificate and National Diploma. (It could be held that, in law, a letter to the board of each school would have been more appropriate.)

The Authority was charged by a new section of the Education Act in 1990 to build the Framework, and a model was canvassed in a public discussion draft document in 1991. Principles underpinning the Framework are the setting-up of an extensive bank of separate achievement-oriented unit level standards, without overlap, and provision for portability by the learner of all unit standards passed (and recorded on a National Certificate), across providers and into more occupation-specific qualifications.

In 1993, principals were advised that, to entitle their school to assess and award credits towards the National Certificate and National Diploma, accreditation of their school by the Authority would be required. Applications would need to be based on school-wide policies, and the school would need to have 'quality management systems' in place. Schools would be subject to a three-year monitoring cycle, undertaken by Authority analysts or specialist teachers under contract to by the Authority. The accreditation would normally be by documentation analysis.

The notice of 23 July incorporated an Education Gazette notice of agreement by the CEOs of the Ministry and the Authority, that the Ministry would manage a programme for the writing of twenty-six National Curriculum Statements over the next two years within the seven essential learning areas, and that this would permit the Authority to commission immediately afterwards the writing of unit standards in these areas of the curriculum at levels appropriate to senior secondary school.

Issues arising

Of concern to schools are the issues of information overload, and of the coordination of developmental tasks, with the implied loadings of consultation if there is to be practitioner input. In particular there is the issue of multiple accountabilities, with a second monitoring of school practice, for 'non-conventional subjects', to supplement that of the Education Review Office.

Of equal interest to school leaders is the coordination or dislocation between current school practice of increasing multi-level study by individual students – and the Authority's sponsorship of a modular pattern of unit standards for the Qualifications Framework – both perceived to have a vertical orientation – and the New Zealand Curriculum Framework's thrust of coverage of a range of essential learning areas – a horizontal dimension.

The resolution of these matters is still not apparent to school managers. Confusion also appears to persist between the notion of unit standard (an assessment measure) and unit of study (a component of a broader curriculum statement dealing with the programme for the development of knowledge, skills and attitudes). The compatibility of these parallel concepts, and the limitation of potential backwash from assessment into curriculum and pedagogy, are also not yet apparent to school managers, and in late 1993 were matters of escalating concern. By 1995 schools were trialling unit standards in mathematics and geography and the full system was planned to be operational by 1998 but a new Government in 1996 announced a full review.

Requirements of the Public Finance Act, 1989

Boards of Trustees are required to render account to their communities and, in an Annual Meeting, table a Financial Report whose format increasingly coincides with the reports required by the Public Finance Act of all Crown Entities, government departments, and State Owned Enterprises.

The reports are subject to scrutiny by the Auditor-General and must be lodged, after audit, with the Ministry of Education. The 1992 amendment to the Public Finance Act provides that, as an extra level of accountability the Ministry will forward a copy of all relevant reports to the electorate MP. The same amending act provided that, from 1994, by each 30 June the Minister of Education will table in the House a report on the outputs purchased by the Crown from the Combined Schools Sector in the previous school year, together with comment on the quality of the management systems and on the outcomes measured as learning achievement. In assisting the Minister, the Ministry will draw on its databases, and on those of the Education Review Office and the New Zealand Qualifications Authority.

Issues arising

An issue of concern to boards is that the reporting model requires that each year in advance they set key objectives. In 1992 the Audit Office tagged many sets of 1991 school board accounts, noting lack of specificity in their statements of service performance on the desired quantity and quality of their output objectives. This led in turn to unsatisfactory reporting on the producing to specification of the outputs which had been purchased by the state with the funding it had made available to each board.

The Ministry, in 1993, through its Contracts Management Section, as part of its school development programme, let a contract for a training pilot of principals and trustees in the development of statements of service performance to a standard that will meet Auditor-General requirements – and in the interim this requirement on the boards has been relaxed until 1997.

It is of interest to both boards and Ministry that the new Combined Schools Sector Report will require aggregation of data, which could lead to requests for standardisation of reports – and of performance measures. The production of the initial report in 1994 has been described in an article to appear in 'International Studies in Educational Administration' (Rae, in press). The 1995 and 1996 reports were also produced on time, with significant media interest on inter-school comparability.

DISCUSSION

Evolving accountabilities for New Zealand schools

The Auditor-General has voiced his approval, as financial watchdog for Parliament, of the clarification of accountability measures for education that has taken place in New Zealand (Cameron, 1992). In his outline:

- A Charter approved by the Minister of Education forms the contract [sic] between the Crown and the board of trustees for the services to be delivered by the school
- Annual Financial Statements report to the Ministry of Education and to the community on the financial operations and financial position of the school, on the achievement of targets set, and on the resources deployed to meet them
- The audit of these statements is the responsibility of the Auditor-General
- The audit of educational effectiveness in the meeting of Charter objectives is the responsibility of the Education Review Office.

Boards and principals perceive, however, some overlap, and note that education objectives are set within a financial planning context, which they find problematic. They are also aware that it is an evolving context of curricular and qualification frameworks that needs to be acknowledged, in any requiring of each school that is set appropriate objectives.

Of a more general strategic concern is the contrast between specificity of requirements on boards of financial planning and reporting processes and the ambiguity concerning the school's charter. The charter of every school now has a major deemed component not to be found in the document at the school, but in the guidelines statement in the Education Gazette. A variant of Gresham's Law would say that the more precise procedure will drive out the less precise.

Accountability has been more broadly described in the past. To the NZEAS national conference of 1983 on 'Educational Accountability in a Multicultural Society', Renwick, as Director-General, proposed dimensions of professional and moral accountability – accountability to an internalised professional code of conduct and ethics; and an ability to explain one's actions and decisions as a teacher and as an educational administrator. His definition proposed the ability to give an account as well as to render account.

Accountability in the discourse of today could be considered to be more narrow and more technical. Scott (1993), however, affirms that the required statements of service performance are an accountability device more acceptable for 'not-for-profit' organisations than the standard financial report. They require the organisation to specify the nature of its service, the targets and desired quality for its service delivery, and at the end of each year to evaluate its performance. The procedure is in fact close to the Renwick definition of accountability as the 'giving of an account' – the ability to examine and explain one's decisions and actions.

The accountability frameworks, and the basis for defining effectiveness (the meeting of appropriate goals) and efficiency (the meeting of those goals in the most appropriate manner), thus continued to evolve, in the fourth year of 'Tomorrow's Schools', with components that would continue to be erected over at least the next two years. There are issues, amid ongoing change, of the maintaining of morale across the schools, of steerage from the centre, and of the centre's reliance of necessity on input, lay and professional, at the school level. There will need to be recognition by the centre that schools are crowded, compulsory locations for social exchange and learning – and for the implementation in detail of its grand designs.

An additional pressure on schools since 1989 has been the freeing-up of enrolment procedures to create choice in an 'education market' – in the proclaimed interest of desired responsiveness, accountability and school improvement. Issues of choice and equity embedded in these enrolment policies are discussed by Codd (1993) who contrasts the Utilitarian Market-Liberal's concept of education as 'preferred good', to be competed for, with the Rawlsian concept of education as a 'primary good', its possession essential if a citizen is to participate in society and make appropriate life choices, in a manner that accords with social justice.

Codd also explored the concept of education as 'positional good' – in a market imperfect on both the supply and demand sides – i.e., the more choice in education some possess, the less choice is available to others. A most telling proposition in the Codd essay is the suggestion that a belief in the market establishing quality and responsiveness in schools, as some succeed and others fail, is in fact a belief that students may attend failing schools. That this is unsatisfactory even to Utilitarian Market-Liberals is suggested by the creation in the 1989 restructuring of an Education Review Office as a separate and single-purpose department of state, and the initial focus of the Office in its revised outputs of 1992–3 on Assurance Audits.

Issues of school effectiveness and school improvement

A range of international models can be studied to interpret New Zealand's evolving practices on achieving and assessing school effectiveness and accountability.

Shipman (1990: 65–6) proposed five models for the assessing of school effectiveness (see Fig. 7.6). He suggested, however, that at best they supply only hunches on the way schools work, and that social and cultural realities are more complex.

The output model

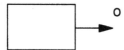

This is *ex post facto* after-the-event research. There is no way of knowing what caused the outputs in the school.

The process–output model

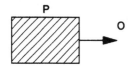

Now the outputs can be related to different school processes. But differences among intakes and their environment could still be major influences.

The input–output model

The before-and-after design is very popular. But it gives no information on what may have caused any differences in the result.

The input–process–output model

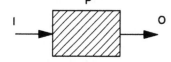

Now the progress (output less input) of pupils can be related to what went on in school.

The context–input–process–output model

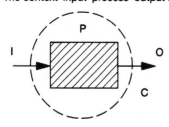

Now environmental factors can also be taken into account at input and output, and progress attributed to the school.

Figure 7.6 Models for assessing school effectiveness (from Shipman 1990)

1 With a simple output model, there is no way of knowing what caused the outputs. The league table model is deficient in explanatory power.
2 Even with a process–output model, differences across school intakes could be a significant factor.
3 An input–output model leaves school processes as a 'black box'.

4   In an input–process–output model progress is related to what happened within the school.

5   Only in a context–input–process–output model can environmental factors be taken into account in seeking to establish the progress attributable to the school.

This final model is that adopted by the Education Review Office in its 1993 trials of Effectiveness Reviews.

McPherson (1992) critiqued the concept of 'league tables' as providing information of assistance in an 'education market'. He modeled the relative ranking of six schools after four adjustments of students scores – for gender, for ability at age 12, for family background, and for family background of the students (see Fig. 7.7).

He comments that a good indicator system will:

* take account of different needs and uses
* be as simple as possible while recognising the individuality of pupils, families and schools
* prefer measures of stability and of change in performance to single snap-shots
* have built-in means of monitoring and improving its validity.

The Scottish Office Education Department has defined an effective school as 'one in which the pupils progress further than might be expected from consideration of its intake' (Mortimore, 1991: 281). The McPherson model can be located within this tradition. The model also suggests, however, the sophistication of assessment procedures required, to permit valid comment on such effectiveness.

Mortimore (1991) and Reynolds (1993) have both pleaded for synergy from linking school effectiveness research and school improvement research. A table by Reynolds distinguished key characteristics of the two fields – focus on organisation in work on school effectiveness, focus on process in school improvement; quantitative, qualitative; data driven, rarely empirical; based on research knowledge, based on practitioner input.

He proposed as strategies to release the synergy:

* staff development
* inquiry and reflection
* leadership
* coordination
* planning.

Mortimore (1991: 224) suggested that schools are likely to improve if:

* most staff and the head agree on a clear mission for the institution
* a systematic audit of current strengths and weaknesses is carried out
* an outside agent is involved

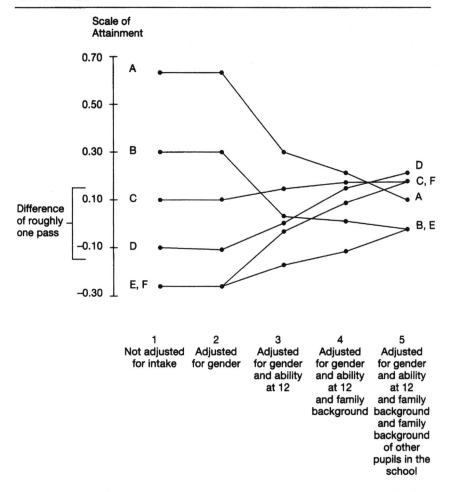

Figure 7.7 Average pupil attainment in six schools unadjusted for pupil intake, and with four adjustments (from McPherson 1992)

- the implementation of the change plan is supported by the appropriate external authorities
- an evaluation of progress is used formatively to support the implementation.

In a paper to the CCEA Hong Kong Conference (Rae 1992), it was noted that the Mortimore model accords with New Zealand experience with the 'Professional Development Cycle' of Prebble and Stewart (1985) and the use of a developer across a cluster of schools to promote school–community interaction for curriculum development of the CRRISP Project (1989–90; Ramsay et al., 1993). It is also the model used in the sequence of school and principal development contracts awarded from 1990 to the present day by the Ministry Curriculum Functions Division (Ministry of Education, 1992; Rae, 1994).

'Hear Our Voices', the final report of the Monitoring Today's Schools team from Waikato University, contracted by the Ministry of Education to monitor the restructuring through 1990 to 1992, has commented on the issue of school effectiveness, on the basis of surveys of views of trustees, principals and teachers (Mitchell, 1993: 121):

> If we accept that the final judgement as to the success or failure of school reforms must be based on the quality of knowledge, skills and dispositions acquired by the students, then it must be said that the jury is still out on Tomorrow's Schools. The question that must be addressed however is whether it was ever appropriate to expect the reforms to bring about improved educational standards. What are the grounds for expecting such an outcome?

The report notes that the Picot Report Task Force (1988: 98) posited an improved standard of educational outcomes from the reformed structures, arising principally from institutions' increased clarity of focus and their ability to manage their own resources. 'Hear Our Voices' notes that behind these explicit and positive comments lay 'unstated but clearly implied more negative motivations' – i.e. fear of parents withdrawing their children from the learning institution, and fear of negative evaluations from the Review and Audit (sic) Agency.

The Waikato team observe that the Picot analysis is close to that of the American commentator Newman (1993), who saw the value in improved efficiency and effectiveness in schools to be derived from a greater sense of ownership and responsibility for quality, which would inspire greater commitment by staff to do a good job. Newman affirmed, however, that a focus on organisational structures was not of itself sufficient for enhanced educational outcomes, and presented a case for 'infusing restructuring with a powerful commitment to an educational vision'.

This section in the Waikato team's report, therefore, concludes that the drive for enhanced educational outcomes lies properly at the heart of a second reform initiative which will focus on the curriculum and its assessment (Mitchell, 1993: 122):

> [Discussion of the] commitments and competence [to] be nurtured in the New Zealand education system . . . is a critical task and a significant beginning has been made in addressing it through the recently published New Zealand Curriculum Framework. To a large extent it and the proposals regarding national monitoring set the agenda for the second wave of reforms.

CONCLUSION

In August 1993, towards the end of the winter term, two educational news items were broadcast consecutively on the national midday radio bulletin. In one the president of the secondary teachers union (PPTA) was calling for the contract appointment of a coordinating director-general to manage the introduction of curricular reform and the new qualifications framework; in the second the School Trustees Association was taking an injunction against the Minister of Education who, on advice from the Education Review Office, had dismissed the board of a rural school of thirty-one pupils, and proposed to have installed a commissioner who would prepare for fresh elections.

Two weeks later the Minister of Education addressed the first issue, that of coordination, in his speech of 24 August to the Annual Conference of the secondary teachers union, stating, 'I will coordinate the work of the New Zealand Qualifications Authority with that of the Ministry of Education and strengthen their communication with you so that we can all work towards a common vision.' In terms of current legislation, and in line with the theories explored early in this paper, the Minister is technically correct – he alone has the power to require this coordination. No senior officer within the public service has the power to compel cooperation of the two Crown entities named.

This development can only be described at this close range as a very proactive 'strategic withdrawal' to the core business of the state (to paraphrase Nash, 1989). It is an interesting blurring of the distinction between policy and administration promoted by Director-General Ballard and the Implementation Unit in 1989, between governance and management as promoted by the Lough Report in 1990, and between outcomes and outputs as found in the Public Finance Act of 1989. It could also be seen as the triumph of political initiative over Public Choice theory, and Principal–Agent theory over managerialism.

On the second issue, concerning ministerial use of a statutory discretion, the requested injunction was not granted. Eventually, the Minister's action, because he had sought and considered advice, was upheld.

1993 also saw a national election in New Zealand, which almost produced for the first time in 65 years a minority government, and a referendum which has determined that a new form of parliamentary electoral process will apply from 1996. Both events were able in their consequences to significantly impact on the roles of the state at the centre and on policy and management practices for New Zealand schools from the beginning of 1994.

Two significant forums were convened in Wellington in November 1993, to fall unknowingly into the hiatus between the election and the final declaration of results. The first considered the formation of a New Zealand Teaching Council, at a meeting sponsored by the Teacher Registration Board with support from all the teacher unions and the New Zealand Council of Teacher Education; the second considered the establishment of an Industry Training Organisation (ITO) for education, with sponsorship by the Education Training and Support Agency in terms of the Skill New Zealand policy under the Industry Training Act 1992. This second initiative had support from the New Zealand School Trustees Association as an employer organisation required in terms of the legislation to drive the ITO, if and when established. The ITO concept also had the support of the unions, who proposed a structure that would bring together the employers, the unions, the Government agencies, and the providers of professional training.

One significant recommendation of the 1988 Picot Task Force (which had disappeared by the time of the publication of Tomorrow's Schools) was for an Education Policy Council, a recommendation for a coordinating body which signalled the task force's recognition of the number of State agencies that were to emerge, and a recommendation to which Brian Picot alluded in his retrospective commentary in April 1993 already referred to in this chapter.

An obvious motivation for protagonists at both forums was a desire for a greater slice of the influence pie in the setting of education agendas, given the strategies for management of public policy driven by the competing theories that have held sway since 1988. Equally potent among the participants, however, was a deeper wish to locate a clear focus for the development of education policy, given the destruction of the earlier umbrella organisation, the Department of Education, and the increase in the number of players in the education field. By the end of 1996, neither proposal has yet been fully implemented. The Teaching Council has been launched, but with limited membership and impact, and the Education ITO has not been launched at all.

In summary, this chapter has proposed that devolution of management in the New Zealand education system has been evolving through nearly ten years. Devolution is currently incomplete and is responding to the increasing attention falling on curriculum change and assessment of learning. The devolution has been marked by increasing accountabilities placed upon school managers, by a centre which is finding structural coordination a continuing challenge, and by thrusts towards coordination both inside and outside Government policy. The final cameos indicate that countervailing and simultaneous thrusts toward devolution and toward centralisation will indeed persist within restructured educational administration in New Zealand.

NOTES

1 This chapter is the personal commentary of a participant observer. It is not to be taken as a statement of Ministry policy, nor as a statement of policy of the Minister of Education in New Zealand.

2 The flower stalk at the heart of the New Zealand flax bush provides nectar, and a singing platform for the bellbird. The flax bush provides leaves and fibre for Maori kits and weaving, if plucked in a manner which conserves the growing heart. The choice of epigraph, a traditional Maori song, could suggest the self-managing school is a flax bush under potential threat.

REFERENCES

Aitken, J. E. (1993a) 'Education Review Office: Effectiveness Reviews', *NZ Educational Gazette*, 72(10), Wellington: Learning Media.
—— (1993b) 'Educational Leadership and Today's Schools: Speech to NZEI Waikato Principals Council', Wellington: Education Review Office (Mimeo).
Barrington, J. (1991) *Report to the Ministry of Education. OECD: Education Evaluation and Reform Strategies*, Wellington: Ministry of Education (Mimeo).
Beare, H. and Boyd, W. Lowe (eds) (1993) *Restructuring Schools: An International Perspective on the Movement to Transform the Control and Performance of Schools*, London: Falmer Press.
Beeby, C. E. (1992) *The Biography of an Idea: Beeby on Education*, Wellington: NZCER.
Boston, J., Martin, J., Pallot J. and Walsh P. (eds) (1991) *Reshaping the State: New Zealand's Bureaucratic Revolution*, Auckland: Oxford University Press.
Cameron, W. (1992) *Report on the Accountability of State Schools*, Wellington: Audit Office.
Chapman, J. (1991) *The Effectiveness of Schooling and of Educational Resource Management*, Monograph No. 1: A Conceptual Framework, Paris: OECD.
Codd, J. A. (1993) 'Equity and Choice: the paradox of New Zealand Education reform', *Curriculum Studies* 1(1), pp. 75–90.
CRRISP (1989–90) *Reports 1–5*, Hamilton: Curriculum Review Research in Schools Project Project, University of Waikato.
Cusack, B. O. (1992) 'A Theoretical Analysis of Policy Production: The Picot Reforms in New Zealand', unpublished PhD thesis, Armidale: University of New England.
Cuttance, P. (1992) 'Evaluating the effectiveness of schools', in D. Reynolds and P. Cuttance (eds), *School Effectiveness; Research, Policy in Practices*, pp. 1–24, London: Cassell.
Dale, R. and Jesson, J. (1993) 'Mainstreaming Education: the role of the State Services Commission', in *New Zealand Annual Review of Education 2: 1992*, pp. 7–34. Wellington: Victoria University of Wellington.
Education Implementation Team (1990) *Today's Schools: A Review of the Education Reform Implementation Process*, Wellington: Government Printer.
Goff, P. (1990) 'National Education Guidelines', supplement to *NZ Education Gazette*, 1 February.
Hargreaves, D. H. and Hopkins, D. (1991) *The Empowered School: The Management and Practice of Developmental Planning*, London: Cassell.
Harrison, R. (1993) 'The Powers, Duties and Accountabilities of School Boards of Trustees', in *Education and the Law in New Zealand: Seminar Papers*, pp. 62–98. Auckland: Legal Research Foundation.
Lange, D. (1988) *Tomorrow's Schools: The Reform of Education Administration in New Zealand*, Wellington: Government Printer.
Lauder, W., Middleton, S., Boston, J. and Wylie, C. (1988) ' "The Third Wave": a critique of the New Zealand Treasury's Report on Education', *NZJES*, 23(1), pp. 15–34; *NZJES*, 23(2), pp. 115–44.

Levacic, R. (1993) 'Local Management of Schools as an organisational form: theory and application', *Journal of Education Policy*, 8(2), pp. 123–41.

McPherson, A. (1992) 'Measuring Added Value in Schools', reprinted in *Set No 1*, 1993.

Middleton, S., Codd, J. and Jones, A. (eds) (1990) *New Zealand Education Policy Today: Critical Perspectives*, Wellington: Allen and Unwin, and Port Nicholson Press.

Ministry of Education (1990) *Quality Education for All According to their Needs. Brief to the Incoming Government*, Wellington: Ministry of Education (Mimeo).

—— (1992) 'Principal Development and Curriculum Leadership', *Curriculum Update*, 4(1), October.

—— (1993a) 'Assessment in the New Zealand Curriculum Framework', *Curriculum Update*, 5, 15 April.

—— (1993b) *The New Zealand Curriculum Framework: Te Anga Matauranga o Aoteoroa*, Wellington: Learning Media.

—— (1993c) *Three Years On: The New Zealand Education Reforms 1989–1992*, Wellington: Learning Media.

—— (1993d) *Education for the 21st Century: A Discussion Document*, Wellington: Learning Media.

Mitchell, D. (1990–93) *Monitoring Today's Schools. Reports No. 1 to No. 17*, Hamilton: Monitoring Today's Schools Research Project, University of Waikato.

—— (1993) *Hear Our Voices: Final Report of Monitoring Today's Schools*, Hamilton: Monitoring Today's Schools Research Project, University of Waikato

Mortimore, P. (1991) 'School Effectiveness Research: Which Way at the Crossroads', *School Effectiveness and School Improvement*, 2(3), pp. 213–29.

Nash, R. (1989) 'Tomorrow's Schools: State power and parent participation', *NZJES*, 24(2), pp. 113–38.

Newman, F. (1993) 'Beyond common sense in Educational restructuring: The Issues of content and linkage', *Educational Researcher*, 22(2), pp. 4–13.

New Zealand Qualifications Authority (1991) *Designing the Framework. A Discussion Document about Restructuring National Qualifications*, Wellington: NZQA.

—— (1993) *Quality Management Systems for the National Qualification Framework*, Wellington: NZQA.

O'Brien, T. (1990) 'A Critical Analysis of the Reform of Industrial Relations for Primary Teachers in New Zealand', unpublished MPP thesis, Wellington: Victoria University of Wellington.

O'Rourke, M. (1993a) 'The New Zealand Curriculum Framework', *NZ Education Gazette*, 72(6), pp. 1–2.

—— (1993b) 'National Education Guidelines', *NZ Education Gazette*, 72(8), pp. 3–4.

Peters, M. (1993) 'Starship Education: Enterprise Culture in New Zealand', *Access*, 11(1), pp. 1–12.

Philips, D. (1993) 'Curriculum Development in New Zealand', *Educational Review*, 45(2), pp. 155–64.

Picot, B. (1993) 'Picot Report Revisited – five years on', *Eduvac*, 4, 132, Auckland: Kaha Media.

Principals Implementation Task Force (1990) *A Guide to Educational Objectives; A Guide to Governance and Management; A Guide to Financial Management; A Guide to Property Management; A Guide to Personnel Management*, Wellington: Ministry of Education.

Rae, K. A. (1990) 'The Education Officer in New Zealand', in W. Walker, R. Farquhar and M. Hughes (eds), *Advancing Education: School Leadership in Action*, pp. 170–87. London: Falmer Press.

—— (1991a) 'Te Ao Hurihuri – "Tomorrow's Schools": Administrative Change and the Consequences for Educational Administration and Supervision', in P. Ribbins, R. Glatter, T. Simkins and L. Watson (eds), *Developing Educational Leaders*, pp. 40–56. Harlow: Longman.

—— (1991b) 'Industrial Relations for New Zealand Teachers', *Access: Critical Perspectives in Educational Policy*, 10(2), pp. 21–34.

—— (1992) 'Te Wero – "Tomorrow's Schools in the Third Year": The Challenge for Educational Administrators in New Zealand', paper prepared for the CCEA Regional Conference in Hong Kong, Wellington: Ministry of Education (Mimeo).

—— (1994) 'Te Wero: The Challenge of School Development in Tomorrow's Schools', *Studies in Educational Administration*, 59, Summer, pp. 33–40.

—— (In press) 'Devising New Measures to Report on Tomorrow's Schools', *International Studies in Educational Administration*.

Ramsay, P., Hawke, K., Harold, B., Marriott, R. and Poskitt, J. (1993) *Developing Partnership: Collaboration Between Teachers and Parents*, Wellington: Learning Media

Reynolds, D. (1989) 'School Effectiveness and School Improvement: A Review of the British Literature', in D. Reynolds, B. Creemers and T. Peters (eds), *School Effectiveness and Improvement: Proceedings of the First International Congress, London, 1988*.

—— (1992) 'School Effectiveness and School Improvement: An Updated Review of the British Literature' in D. Reynolds and P. Cuttance (eds), *School Effectiveness; Research, Policy in Practices*, pp. 1–24, London: Cassell.

—— (1993) 'Linking School Effectiveness Knowledge and School Improvement Practice: Towards a Synergy', *School Effectiveness and School Improvement*, 4(1), pp. 37–58.

Reynolds, D. and Packer, A. (1992) 'School Effectiveness and School Improvement in the 1990s', in D. Reynolds and P. Cuttance (eds), *School Effectiveness; Research, Policy in Practices*, pp. 171–87, London: Cassell.

Scott, D. (1993) 'Statements of Service Performance: A Measure of School Effectiveness', paper delivered to Wellington Branch, NZ Society of Accountants, Wellington: College of Education (Mimeo).

Shipman, M. (1990) *In Search of Learning: A New Approach to School Management*, Oxford: Blackwell Educational.

Smith, A. L. (1992) 'Reviews and Audits of Schools and Early Childhood Services by the Education Review Office', *NZ Education Gazette*, 2 June, pp. 4–5.

Smyth, J. (1992) 'Teacher Work and the Politics of Reflection', *American Educational Research Journal*, 29(2), pp. 267–300.

—— (ed.) (1989) *Critical Perspectives on Educational Leadership*, Lewes: Falmer Press.

Stewart, D. and Prebble, T. (1985) *Making it Happen: A School Development Process*, Palmerston North: Dunmore.

Task Force to Review Education Administration (1988) *Administering for Excellence: Effective Administration in Education*, Wellington: The Task Force.

Treasury, The (1987) *Government Management: Brief to the Incoming Government, vol. II: Education Issues*, Wellington: The Treasury.

Part III

The impact of restructuring on schools and school systems

Chapter 8

Underlying the chaos
Factors explaining exemplary US elementary schools and the case for high-reliability organisations[1]

Sam Stringfield

The United States is perpetually awash in 'new' and self-proclaimed 'highly effective' programs for improving students' academic achievement. The now-defunct National Diffusion Network, for example, disseminated 195 'educational programs that work' in 1992. Some used computers, some did not; some, through 'whole-school-restructuring' designs or otherwise, involved the whole school, some did not; some were phonics-based, others 'whole-language'; and so on. The evidence that most of these programs 'work' has always been modest, and evidence of generalisability of effects is, for the majority of programs, non-existent. In short, chaos reigns. Chaos theory (Gleick, 1987) postulates that, by stripping off the apparent orderliness of the universe of 195 often utterly incompatible programs, one sees chaos, but that beneath that chaos can be found a different level of order.

This chapter attempts to find that order underlying successful elementary school improvement efforts. By examining richly detailed, longitudinal descriptions of four schools' reasonably successful efforts to implement very different improvement programs, the chapter examines common elements from the perspective of High-Reliability Organisations (Roberts, 1993; Stringfield, 1995). Data indicate that *differing* implementations among the four schools share *common* characteristics. Those characteristics are shared with other organisations charged with maintaining very high reliability while achieving different goals within society. Implications of the findings for improving schooling are examined.

THE FOUR LONGITUDINAL CASES

Each of four schools was followed for between two and eleven years during studies funded by the Louisiana Department of Education, the Kellogg Foundation, the Abell Foundation, the Center for Research on Effective Schooling for Disadvantaged Students (CDS), or the Center for Research on the Education of Students Placed At Risk (CRESPAR). Short descriptions of the schools and their improvement efforts follow.

Frances Scott Key Elementary School

In the late 1980s, Frances Scott Key Elementary School served an inner-city Philadelphia neighbourhood comprised of more than 70 per cent first generation immigrants from refugee camps in Southeast Asia, and about 30 per cent African-American students. Over the subsequent ten years, those percentages have approximately reversed, with the majority of students today being African-American. Many of the Asian students had never known life outside a refugee camp and had never been to school before coming to Philadelphia. The school had a history of very poor academic performance (Slavin and Yampolsky, 1991), a condition that was not regarded as unusual for a school serving inner-city immigrant and poor minority students. Under the direction of a new principal and with a supportive central administration, Key Elementary School was one of the first to adopt the 'Success for All' program (Slavin *et al.*, 1990, 1992, 1996a, b). Though implementation proved difficult, results have been dramatic (Slavin *et al.*, 1996a). Five years of individual-student-level data-gathering by the Success for All team resulted in an unusually complete set of longitudinal outcome data. Using the students of a carefully demographically matched, physically nearby school as controls, Slavin *et al.* (1996a) found that, on average, Asian-heritage Key Elementary School fifth graders, who had attended the school throughout, averaged nearly three academic years greater reading achievement than well matched controls (median effect size = +1.44). Non-Asian, largely African-American, fifth grade students averaged reading scores that were more than two years more advanced than their matched controls (median effect size = +.78). In addition, local evaluation data, and two sets of detailed case study data over a six-year period, have been analysed. Case study data have consistently indicated an orderly climate at the school, students with clearly positive attitudes and high on-task rates, and positive faculty attitudes toward the program and dramatically high reading and mathematics achievement gains (Rossi and Stringfield, 1995; Stringfield *et al.*, 1996).

The results at Key Elementary School are unusually well documented, but not unusual in size among Success for All schools (Slavin *et al.*, 1996a, b). What components contribute to such success? Slavin *et al.* (1996a) now list ten major components of all Success for All projects:

1 A reading curriculum based on research on effective practices in beginning reading, and on effective uses of cooperative learning Students attend heterogeneous classes throughout the day, but are grouped homogeneously across grades in grades 1–3 for reading instruction. This regrouped reading session lasts for 90 minutes every morning. Paired reading and heterogeneous cooperative learning are components of the reading program.

2 **Eight-week reading assessments**   Every eight weeks, reading teachers assess all students' progress in the reading program. Results are combined with teachers' assessments to determine who is to receive tutoring, to make changes in students' reading groups, and to suggest other strategies for addressing the needs of individual students.

3 **Reading tutors**   One-to-one tutoring is provided for first grade students who are in danger of falling behind in reading. This is consistent with the program's goal of preventing reading problems before they are exacerbated.

4 **Preschool and kindergarten**   Most Success for All schools provide a half-day pre-school (age 4), and/or a full day kindergarten (age 5), for eligible students. The curriculum emphasises the development and use of language, and academic readiness.

5 **Family support team**   Viewing parents as essential to students' success, Success for All requires the development of a family support team at each school. At the least, the team includes a school administrator, a community liaison, a counsellor (if available at the school), the Success for All facilitator, and others deemed appropriate to the task. The family support team serves functions that range from welcoming new families into the school, to coordinating services for families, to teaching parents to read developmentally appropriate materials to their children every night.

6 **Program facilitator**   Every Success for All school has a program facilitator who works with the principal on planning the program and scheduling problems, and visits classes and tutoring sessions to help teachers with individual problems.

7 **Teacher training**   Teachers receive detailed teachers' manuals supplemented by three days of in-service training at the beginning of the school year. Initial training focuses on the program overview, the initial reading curriculum, and cooperative learning techniques. Tutors receive two additional days of training on tutoring strategies and reading assessment. Additional in-service presentations are made throughout the year by the facilitators, all featuring extensive classroom follow-up, coaching, and group discussion.

8 **Advisory committee**   The building principal, program facilitator, teacher representatives, parent representatives, and family support staff meet regularly to review the program's progress and to solve emerging problems. Grade-level teams meet in addition to this whole-school team.

9 **Special education**   A goal of Success for All is, to the greatest extent possible, to address the needs of every child in the regular classroom, without labelling the child. On the rare occasions when such special services are required, the Success for All team attempts to serve the child in such ways as to not disrupt their regular classroom experiences.

10 **Relentlessness**   Over the past year, the Success for All team has become more explicit in stating that 'relentlessness' regarding solving the problems facing each child is a major component of Success for All. If one strategy doesn't succeed, the various teachers and teams are to engage in a relentless search for what will work for the child.

To one degree or another, all ten of these components have been implemented and observed at Key Elementary School. Over the years, the school has experienced a significant turnover in teaching staff, has been served by two principals, and has experienced shifts in the demographic make-up of the school. Yet multiple evaluations over several years have found that the school successfully 'turned itself around', and produced dramatic rises in mean student achievement.

Barclay School

Barclay School serves a 97 per cent African-American community in Baltimore, Maryland. Eighty per cent of students receive free or reduced-price lunches, a traditional US measure of poverty in schools.[2] In the late 1980s, the African-American principal had become very concerned that scores on district tests had fallen over several years, and that student discipline had suffered notable declines. Together with a parent–community organisation, she lobbied the district administration to allow the school to adopt the curriculum and instructional program of a nearby, highly regarded private school. After two years of negotiation, the district allowed Barclay school to adopt the Calvert School program.

The Calvert School curriculum was developed nearly a century ago to serve children of considerable affluence. It features whole-group instruction in texts, some of which have been out of print for years. Where 'Success for All' is a 'state of the art' program, Calvert could be thought of as the 'old time religion' of education.

Calvert's insistence that their program be implemented one grade at a time, beginning with first grade, created an excellent, within-school control group for studying the program's effects. The control group for the Barclay/Calvert program has been the Barclay School cohorts in front of the Calvert program. Extensive quantitative records have been available, in addition to detailed field notes gathered each year (Stringfield, 1994). In addition to local measures, the evaluation has featured an additional norm referenced test, independent of local school district control.

Over four years of implementation, during which Barclay has begun with kindergarten and first grade and added one Calvert grade per year, results have been dramatic. Whereas in grade four previous Barclay cohorts had averaged between the 20th and 26th percentiles on the Total Reading portion of the Comprehensive Test of Basic Skills (CTBS, the nationally normed test used in Baltimore), the first cohort of Barclay/Calvert students achieved mean reading achievements at the 55th percentile. In general, cohorts two through four were scoring even higher, with the second cohort finishing grade three at the 59th percentile, and the fourth cohort finishing grade one near the 70th percentile. Nationally, Tests of Language Arts told a similar story. Where the typical pre-Calvert Barclay cohort had averaged between the 20th and 30th percentiles nationally, the first Barclay/Calvert cohort scored near the 60th percentile, and the three subsequent cohorts, measured at grades three, two and one respectively, all scored above the 60th percentile. On the spring 1994 administration of the CTBS mathematics test, all four Barclay/Calvert cohorts (grades one–four), scored above the 60th percentile nationally. Again, these scores were well above pre-Calvert Barclay peers, many of whom were the older brothers and sisters of the Barclay/Calvert students.

Teachers described the effects on their students and themselves as 'miraculous'. Using a very different program than Success for All, the Barclay School achieved similarly striking results. A description of the key components of Barclay/Calvert follows:

A more stimulating, more demanding, more fully articulated curriculum for all students   Talks with Calvert teachers and administrators almost inevitably turn to discussions of content. In virtually every area, the Calvert curriculum is more demanding and more intellectually stimulating than that provided by the Baltimore City curriculum. The students read much more, the topics covered are more advanced, they study great artists from around the world, beginning in first grade, and so on.

In part because Calvert also offers a home study curriculum, the courses and lessons are described in great detail in teachers' manuals. Individual teachers are encouraged to vary presentations, but content coverage is nonnegotiable.

The specific reading and mathematics curricula would strike many education professors as 'traditional'. The history, sciences, arts, and geography content places emphasis on 'the classics' from diverse cultures, and bears a resemblance to that advocated by the Core Knowledge Foundation (Hirsch, 1988; Core Knowledge Foundation, 1995).

Writing every day   Both at Barclay and Calvert, students write every day. Their initial drafts may be filled with errors, and that is acceptable, but students must correct all of their errors through repeated writing, so that, by the end of the week, all students have produced error-free text. A first-grade (age six) paper might be on the topic, 'I like my house', and take only eight lines. A third grader's paper might be on Egyptian ruins and take a page and a half. Both will begin with a topic sentence, have supporting detail, and, by Friday of the week, be error-free.

A full-time program coordinator   School principals in the US have full-time jobs. The implementation and sustaining of this major set of changes was seen by the Barclay and Calvert principals as requiring a full-time program coordinator. That person leads staff development activities, visits classrooms, models lessons, coordinates academic work within the school and between the school and homes, and coordinates activities between Barclay and Calvert.

Initial, and ongoing, focused staff development   The implementation design for Barclay/Calvert called for the Calvert curriculum to enter Barclay at kindergarten and grade one only, then expand one grade per year, as students move forward. This was based on the Calvert assumption that the more advanced grades' curricula were simply too advanced for traditionally-prepared students. As each new grade's teachers (and any teacher moved into Barclay's earlier grades) prepared for the program, they were provided with a two-week summer training course on the philosophy and particulars of the Calvert curriculum. The coordinator then came into classes throughout the year and modelled lessons, providing feedback and other support.

Regular folder checks   In every Calvert and Barclay/Calvert classroom, a bulletin board at the rear of the class is given over to student folders. The first day of the month, all students create a piece of artwork that becomes the cover for the month's folder. The folders are displayed in alphabetical order. Each student's folder contains writing, mathematics, geography, history, spelling, and other tasks. All contents of folders are corrected by students until they contain no errors. Folders are checked and counter-checked by the students themselves, by teachers, the coordinator and/or principal, and by parents. The folders serve several valuable functions. First, they keep the school's focus on students' productions. Although Calvert's curriculum and methods predate 'constructivist' theories by nearly 100 years, the two share a focus on the students' productions, the students' learning, the students' work.

Calvert insists upon 100 per cent accuracy. Over time, students become increasingly proficient in turning in very nearly error-free work the first time, because it saves time spent in corrections over the week.

Finally, the folders and folder checks provide a ready source of multi-way accountability. Parents and the principal can be sure that assignments are being made and corrected, and that students are doing their work. The coordinator and teacher can discuss problems, not in the abstract, but while looking at a long-term record of a student's progress. (Previous months' folders are stored and made into a 'book' of accomplishments at the year's end, and therefore remain available for discussion.)

Making sure things work   In some ways the hardest-to-observe component of the Calvert program is a determination that all of the pieces will be in place and work. It is hard to observe because it simply happens. In US education, in more ways than are immediately obvious, a considerable amount of 'normal practice' derives from an assumption that something coming before or about to happen will not work for lack of simple components: the materials won't be available on the needed day, the school will run out of paper for students before the end of the year, the overhead projector's light won't work, or the video player won't work. It is not that these things *usually* don't work; it is, rather, that a teacher *can't count on them* working this time, and therefore she schedules around the possibility of uncorrected system failure. In Baltimore, and most school districts, it has not been historically unusual for the state or district to mandate a new history series, and then not provide the books until the second semester of the year. Similar examples abound. At Calvert, and at Barclay/Calvert, great efforts have been expended to be sure that teachers, and by extension, students, can succeed the first time. Books arrive on time. The school doesn't run out of paper. When the air conditioner for the computer room failed, and the school district didn't get a technician to the building for weeks, Barclay/Calvert persons were able to secure assistance through non-traditional routes. While the school system's system failed (and no one seemed surprised), Barclay's unusual system worked.

At Calvert, and at Barclay/Calvert, it is considered important that things work. The results have been clear.

Aynesworth Elementary School

Aynesworth Elementary School in Fresno, California, served an impoverished, more than 90 per cent minority (Mexican-American, Asian-American and African-American) community. Aynesworth had for several years consistently scored at the extreme upper end of the expectancy band on the state's California Assessment Program.

A two-year case study of the school (Hepler *et al.*, 1987), indicated that the school's locally developed 'super kids' program and energetic principal were at the heart of the unusual student success. The curriculum was not extraordinary, and was fairly 'California-standard'. However, the following points were nearly unique to the school.

Initial diagnosis   Every entering student underwent extensive testing before being assigned to a class. The diagnosis included several individually administered reading and mathematics tests. Based on these data, all students were individually assigned to classes.

Each student's progress was re-evaluated on a quarterly basis   The faculty had developed non-standardised reading and mathematics tests to determine the extent to which students were making sufficient progress.

Students not making progress were 'staffed' by a multi-teacher team   The team met quarterly. If a student was making extraordinary progress, he or she was bumped forward. If a student was making substantially less progress than expected, the team discussed instructional and curricular options with the teacher. If requested, peer teachers would observe the student. If a ready answer was not found, the student was re-tested.

High expectations (for students and staff)   Throughout the school were signs declaring 'Aynesworth: Home of the Super Kids!' The principal and staff seemed strikingly and even stridently committed to the proposition, 'All our students are super. All our students can learn. If one way won't get them there, we'll just try another and another until we find a way.'

A common-sense, 'can do' search for success   In two years of observations, this author never heard a reference to a consistently research-based method. Rather, Aynesworth's 'super kids' was a 'home brewed' innovation. The principal and faculty continuously tried new interventions. If they worked in forwarding student achievement, the group discussed the innovation, and standardised it throughout the school. If the innovation didn't work, the faculty simply moved on. But the experimental nature of their search for success never stopped. The central office tried to be supportive of Aynesworth, and often simply stayed out of their way, or looked the other way when a district rule was inadvertently broken.

Roosevelt Elementary School

Roosevelt Elementary School's case has been described in *Schools Make a Difference* (Teddlie and Stringfield, 1993). The school is in an isolated rural area of Louisiana. The district, like the land, is dirt poor. There has been no significant budget for systematic school improvement or staff development in the memory of any of the staff. The district office, in a small, impoverished town fifteen miles away, was largely content to ignore this isolated outpost serving a 100 per cent African-American, high poverty community. In the school's old building, without air-conditioning, on the sweltering delta of the Mississippi River, a slow-moving, energy-conserving style of schooling was adopted of necessity. Yet during the planning of the Louisiana School Effectiveness Study (1983), Roosevelt was one of the clearest, most stable positive outliers (e.g., schools scoring well above expectation) in the 10+ prospective school districts. A team of researchers visited the school and gathered detailed quantitative and qualitative data during the fall and spring of the 1984/5 and 1989/90 school years. The longitudinal data clearly indicated that Roosevelt was performing well above similar schools in the region, both on locally administered and on LSES-administered tests. Attendance levels were unusually high, and staff morale was strong. Multiple observations made between the fall of 1984 and the spring of 1990 detailed the following characteristics of Roosevelt Elementary School:[3]

All classes covered all content mandated by the school district   As a result, teachers receiving students the following school years experienced very few 'surprises' at learning, for example, that an entire class had not covered one portion of the mathematics curriculum.

While the teaching staff displayed few 'modern' or 'trendy' techniques, they had almost no glaring weaknesses

The principal gave the appearance of an easygoing fellow, but in fact held firm standards for both students and staff   Across eighteen days of observation, no observer ever heard the principal raise his voice or saw him move rapidly, yet he maintained a firm bottom line. If a teacher was not moving a class forward in an area, he quietly visited the class, and later discussed the issue with the teacher. If a student was having trouble (or making trouble), the teacher, principal, parent, and student calmly met and discussed options. Over time, this policy produced a school in which problems were minimal.

Compensatory education (at that time called 'Chapter 1' in the US) staff were strategically deployed so that any potentially debilitating problems were addressed as quickly as was practical   Federal compensatory education money was the closest thing to a 'luxury' in this high-poverty community. The school took full advantage of these funds. Chapter 1 teachers were deployed in a much more flexible manner than was typical in other parts of the state. In virtually every observed case, the deployment made a kind of educational 'common sense'.

Unlike Aynesworth, Key, or Barclay, at Roosevelt no specific or labelled 'program' could be identified. Nor was there any money to bring in programs, or any attempt to find money for such. The texts and district curriculum guides were standard district issue. In only one grade could the teaching be described as exceptional, and there were virtually no 'modern' teaching techniques in use. Yet like Aynesworth, Key and Barclay, the results at Roosevelt were clearly exceptional.

HIGH-RELIABILITY ORGANISATIONS

The first section of this paper has tried to make clear that, much more than most reports in school effectiveness and school improvement discuss, there is something approximating chaos in our field. Schools that produce exceptional results do so using 'programs' and not; they do so with extraordinary and ordinary principals; they do so with staffs that are remarkable (see, e.g., Mentzer and Shaughnessy, 1996) and more typical; they import completely new curricula, or use the local standard. Those schools that do use externally-developed programs often succeed with programs containing components that other successful programs specifically attack as 'ineffective'. Considerably beyond the examples provided in the previous section, the range of designs for improving schools is dramatically diverse, and often contains constructs that are apparently mutually exclusive (see, e.g., Herman and Stringfield (1997); Stringfield, Ross & Smith (1996)). Chaos.

As in chaos theory, below the chaos there is a different level of order. To understand that order, the four cases have been re-examined in light of the emerging field of research on High Reliability Organisations (HROs) (Pfeiffer, 1989; Roberts, 1990, 1993; LaPorte and Consolini, 1991; Stringfield, 1995). Traditional organisational management theory is built on repeated trial and error, leading to gradual improvement. The HRO field is evolving through studies of groups that are assigned the stunning task of operating correctly the first time, every time, and honouring the absolute avoidance of catastrophic failure – *trials without errors*. Air traffic controllers, operators of regional electric power grids, and persons charged with certain functions on nuclear aircraft carriers, are just a few of the many groups currently operating under *trials without errors* requirements. As LaPorte and Consolini (1991) have noted, these organisations are 'working in practice but not in theory'. In the following section, I will briefly discuss characteristics of high-reliability organisations, with notes on how those characteristics are visible in the four seemingly quite different schools described earlier.

HROs require clarity regarding goals   Staff in HROs have a strong sense of their primary mission.

All four of the schools described in the first section of this chapter had successfully moved to a clear understanding of a finite set of goals. That set of goals invariably included unusually strong academic progress for all students.

The evolution of HROs requires a perception, held by the public and the employees, that failures to achieve the organisation's core goals would be disastrous   Mid-air collisions of aircraft are disastrous.

Most parents are increasingly aware that the relationship between level of education attained and long-term ability to provide for one's family has become much tighter during the past 25 years. Increasingly, children who do not successfully complete a secondary education are effectively shut out of well-paid career paths. Overwhelmingly, prisons are filled with high-school drop-outs. Parents are increasingly aware of the costs of school failure, and want all of their children to succeed in school. As the former principal at Aynesworth was fond of repeating, 'Our parents send us the very best children they've got!' All of the four case study schools were permeated by a belief that it was their school's job and duty to see to it that all of their students succeeded academically. In each school, when one student was detected having academic trouble, a group of adults, often including the parent(s) and principal, was called into action.

High-Reliability Organisations are alert to surprises or lapses   Small failures that can cascade into major failures must be monitored carefully. All of us make dozens of small mistakes a day. In HROs, areas in which mistakes can cascade are monitored very closely.

Success in monitoring basic reading and math skills is absolutely critical to students' long-term success in school. It takes a young child years to learn that he or she is not a skilled reader. During that time, several adults over literally hundreds of occasions will have observed small failures in the student's learning. It is not critical to catch any one error; however, it is critical to avoid cascades.

All of the four schools have straightforward, often very 'low-tech' systems in place for early detection and regular monitoring of students' problems in learning to succeed in basic school subjects. In every case, those systems worked well. This leads to the next point.

HROs build powerful databases on dimensions highly relevant to the organisation's ability to achieve its core goals   Those databases are:

(a) relevant to core goals
(b) data-rich, with triangulation on key dimensions

(c) available in real time (before cascades develop), and
(d) regularly cross-checked by multiple concerned groups.

At Barclay (and Calvert), student folders focus all participants' energies on students' productions. In Success for All, the testing every eight weeks, combined with follow-up meetings among the grade-level teams, the coordinator, and tutors (at grade one), keep faculty and, when necessary, parents fully aware of all students' progress. At Aynesworth, the initial and follow-up testing, combined with a great deal of attention to teachers' ongoing judgements, served the same function. Roosevelt was, by American standards, a relatively small school in a stable community. The principal sustained an informal, but exacting, awareness of the progress of each child. If a child was having trouble, previous teachers might be called in to assist in finding a solution. In all cases, a real-time, data-rich environment was created, maintained, and regularly accessed.

The flight of time is the enemy of reliability. Error cascades gain speed quickly. Therefore, several HRO characteristics deal with the reality that time flies very rapidly.

HROs extend formal, logical decision analysis   This is based on Standard Operating Procedures (SOPs), as far as extant knowledge allows. In a real-time environment, the time required for reflective professional judgement must be regarded as a scarce resource. Standard operating procedures allow professionals to move rapidly past some issues in order to focus their professional judgements on anomalies.

Success for All researchers and developers conduct ongoing evaluations of 'what works' in elementary schooling, and modify the program accordingly. The Aynesworth principal actively encouraged his staff to try new things, and when something clearly worked in a class, the entire faculty was brought together to discuss whether this new component should be implemented schoolwide. The efforts were not always 'research-based', but the process by which they were implemented was always open, thoughtful, and logical.

HROs have initiatives that identify flaws in Standard Operating Procedures   They nominate and validate changes in those procedures that have proven inadequate. Things change. A perfectly adequate procedure at one moment in time may prove inadequate at another. Yet the need for some standardised procedures is clear. HROs resolve this tension by honouring those that identify flaws in current SOPs and nominate improved procedures. Toyota Motor Company, maker of one of the most reliable lines of automobiles on earth, perpetually seeks suggestions from all of its employees. In an average year, the company receives and considers over

2,000,000 suggestions for improvements. Most are never widely implemented. But after careful evaluation, some of the suggestions *are* widely implemented and contribute to the company's enviable reputation. Many lead to oral, written, and other rewards for janitors, line workers, and middle and top executives.

Aynesworth's principal and faculty never stopped searching for better ideas. Ideas from cooks and special education teachers, janitors and secretaries, were all openly discussed in faculty meetings. When one was agreed upon, it was double-checked for implementation, and followed by all staff.

When Success for All schools believe they have a better idea, they bring it to the entire group's annual meeting in Baltimore. It is discussed, often widely copied, and, where clearly proven, universally adopted.

The Calvert curriculum undergoes constant refinement. Barclay has experimented with components of the Calvert curriculum, added Barclay's own refinements, experimented with 'what works at Barclay', and made adjustments accordingly.

Because no set of SOPs, however refined through practice, can anticipate all contingencies, HROs must rely on individual professional judgement, regardless of the person's position or rank. Therefore:

HROs recruit extensively   There is no substitute for a competent, smoothly functioning staff. The probability of such a group coming together by chance is very low.

The principals at all four schools developed and nurtured very active informal networks for identifying promising potential staff. A common theme among them, and among most of the principals in 'positive outlier' schools in the Louisiana School Effectiveness Study (Stringfield and Teddlie, 1991) was an acknowledgement of the formal procedures for recruitment, and an extensive description of their schools' additional, informal methods.

HROs train and retrain constantly   The principals in the four cases all shared a belief that all teachers (and principals) can improve. While the one Louisiana school was hard-pressed to provide intensive, ongoing, formal staff development, the principal sought out informal methods for finding and spreading 'things that work'. The others found ways within their budgets to appoint at least part-time program coordinators, who provided initial training, modelled desired techniques in classes, observed, and provided non-evaluative feedback. This is precisely the sequence of professional development steps that Showers, Joyce & Bennett (1987) identified as bearing real changes in classroom practices.

HROs take performance evaluations seriously   If a system must rely on professional judgement, then repeated, egregious failures of professional judgement cannot coexist with long-term high reliability.

During interviews, all of the principals were asked about the potentially touchy issue of performance evaluations. All reported that they had strong teachers. After further probes, all reported having moved several teachers and other staff out of their schools. The process was invariably handled carefully and professionally, but in each case the principal had made the annual evaluation process a serious one (i.e., there were no 'rubber stamped' evaluations), and all had moved more than one former teacher out of their school. None of the principals were regarded by their faculties or their supervisors as 'mean' or 'vindictive' or 'tough for its own sake'. However, each maintained a firm bottom line.

In High-Reliability Organisations, monitoring is mutual without counterproductive loss of overall autonomy and confidence   Success for All sends out monitors to all of its schools. The nature of Success for All teaching and teaming is such that teachers become much more aware of one another's actions.

Through the regular checking of student folders, the Calvert program makes the principal much more aware of individual students' and teachers' current strengths and limitations. Similarly, if the principal falls behind in monitoring, all of the faculty soon know it. At Aynesworth, observers reported the perception that virtually all teachers were regular visitors in other teachers' classes, helping out and learning new things. The principal at Roosevelt was quick to suggest to any one teacher that he or she might benefit from observing in another's class. There can be very little 'close my door and teach my way' in a highly reliable school. Principals and teachers in the four schools found ways to open their doors and feel that they were, if anything, more professional as a result.

In each case, it could be argued that part of the eventual positive effect was derived from simply making the student aware that he or she would be noticed. The same could be argued about the parent(s), the teacher, and the program itself. But the clear message was that long-term failure could not be afforded, and that long-term success required that all parties contribute skilfully. Multi-way accountability was in place, and virtually everyone involved appeared to take pride in that fact.

HROs are hierarchically structured, but during times of peak load, HROs display a second layer of behaviour that emphasises collegial decision-making regardless of rank   This second mode is characterised by cooperation and coordination. At times of peak activity, line staff are expected to exercise considerable discretion. Especially during times of peak performance, staff are able to assume a close interdependence. Relationships are complex, coupled, and sometimes urgent.

In each of the four case study schools, the role and perceived legitimacy of the principals went unquestioned. However, one of the shared characteristics of all four schools was that the principals and staff all assumed a close interdependency. Teachers and aides clearly perceived that they were 'empowered' to act when action was needed. At each of these schools, teachers talked with joy and pride about the extent to which they felt they could rely on each other, and how certain they were that trust was reciprocated.

Getting rid of hierarchy in education may not be an important goal. Allowing exceptions to hierarchical rules and communication patterns at moments when that side-stepping of hierarchy can save a student from illiteracy may be what is needed.

In HROs, key equipment is maintained in the highest working order   Responsibility for checking the readiness of key equipment is shared equally by all who come in contact with it.

As noted earlier, at Barclay, things worked. At Aynesworth, if an equipment problem recurred, the principal, the teacher, the librarian, and, if necessary, the janitor, met and devised methods of ensuring that equipment worked.

HROs are invariably valued by their supervising organisations   Each of the four principals and faculties took steps to make sure that their supervising school district understood the actions their school had taken to reach excellence. When interviewed, district personnel often referred to Aynesworth, Barclay, Key, or Franklin in what otherwise might be regarded as uncommon detail. It was obvious that the schools actively fostered a close working relationship with their districts.

Short-term efficiency takes a back seat to very high reliability   In the unstable environment that is American educational finance, all four schools found ways to protect their core activities. Some things would not be compromised. By budgeting proactively, by keeping track of expenses, by keeping superiors appraised of the schools' needs, and occasionally by writing grants, the schools managed more often than not to find ways to protect themselves from the most arbitrary of cuts.

In the rare cases where a cost-saving measure was imposed from above and the school was unable to work successfully around the cut, the results were almost immediately obvious. These schools were working at high levels of efficiency. Mandated cuts, aimed at typically non-existent 'fat', almost invariably struck meat and bone.

SUMMARY

A cursory look at school improvement efforts could lead a rational observer to conclude that the situation is chaotic. However, in chaos theory, there is order beneath the apparent chaos. This chapter has presented four case studies of very different, successful, school restructuring efforts. At first brush, the differences might be seen to outweigh the similarities in method. However, in each school the underlying principles of high-reliability organisations were at work.

No one school's faculty would describe their school as a perfect or completed effort. Similarly, no one of the schools displayed all of the characteristics of highly reliable organisations. But the majority of HRO characteristics were present in all of the schools.

While there are many interesting ideas for school reform afield, most have travelled from school to school poorly. The exemplary schools examined in this chapter demonstrate one fact. To the extent that measurable improvements in students' outcomes at all schools is one of a finite number of goals of school improvement, the high-reliability organisational characteristics can serve to guide implementations of diverse, potentially valuable, restructuring efforts.

NOTES

1 Funding for various portions of the research described here has been provided by the Center for Research on Effective Schooling for Disadvantaged Students (CDS, grant # R117R0002) and the Center for Research on Education for Students Placed At Risk (CRESPAR, grant No. $117D-40005), both funded through the Office of Educational Research and Improvement (OERI) of the US Department of Education; Educational Reforms and Students At Risk (Rossi and Stringfield), also funded through OERI; the Kellogg Foundation of Battle Creek, Michigan; and the Abell Foundation of Baltimore, Maryland. However, all opinions expressed are the author's alone.
2 Barclay's free lunch percentage is 15 per cent above the district average, and fully 55 per cent above the state average of 26 per cent. Barclay serves a high-poverty community in a high-poverty city.
3 Roosevelt was re-visited as part of the next follow-up of LSES schools, during the 1995/6 school year. Study-specific test data were not available as this chapter went to press, but attendance rates and scores on locally-administered tests remained high. Qualitative observations at Roosevelt were remarkably consistent with those from 11 and 6 years earlier.

REFERENCES

Core Knowledge Foundation (1995) *Core Knowledge Sequence*, Charlottesville, VA: Core Knowledge Foundation.

Gleick, J. (1987) *Chaos: Making a new science*, New York: Viking.

Hepler, N., Stringfield, S., Seltzer, D., Fortna, R., Stonehill, R., Yoder, N. and English, J. (1987) *Effective compensatory education programs for extremely disadvantaged students*, Portland, OR: Northwest Regional Educational Laboratory.

Herman, R. and Stringfield, S. (1997) *Ten promising programs for improving schools serving students placed at risk*, Arlington, VA: Educational Research Service.

Hirsch, E. D. (1988) *Cultural literacy*, New York: Random House.

LaPorte, T. and Consolini, P. (1991) 'Working in practice but not in theory: Theoretical challenges of "High-Reliability Organizations"', *Journal of Public Administration Research and Theory*, 1(1), 19–48.

Mentzer, D. and Shaughnessy, T. (1996) 'Hawthorne Elementary School: The teachers' perspective', *Journal of Education for Students Placed At Risk*, 1(1), 13–24.

Pfeiffer, J. (1989) 'The secret of life at the limits: cogs become big wheels', *Smithsonian*, 20(4), 38–48.

Roberts, C. (1990) 'Some characteristics of High Reliability Organizations', *Organizational Science*, 1(2), 1–17.

Roberts, K. (1993) *New challenges to understanding organizations*, New York: Macmillan.

Rossi, R. J. and Stringfield, S. C. (1995) *Educational reforms and students at risk: Final research report, vols I–III*, Washington, DC: Office of Educational Research and Improvement, US Department of Education.

Showers, B., Joyce, B. and Bennett, B. (1987) 'Synthesis of research on staff development: A framework for future study and a state-of-the-art analysis', *Educational Leadership*, 45(3), 77–87.

Slavin, R. E., Madden, N. A., Dolan, L. J. and Wasik, B. A. (1996a) 'Success for All: A summary of research', *Journal of Education for Students Placed At Risk*, 1(1), 41–76.

—— (1996b) *Every child, every school: Success for All*, Thousand Oaks, CA: Corwin.

Slavin, R. E., Madden. N. A., Karweit, N. L., Dolan, L. J. and Wasik, B. A. (1992) *Success for All: A relentless approach to prevention and early intervention in elementary schools*, Arlington, VA: Educational Research Service.

Slavin, R. E., Madden, N. A., Karweit, N. L., Livermon, B. J. and Dolan, L. J. (1990) 'Success for All: First year outcomes of a comprehensive plan for reforming urban education', *American Educational Research Journal*, 27, 255–78.

Slavin, R. E. and Yampolsky, R. (1991) *Effects of Success for All on students with limited English proficiency: A three-year evaluation*, Baltimore, MD: Johns Hopkins University, Center for Research on Effective Schooling for Disadvantaged Students.

Stringfield, S. (1994) *Fourth-Year Evaluation of the Calvert School program at Barclay School*, Baltimore, MD: Johns Hopkins University, Center for the Social Organization of Schools.

—— (1995) 'Attempts to enhance students' learning: A search for valid programs and highly reliable implementation techniques', *School Effectiveness and School Improvement*, 6(1), 67–96.

Stringfield, S., Herman, R., Millsap, M. and Scott, E. (1996) 'The three-year effects of ten "promising programs" on the academic achievements of students placed at risk', paper presented at the meeting of the American Educational Research Association, New York, April.

Stringfield, S., Ross, S. and Smith, L. (eds) (1996) *Bold plans for school restructuring: The New American Schools Development Corporation models*, Hillsdale, NJ: Lawrence Erlbaum.

Stringfield, S. and Teddlie, C. (1991) 'Observers as predictors of schools' multi-year outlier status', *Elementary School Journal*, 91(4), 357–76.

Teddlie, C. and Stringfield, S. (1993) *Schools make a difference: Lessons learned from a 10-year study of school effects*, New York: Teachers College Press.

Chapter 9

Systemic reform
A case study on restructuring one American public high school

Judy Codding

As we approach the twenty-first century, more students than ever before in the United States need to be educated to higher levels, so that they can:

- participate in the American democratic system
- develop strong moral and ethical values and the ability to reach their potential
- compete successfully in the increasingly technological job market.

Many people in the United States have come to recognise that early efforts with reform of public education at the start of the 1980s were not successful enough. The impetus for these attempts was primarily economic. People from all walks of society concluded that the United States was on the verge of being displaced as a major player in the world economy. The belief that it was falling behind other industrialised powers in development, productivity and quality was a theme echoed in many national reports during the 1980s, including the *Carnegie Forum, Education Commission of the States,* the *National Commission on Excellence in Education,* the *National Governors Association,* the *National Science Board* and others. It did not take reformers long to draw the connection between this economic impetus and the educational system. Many people drew the conclusion that it would be up to schooling and a successful system of education to restore the economic pre-eminence of the United States.

It has become increasingly obvious that, if we are to succeed in helping our students reach these higher performance levels, we must radically change the way our schools and school systems do business. This will include:

- developing a standards-driven system with results-based accountability
- making instructional and organisational changes to allow students to reach these higher levels
- strengthening curriculum at every level
- providing effective support for all students
- establishing an environment of professionalism for school faculty
- initiating effective parent, business and community involvement.

THE AMERICAN REFORM AGENDA

There is a growing consensus across the United States on what the principles of a new educational system should be. Although they take different shape in different states and communities, the underlying principles of the new American reform agenda seem to be as follows:

High standards for all students

In order to lead fulfilling, productive lives in the twenty-first century, all young people need to achieve at levels currently reached by only a small minority. Accomplishing this requires a change in beliefs as well as policies and practices. For decades, the American education system has acted on the belief that only a few students are capable of complex skills and knowledge; we have set high expectations for those few and allowed the rest merely to get by. From what we have learned from cognitive research and from our analysis of society and the economy, however, we now understand that the prevailing belief is dangerous and wrong. All young people can and must learn and learn well.

It is not enough to believe that all children can learn – that idea has become something of a mantra among American educators – we need to act on that belief. That means setting standards for student performance in core subjects that is as high as those the best-performing countries expect their students to reach, and then building a system that expects all but the most severely disabled students to attain those standards. And it means creating a system for assessing student performance that is true to the standards we require, one that will not only measure performance but improve it by setting clear expectations and offering students opportunities to engage in challenging tasks.

Redesigned learning environments

The cognitive revolution of the past two decades has taught us much about how children learn best, and these findings imply a fundamental redesign of learning and teaching. The traditional reliance on lecturing, seatwork and low-level skills and knowledge will not work. We now know that students learn best when they actively construct knowledge based on what they already know; when they use their knowledge to solve real problems; when they produce authentic products and performances for real audiences; and when they know what the expectations for performance are and continually strive to attain those expectations. Applying these ideas calls for a different view of how learning and teaching takes place in schools.

The redesigned learning environment starts with the standards for student performance. The curriculum and instructional program is explicitly designed to lead to high performance against these standards. Students are active and engaged in projects that are tied to standards. They are constantly asking questions, analysing problems and speaking and writing to build on and extend their knowledge. And teachers function more like coaches, modelling expert performances and guiding students toward improving their own learning. Teachers thus know their students well, both as learners and as individuals, and the school is organised to enable them to provide whatever help they need to enable all students to meet high standards.

The learning environment also extends beyond the classroom. For decades, schools have acted almost as if the world outside did not exist. However, students do not come to school as empty vessels, waiting to be filled. They know a great deal about the world and they learn best when what they learn connects with the world they know. Therefore the redesigned learning environment includes links to the community and the workplace to help develop students' abilities to solve problems and communicate effectively – the kinds of skills they will need when they enter the workforce. And it includes technologies that enable students to communicate with peers and experts far beyond the school walls and to gain access to, and manipulate, information in ways not possible even a decade ago.

Support for children and families

The dramatic social and economic changes that have swept through American society in recent years have profoundly affected the ability of schools to educate children. As more and more young people come to schools hungry, fearful and abused, from homes with one or no parents, teachers can no longer expect that all of their students arrive at school ready to learn, and that once they are there they are all alert and engaged in their schoolwork.

This does not mean that schools need to take on the job of ensuring the health and well-being of children and families; the mission of schools must remain the education of young people to high levels. Nevertheless, schools must be part of the solution. The education system cannot make good on its promise of enabling all students to achieve at high levels until the issue of support for children and families is addressed. Following the African adage, 'It takes a whole village to raise a child', addressing this issue requires collaboration among a host of agencies and organisations – including schools – that provide support for children and families, setting goals for improvement and identifying and creating the services and supports needed to achieve those goals.

Organising for results

To an observer from outside the United States, the American education system must seem extraordinarily diffuse: a small federal department with a limited mandate; fifty state agencies, each with its own constitutional authority; and more than 14,000 local school boards, some overseeing only a handful of schools. To teachers and principals in schools, however, the system is stiflingly bureaucratic. These educators live under a plethora of rules that govern much of their activity and constrain their ability to do what they consider best for their students.

This bureaucratic structure is in many ways a legacy of the industrial model under which the school system was designed. In that model, management makes all the important decisions, which those at the front line carry out. The workers, moreover, are held accountable for how faithfully they follow the rules, not by how well the product turns out – or, in the case of schools, how well students learn.

As industrial firms are finding out, and as education systems and other public agencies are beginning to see, the old model does not work very well, either for the firm or for its employees. Quality suffers, and employees miss out on the opportunity to work as true professionals, with skills and knowledge that are valued. These firms are moving to a new model, one organised for high performance. In a high performing organisation, the focus is on results: what the organisation wants to achieve. It sets clear goals and develops ways of measuring progress toward the goals. It then leaves it up to the professionals closest to the customer to figure out how to achieve the goals, while providing the support and professional development they need to do their jobs well. And the organisation provides appropriate incentives to ensure that the professionals achieve their goals.

Organising education systems for high performance – setting goals for student learning and allowing teachers and principals to determine how to meet the goals, while holding them accountable for results and supporting them along the way – will not, by itself, enable all students to reach high standards of performance. But it is an essential step, particularly if we want all students to meet that goal. It is not enough to create a few good schools. The system must be organised for high performance so that large numbers of schools, not just a few, routinely produce high levels of student performance.

Parent and public engagement

The structure of public education in the United States makes it imperative to engage parents and the public in the education of their children and particularly in the reform effort itself. These are the public's schools, and educators need the public's 'permission' to change them, especially to make changes of the magnitude we consider necessary. At the same time, we know from abundant experience that parents' engagement in children's learning is a vital ingredient in student success. Children spend far more of their time out of school than in school, and children will not achieve at high levels if learning takes place only between 8 a.m. and 3 p.m., Monday through Friday, nine months a year.

The first step in engaging parents and the public is listening to them and making sure that their concerns are addressed. We know from surveys conducted over the past few years that the public is most concerned that students learn basic skills and that schools are safe and orderly. Yet some school reformers talk as if basic skills are unimportant as long as students can think and reason – as though there was a contradiction between the two. And discipline has hardly made it on to the reform agenda. But we ignore these issues at our own – and our children's – peril. We need everyone – parents, taxpayers, teachers, administrators and students – to accept their share of the responsibility for students' achievement and to do their part to ensure that all students achieve at high levels.

RESTRUCTURING AN AMERICAN URBAN HIGH SCHOOL

In the past two decades, the major question has shifted from 'Do schools make any difference?', to the far more hopeful 'What characteristics of schools are associated with what desirable outcomes for students, teachers, principals, parents and communities?' It is the latter question that is grounding the rethinking and remaking of at least one urban high school in the United States.

Restructuring the schooling experience of high school students is hard work. This hard work, however, was urgently needed at Pasadena High School (PHS), a school located near the Rose Bowl in southern California. Like many other high schools, PHS had a successful and strong academic program twenty-five years ago. Yet this strength had faded over the years for many reasons. The student body had changed dramatically from an Anglo, middle-class population to an ethnically diverse student population, many of whom came from disconnected home lives and lived in poverty.

The staff had become trapped in recalling the 'good old days', rather than responding to the needs of current students. Despite pockets of good teaching, most teachers did not know their students either as people or learners; most students were docile and only marginally engaged in the academic life of the school. It became clear that PHS was not working for most of its students.

Student performance

In the late 1980s, the performance profile for students was dismal. The school had a dropout rate of at least 36 per cent for the 1988 senior class, a class where approximately 75 per cent of students were from the three lowest economic levels. Of the students who stayed in school, 40 per cent received 'D' or 'F' grades in the core subjects and only 13 per cent had completed the academic requirements to enrol in a state university. Test scores were very low. Attendance was a major problem. In fact, academic performance went hand-in-hand with the declining average family incomes of students.

Students entering the school had serious problems. The typical student was 2.3 years below grade level, and 30 per cent of entering students were 'socially' promoted from the 8th grade. Personal and social problems as well as poor academic performance kept too many students from success; too many were involved in drugs, became pregnant or experienced instability at home. By the more important standard of helping students engage in a thinking/meaning-centred curriculum, most of the students were seriously lacking.

The schooling experience for students was clearly a fundamental part of the problem. For many students, school was alienating rather than engaging. Many of the teachers talked *at* students, and many were not knowledgeable about current pedagogy. The school structure supported a student's docility and failure rather than success. In short, Pasadena High School had become an urban, comprehensive high school that was not working for its students.

Consequently, a radical restructuring effort, which forced administrators and faculty to rethink both what education is and how the school could support powerful learning for students, was called for. This included examining basic beliefs about teaching, learning, the nature of adolescence, and the kinds of learning environments most appropriate for students. PHS could not be redesigned piecemeal because everything important within the school affected everything else. The school drew heavily on the Nine Common Principles of the Coalition of Essential Schools, the work of the National Alliance for Restructuring Education and the report of the Commission on the Skills of the American Work Force, 'America's Choice: high skills or low wages'.

These works helped determine the nature and direction of the restructuring efforts at Pasadena High School. The goals of *America 2000*, which are reflected in PHS's restructuring efforts, appropriately focus on preparing all students to meet national standards in core subjects and world-class standards in the workplace; on heightened professional standards for teachers; and on more clearly defined accountability measures both for students and for schools. Leaders at PHS understood that this would require completely new educational paradigms which rethink and redesign the ways in which learners interact with each other, their teachers, and their environment.

School vision

Pasadena High School has developed an integrated vision, focusing on students and their future. Three outcomes of quality citizenship, productive worklife and literacy in its broadest sense are the vital sources for PHS's vision and the objectives around which grades 9–12 are organised. The school developed a five year restructuring plan which calls for all its students to achieve the following outcomes to the best of their ability.

Quality citizens in a changing society

The school believes that good citizens need:

- a clear sense of values, experience in ethical reflection and decision-making, and internalised norms of fairness, honesty, and respect
- understanding of the similarities and differences in our American culture
- vital knowledge and patterns of thought that allow them to analyse and propose solutions to essential societal issues
- ability to work productively in groups
- successful experience in community service and community participation.

PHS is committed to seeing that all students leave the school with these qualities, experiences and insights.

The coursework, advisories, governance structures and school norms set the base for a student's culminating exhibition in this area: the Senior Community Service project. To graduate, each senior must demonstrate two aspects of the Community Service Project:

- a track record of informed and ethical analysis of social issues leading to a proposed solution
- a community service project and the reflection/perspective which the student brings to bear on this project.

To prepare for the Senior Community Service project, ninth grade students begin a portfolio and reflective self-analysis, and undertake community service.

Productive worklife in the twenty-first century

About half of America's youth do not go to college, but they receive little assistance in making the transition from school to work. Upon leaving school, many flounder in the labour market, secure low skill jobs, jobs with few opportunities for advancement, or remain jobless. The school's vision is that all its students will demonstrate that they are prepared for a productive worklife where they

- can integrate academic and applied knowledge and use this knowledge in practical ways
- have habits of initiative and responsibility
- have a personal plan for the future.

New academic foundation: literary thinking and communication skills needed for higher education and life-long learning

The PHS plan calls for all its urban, multicultural students to leave the school with a set of strengths very different from those provided by most comprehensive high schools. These are:

- an interdisciplinary, concept-based understanding which is intertwined with communication (written and oral) and thinking (both critical and creative) skills, so the students will express and demonstrate their integrated knowledge and original work
- a very strong track record of knowing how to learn, including how to formulate and solve problems/tasks, how to acquire knowledge from education-based and other relevant sources, and how to better one's work and the work of others.

The PHS focus on literacy in science, mathematics, history, geography and English, on powerful thinking/problem-solving, and on communication skills requires a schooling experience that is very different from the usual high school. Extensive efforts in grades nine and ten are made to ensure that all students receive the support they need to succeed in the core program. The strategies for the eleventh and twelfth grades include requiring students to take rigorous core courses as they pursue work in the academic partnership or the program major of their choice. By 1994, all students were required to complete a Senior Project. The projects require:

- original synthesis of information around some important focus
- multiple-mode communication and defence of the student's work in a public setting
- insightful self-reflection about the process and success of the effort, and how it could be improved.

All aspects of the school are designed directly to support these dimensions of student success. Many pieces of the new vision have been started, but the schooling experience for the students needs to be deepened and integrated. The most significant change occurring at PHS is that the school has become results-driven (in terms of the new student outcomes) so that the students are truly successful, and that all aspects of the school directly support these dimensions of student work.

NEW CURRICULUM AND INSTRUCTIONAL STRATEGIES TO HELP ALL STUDENTS ACHIEVE HIGH STANDARDS

Initially, in the restructuring effort, PHS set out to accomplish three broad goals:

* to create a more personal environment for its students
* to make the student become the worker, the active learner
* to form a partnership with the home and community.

To accomplish these goals, Pasadena High School had to be remade. It had to change the way the school was organised and governed, how the curriculum was developed including the integration of knowledge and skills, the way instruction was delivered and the way students were assessed. In addition, it had to reach out to parents and the community at large.

The restructuring effort began with the entire ninth grade for the 1989/90 school year, and now includes grades nine through eleven, with the twelfth grade as a transition year. The rethinking and reorganisation has led to dividing the school into five learning units or clusters called Houses. One of the five Houses is the International House for bilingual students. Each House has its own teaching team within it. In the ninth grade, fifty students work with two teachers (one in humanities and one in maths/science); in the tenth and eleventh grade, four teachers (two in humanities, one in maths and one in science) work with 120 students. All teachers in a given House have common planning time to discuss student progress, develop curriculum, problem-solve House issues, and meet with parents. Each House has a head teacher, guidance counsellor, and part-time clerical staff. The houses have the following characteristics and focus:

Using one's mind well

Using one's mind well is the integrating force behind a 'thinking' curriculum, for which the California Curriculum Frameworks provide a vital source and base. Curriculum and goals for learning outcomes concentrate on the development of complex understandings rather than on a passing familiarity with or exposure to pieces of knowledge. This has required an interdisciplinary, inquiry-driven core curriculum, because real understanding and problem-solving need an integration of different skills, knowledge and disciplines. It requires a curriculum built around essential questions. A set of questions specific to a given course organises learning by posing problems, the solutions to which derive from the learner's deepened perceptions, complex thinking and a drive toward integrated understanding. Each student bears the responsibility to think, to be thoughtful and to solve problems related to issues linking academics and the world of the intellect and real life experiences. Thus, each student is trained to be both intellectually and practically-minded, with emphasis on the integration of both perspectives.

The student as the worker and learner

Students learn best by being actively involved in their own learning and by doing the work, rather than being the passive recipients of knowledge. The curriculum asks students to work together with more frequent coaching, rather than formal lecturing on the part of the teacher. With this method students do more of the work of learning, while their instructor advises and encourages them. Because it stresses that each student should think well, participate in his own learning, and exhibit mastery of his learning, it is intended that the PHS program will lead to an increased access of all students to an authentic education of high quality.

Personalisation and advisory

Students must feel connection with the school and a sense of belonging. Personalising the schooling and learning environment is a key to improving the attendance and learning outcomes of students. Having each student as a member of a House provides teachers with an opportunity to get to know students well, discuss openly any concerns about students and give students an opportunity to know their peers and teachers well. All House teachers serve as advisers to a group of students and present an advisory curriculum based on the development of self-esteem and of leadership, on the resolution of conflicts and on issues of school governance, decision-making and career opportunities. The school views this as integral to improved academic performance for all students and to their healthy social adjustment.

All students can and must learn mathematics

The recent restructuring effort has pointed out that most of the students enter Pasadena High School as fundamentally innumerate. Beginning in 1992, PHS introduced the Comprehensive Math and Science Program (CMSP), a program supported by the National Science Foundation. The CMSP is a highly structured sequence of maths courses organised to give all students the foundation to master and complete Algebra I and Geometry over a two-year period. In the ninth grade, the designated students (85 per cent of the student population) take two mathematics courses which are arranged in parallel so that students have considerably more time to learn important topics in depth. The parallel arrangement of the two CMSP courses during the first two years allows teachers to utilise the topics in one course to complement and reinforce the topics in the other. This also gives students an opportunity to study important mathematics topics through an interplay of computations, verbal problems and geometric applications.

Authentic student engagement and assessment

Authentic student engagement is required if we expect students to use their minds well. Today, a student's completion of high school is measured by credits accumulated rather than a vision of educational goals which seeks performances in activities that are worthwhile, significant and meaningful; in other words, authentic. A disciplined inquiry that calls for the use of prior knowledge in an integrated rather than fragmented form reflects the goals of an integrated, academic, and apprenticeship program that has value to a student's life beyond simply proving his achievement in school.

PHS has designed assessment tools based on the student's ability to produce rather than reproduce knowledge. Authentic assessment at PHS takes the form of conversation and writing, preparing and building physical objects, and expressing oneself through artistic performances and so forth. Both student portfolios (a collection of student work that exhibits the student's efforts, progress and achievements) and exhibitions (a student's ability to demonstrate mastery in areas that include written and oral communication, personal and civic development, interrelationship of science and technology in society, critical thinking and problem solving, and national and international awareness) are central to the restructuring efforts. The school has already begun to reshape the course of study around portfolios and exhibitions and, therefore, to engage more students in different ways of using what they know. PHS is moving in the direction of not permitting a student to graduate from high school without a definite post-graduation plan approved by his adviser as part of his portfolio.

Transition to adulthood and the world of work

Pasadena High School is developing a program for eleventh and twelfth grade students that provides them with the opportunity to reach out to adult world experiences by integrating academic and applied academic experiences and an apprenticeship program. The school is organising the eleventh and twelfth grade curriculum to allow students to pursue career paths and simultaneously take a sequence of courses that will prepare them either to enter a four-year college, technical preparation program, community college or the world of work. This program is being developed around a two-plus-two cooperative program with associated agencies. Developments include a Graphic Arts Academy, a Visual Arts and Design Academy, and other establishments that focus on Law and Government, Teaching, and Urban Development and the Environment. The program

- integrates academic and applied academic course work while providing all students with community college credit
- involves a wide range of students
- involves the other agencies as full partners in curriculum, governance, staffing and program operation
- provides students with mentors and paid internships both in the summer of the junior year and the second semester senior year
- provides students with the opportunity to complete one year of credit towards an appropriate degree
- guarantees students an appropriate job and/or admission to a tertiary course based on the student's exit performance.

New approaches to improve the quality of teachers, school governance and teacher professionalism

Pasadena High School has developed a comprehensive and integrated decision making and governance process, as Fig. 9.1 indicates.

It has found creative ways to balance the House, department and grade-level decision-making structures which put the decision-making closest to the people who work with the students. Each academy has a coordinating council which includes business partners, members from the industry associations and other agencies, tertiary institutions, and PHS teachers, students and administrators. Common to these interrelated governance structures is a focus on student outcomes and a clear ethical base and sense of decency/fairness for students that underlies the school's decisions and parallels what good citizenship means for students.

Professional collaboration at PHS is increasingly built on new norms of respect/collegiality, continuous improvement, common technical language, and accountability. Because of the House structure, collaboration tends to be among teachers who are collectively responsible for the schooling experience and outcomes of specific students. The differences from the conventional high school are dramatic. House, department, grade-level and team meetings occur within the school day during common planning time, and are major reasons for the success of the restructuring. The school has teachers involved in summer work teams and all core teachers participate in a two-week summer curriculum and instructional institute. Finally, PHS learns by leading. The school is increasingly asked to provide leadership to other schools and districts in all phases of restructuring, and plans to continue to refine its ability to help; and to learn from these interactions.

The school's view of shared governance, collaboration and professionalism leads to two related views about teacher accountability and selection. Each House plays a major role in selecting new teachers, who must 'fit' in with the overall and unique purpose of each House. At the same time, teachers

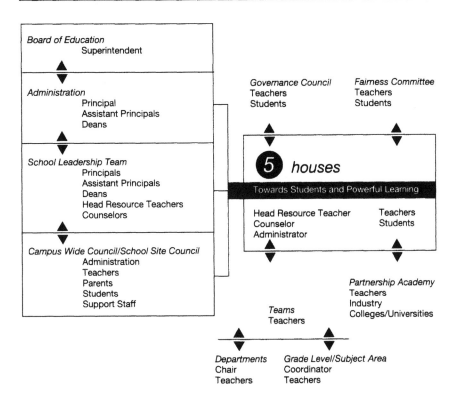

PHS Decision-Making Structure

Board of Education
Superintendent

Administration
Principal
Assistant Principals
Deans

School Leadership Team
Principals
Assistant Principals
Deans
Head Resource Teachers
Counselors

Campus Wide Council/School Site Council
Administration
Teachers
Parents
Students
Support Staff

Governance Council
Teachers
Students

Fairness Committee
Teachers
Students

5 *houses*
Towards Students and Powerful Learning

Head Resource Teacher
Counselor
Administrator

Teachers
Students

Partnership Academy
Teachers
Industry
Colleges/Universities

Teams
Teachers

Departments
Chair
Teachers

Grade Level/Subject Area
Coordinator
Teachers

Figure 9.1 The decision-making structure of Pasadena High School

keep their own portfolios of their work in order to promote positive norms of accountability and continuously to improve.

The House structure allows teachers closely to link planning, program delivery and accountability, and therefore to practise truly as professionals, because at PHS teacher professionalism means expertise in such given areas as subject matter, advisory, areas of pedagogy such as essential questions, exhibitions and assessments, collaborative learning and Socratic Seminars. It is in this context of professionalism that teachers are allowed to work effectively with the whole student. Moreover, these areas of expertise serve as incentives to instruction because their acquisition reflects a measure of professional development as well as enabling the expert in a particular field to provide others with resources, training and advice. The service rendered by these experts should improve the performance of the teachers seeking help, even as it improves the performance of their students.

Professionalism is also closely linked with the nature and the quality of professional development. The staff have attended programs focusing on change and restructuring, and have spent time at other restructuring schools to deepen their knowledge. This provides additional incentives to improve as well as a model for improved academic performance, innovative restructuring and a thoughtful rendering of curriculum and meaning.

Decentralisation of decision-making: some important advantages

Decentralisation of decision-making to the school site (devolution) is at the heart of the debate on the reform movement. As Allan Odden (1995) has stated, the arguments centre on the practice of democracy, constituent influence and control over organisational decisions, ownership of public institutions, trust and organisational accountability. There were many advantages of decentralisation for PHS. These included:

- Participation in decision-making by people at the school led to a feeling of ownership by the constituents, which resulted in greater acceptance of, and cooperation with, the implementation of decisions, and ultimately produced greater satisfaction for the constituents.
- Greater authority at the school level tended to encourage innovation and responsiveness to the needs of the students at the school.
- With greater authority and responsibility came greater accountability. Because of greater participation, the school community was better informed about the school and its activities.
- Parents tended to have more confidence in the school because they were more aware of what was happening at the school.
- When the school had more responsibility for decisions on finance, staffing, attendance, content and organisation, there tended to be a greater emphasis on doing what was best in all areas for children's learning.
- Site-based management and decision-making contributed to an overall professionalisation of the workforce at the school. Most school personnel felt more valued because they believed that their voice counted.
- Under a system of school-based management, accountability for student achievement rested squarely with the school. After all, the people most aware of the diverse problems and needs in a particular school are those working at the school.
- People began to understand the serious financial constraints of the school. Parents, teachers and other school staff became more aware of the costs of programs, the school's financial status and its spending limitations.

In general, the more control PHS had over those aspects of its organisation that affected its performance – the articulation of goals, the selection and management of personnel, the specification of policies – the more it exhibited the qualities that have been found to promote school effectiveness. Advocates for devolution have found support from modern management theory and from activities in the corporate sector. By and large, it has been discovered that the most effective corporations have transformed their businesses by decentralising operations, by pushing decisions down to the level of the organisation in closest contact with a customer, by re-orienting their management philosophy from control to empowerment, by establishing reputations for attention to quality, and by changing their views of workers from property of the company to partners in the corporate undertaking. Many who have worked in schools that have adopted this philosophy have seen the same benefits in schools that corporations have found in their workplaces.

The decentralisation of authority to PHS meant that many of the decisions that had historically been made by state or district personnel were now made by school staff, parents, and by students. The benefits for the students and staff at Pasadena High School fell into five areas:

Goals

Initially, in the restructuring effort at PHS, three broad goals were sought. These were:

- to create a more personal environment for the students
- to make the student become the worker, the active learner; and the teacher, the coach
- to form a partnership with the home and the community.

These goals reflected the most critical issues facing Pasadena High School. The school wanted to develop an integrated vision, focusing on students and their future. With site-based management and decision-making, the school had the authority to decide on the vision and goals that would best meet the needs of students. Decentralisation of authority provided the school with more control over the vision and direction that the school would pursue and the strategies to achieve them.

Budget

Control over the budget was at the heart of the effort to put resources behind what the school felt was important. The ability to allocate resources made it possible to have more direct control over the curricula and personnel. Decentralised budgeting (although there was often not enough funds) gave the school the opportunity to spend money to achieve its goals.

Personnel

Closely connected to budgetary discretion is the importance of control over the defining of roles and the hiring and the development of a school staff. Unfortunately, in the Pasadena school district, the district office still has the power to determine the allocation of teaching positions. However, the school was permitted to select the candidates of their choice; teachers were no longer sent to the school from the district office. Presently, the school is working to get the option to use funds originally budgeted for teachers for other purposes if it so chooses.

Curriculum

The school has the responsibility to implement the California Curriculum Frameworks and to participate in performance assessments. However, it was able to develop its own holistic learning results and to determine the instructional practices appropriate to achieving those results. In addition, it was able to choose the materials thought most appropriate for students. Site-based decision-making allowed the staff and school community to bring greater cohesion to learning for the school's students. At least seven changes occurred as a result of site-based management and decision-making. These were:

1 expanded use of a core curriculum
2 an increase in the interdisciplinary nature of content
3 an emphasis on depth of coverage
4 use of more original source materials
5 enhanced focus on higher order thinking skills
6 expanded methods of student assessment
7 an emphasis on learning outcomes.

Giving teachers more control over the curriculum has allowed the school to shift its focus from teaching to learning.

Organisational structures

Decentralisation made it possible for the school to create the organisational structure it thought to be most appropriate for the students and in support of the established vision and learning outcomes. One result was the 'Houses', each of which developed its own character, personality and organisational structure. None of this would have been possible had the school not had the authority to make decisions about the organisational structure it thought best.

AN ACTION PLAN FOR 'BREAK THE MOULD' CHANGE

Two major obstacles need to be considered within the context in which restructuring at PHS continues to take place: underfunding of public education and the serious problems associated with urban youth in southern California. Both of these obstacles only push the school to work harder on restructuring as the only meaningful response to the dilemma.

Features of the action plan

The action plan builds on the accomplishments of the past, but also enables the school to address specific obstacles to change. The approach features:

- creating a comprehensive vision that is focused on students and results, and is uniformly shared
- using data to support the notion that the current situation must change, yet carefully retaining current strengths that fit with the new vision
- establishing a strategy plan that balances assertive leadership with collective culture and understanding/support for the reform
- building capacity and commitment early and continuously through training, planning and revision based on the school's comprehensive vision
- pushing for results, since results are the most persuasive reason for making long-term commitment.

Major evaluation efforts are linked to each implementation phase. The school plans to focus the evaluation on how it is meeting its developmental goals, and why it is or is not having success as seen by the many stakeholders. Evaluation must be part of the reflection/revision process that is linked to governance and instructional improvement.

Structure of action planning

The school has structured the action plan around:

- Developmental Task Forces (school wide developmental design teams which have a topic focus)
- Developmental Projects (focused improvement efforts with a specific timeframe yet continually integrated with all other aspects of the student's life) which happen within ongoing school structures such as Houses, departments and grade-level groups
- Capacity Building Strategies, including teacher culture enhancements and summer institutes designed to enhance the knowledge, skill and confidence of teachers and to build program coherence
- Implementation Monitoring Strategies that enable the school to keep track of both the big picture and its interrelated parts.

School coach

Additionally, to provide consistent support and feedback, the school has created the role of school coach. David Marsh, Professor of Education at the University of Southern California, has been the school coach from the beginning of the restructuring. He has guided the visits to other schools across the nation, analysed the dilemmas and reflected on the directions the school needs to take. He also has helped the school think about, plan and implement various major phases of the restructuring and build the capacity to get there, especially in getting the change process to work and seeing important next steps in the journey.

Student performance goals

To monitor progress, the school has established collective student goals. These are very demanding, and include goals related to:

- attendance
- academic performance, as indicated by grades, and demonstration of mastery through exhibitions including the Senior Research Project
- graduation (based on student characteristics)
- post-graduate job preparation
- community service
- Higher Education Degree completion.

Evidence of success

While the restructuring effort at PHS is not yet completed, there are already indications that the program is moving in the right direction. Evidence of success can be seen in:

- Standardised Tests: students have increased their reading scores and maths scores on the Stanford Achievement Tests.
- Grades: the percentage of students receiving Ds and Fs in their core classes has decreased from forty per cent to twenty-five per cent.
- Attendance: unexcused absences have declined by over 50 per cent compared to before restructuring begun.
- Dropouts: preliminary results indicate that many more students are graduating. A study done on the ninth and tenth grade years indicates that only seven students out of 600 dropped out of school for the year 1992.

Lessons learned

There are many generalisable lessons from the PHS restructuring effort. These would include the following points.

Have a comprehensive student-centred vision that focuses on results   The vision serves as a broad guideline rather than a specific road map for reform, but covers major elements of a powerful learning experience for students. The results provide the necessary destination.

Involve teachers, yet expand the collective horizons of the planning team   Few schools are equipped to develop all the elements of a comprehensive design for reform, nor should they be expected to have this entire capability. The staff need to visit other schools and engage in sustained staff development, which is critical to the success of the restructuring effort.

Create an opportunity for school leaders to move forward   The reform will probably not have the support of the entire school in the first year. Rather than trying to persuade everyone 'up front', school leaders need to balance pressure to solve school problems and get positive results, with the comfort of time to persuade other staff to participate in subsequent years.

Use data to persuade staff that the current school isn't working, yet honour current good practice and don't blame individuals   In the early phases of the reform, the final design of the restructuring is not settled. What school leaders make clear, however, is that ineffective current arrangements cannot continue.

A strong and visionary principal helps tremendously   Most principals know they need a vision; but it is the comprehensive vision and the experience of working on comprehensive reform that is crucial. Closely linked to this vision is a sense of 'inventing the means, but staying clear about the ends'.

Restructure the school in stages, but make sure that each stage will revitalise major aspects of a given student's life at the school   Serious reforms need the synergistic effects of changing many things about the learning experience of a student at the school.

Revise the structure early   Changes in the structure revise the planning and implementation issues and the conversation about reform. Early implementation may be rocky and difficult, but it helps the staff to:

- learn by doing
- gain time to plan within the school day
- link planning to team-level solutions and accountability
- build momentum for reform.

Meaningful reform attracts positive attention; new teachers, outside resources and networks with significant colleagues   An attractive reform effort can attract the attention of, and funding from, private foundations, the business community, and the educational community. Excellent new teachers can be attracted by the reform effort; and become a major source of energy at the school.

FINAL THOUGHTS

As we begin to enter the twenty-first century, many people in America have now recognised that the foundation of a nation's wealth is really its people, the human capital represented by their knowledge, skills, organisations and motivations. A century ago, a high school education was thought to be superfluous for factory workers and a college degree was the mark of an academic or a professional. By the year 2000, for the first time in our history, a majority of all new jobs in the United States will require post-secondary education and/or training. Many professions will require nearly a decade of study after high school, and even the least skilled jobs will require a command of reading, computing, and thinking that was once necessary only for the professions.

Education and training are the primary systems by which the human capital of any nation is preserved and increased. All children, before they receive a high school diploma, must be able to read and understand sophisticated materials, write clearly, speak articulately, and solve complex problems requiring algebra and statistics. This kind of information has helped bring many segments of the American society to focus on education.

People have concluded that, if a bright future is to be realised, the educational standards that have been established in the nation's schools must be raised dramatically. Simply put, the time spent in school, the curriculum-developed, tests to be taken, all need to be dramatically different from before. Unfortunately, educators and the education system have not revitalised themselves; it is the economic condition of America that has demanded higher standards in schools. The education reform movement of the past decade tended to focus on collateral matters like school structure, governance, finance, requirements, accountability, community involvement and parent choice. These are highly important matters and we must continue to address them as we pursue fundamental change in our traditional system of education. But, critical as they are, they are not the heart of the process; those of us who work and live in schools know that to be the case. The heart of the process is teaching and learning. What are the standards? What should be taught and what should be learned? How is it best taught and how is it best learned? What must teachers do, and what support do they need in order to be most effective? What must students do, and what support do they need to learn most effectively?

We can no longer tolerate the way too many of our young people come to school. It is not possible to separate the way children learn from the way they live. If children arrive in school hungry or fearful, these needs must be addressed if learning is to occur.

The years from birth to about age twenty are a quarter of an average lifespan. The quality of that life very often is in our hands. It is up to us to pursue both our higher standards of achievement and at the same time to help all of our children to develop emotionally, socially and physically, as well as intellectually. We must, in our endeavour to increase the learning performance of all students, also increase their learning opportunities by respecting them and treating them whole. Re-thinking, re-making and restructuring schools with nothing more in mind than higher performance, better outcomes fitted to a global economy, is an absolutely empty exercise. We must put the child's needs at the centre of the process. That must be our mission, in America and in every other place in this world.

REFERENCES

Codding, J. and Tucker, M. (1996) *Organizing for Results*, unpublished paper, Washington, DC: National Center on Education and the Economy.

Gardner, H. (1991) *The Unschooled Mind: How Children Think and How Schools Should Teach*, New York: Basic Books.

Marshall, R. and Tucker, M. (1992) *Thinking for a Living: Education and the Wealth of Nations*, New York: Basic Books.

Martin, J. (1992) *The School Home: Rethinking Schools for Changing Families* Cambridge, Mass. and London: Harvard University Press.

NCEE (1995) *An Orientation to the Design*, Washington, DC: National Center on Education and the Economy.

Odden, A. (1995) *Educational Leadership for America's Schools*, New York: McGraw Hill Inc.

Sarason, S. (1983) *Schooling in America: Scapegoat and Salvation*, New York: The Free Press.

Sizer, T. (1984) *Horace's Compromise: The Dilemma of the American High School*, Boston, New York and London: Houghton Mifflin.

—— (1992) *Horace's School: Redesigning the American High School*, Boston, New York and London: Houghton Mifflin.

The Certificate of Initial Mastery: A Primer (1994) Washington, DC: National Center on Education and the Economy.

The Report of the Commissioner on the Skills of the American Work Force (1990) *America's Choice: high skills or low wages!*, Washington, DC: National Center on Education and the Economy.

Chapter 10

Weaving school and teacher development together

Dean Fink and Louise Stoll

Over the past few years we have attempted to document the evolution of an effective schools project within the Halton Board of Education, located in Ontario, Canada (Stoll and Fink, 1989, 1990, 1992). Now that we both have left the Halton Board, we can look back on this attempted system-wide change process in a somewhat more reflective way than when we were in the midst of its daily challenges. We initiated this reflection when we more recently summarised what we had learned, what we thought we had learned, and outlined areas where we needed help from the research community (Stoll and Fink, 1994). We described our experience as an 'odyssey' because of the twists and turns that the project took from its initiation. We continue this reflection on our 'odyssey' in this chapter by describing how, of necessity, our narrowly defined conception of school effectiveness broadened and deepened and ultimately became woven into the very fabric of the school system.

Since we began in 1986, many school effectiveness projects in other school districts around the world have been abandoned. Many had been imposed on schools and systems and failed to bring quick results. Others failed because schools and systems had no process in place to effect change. The effectiveness literature proved useful in directing the *what* of change; it said very little about the *how* of change. To succeed, it was our view that school effectiveness must be linked to school improvement strategies (Stoll and Fink, 1992). We found, as had others before us, that authentic change is sometimes painfully slow. Sizer described the change process with a simple metaphor:

> a good school does not emerge like a prepackaged frozen dinner stuck for 15 minutes in a radar range; it develops from the slow simmering of carefully blended ingredients.
>
> (Sizer, 1985: 22)

Many schools and systems in the 1980s initiated school improvement activities; most were unrelated to school effectiveness. Once again, results were slow in coming. Politicians and administrators became impatient with the 'slow simmering' of educational change and called for a restructuring or reform of schools and school systems. The terms mean different things to different people, but one thoughtful discussion of restructuring has talked of 'changes in roles, rules, and relationships between and among students and teachers, teachers and administrators, and administrators at various levels from the school building to the district office to the State (or Provincial) level' (Sashkin and Egermeier, 1992: 12). What is missing in the reform movement of the eighties has been a discussion of purpose: school effectiveness for *what* purpose; school improvement for *what* purpose; restructuring or reform for *what* purpose? (Stoll and Fink, 1996). Holly (1990) summarises this dilemma when he describes the three waves of reform in the 1980s: school effectiveness, 'doing the same but more'; school improvement, 'doing the same, but better'; and restructuring and total redesign.

In 1988, we defined excellence in very broad terms. The Halton project's mission stated:

Student achievement and self concept will be enhanced by providing:

- a process for schools to assess their effectiveness as related to validated characteristics;
- a system of planning to effect change.

(Halton Board, 1988a)

In essence, we started with a school effectiveness approach that soon blended with school improvement strategies. By 1992, however, we realised that our journey through school effectiveness to school improvement had actually resulted in a profound restructuring of the teaching–learning process in Halton. We had begun to experience Murphy's prophecy of 'fairly radical changes in the design and unfolding of learning experiences' (Murphy, 1992: 99).

Thus, in 1994, 'excellence' in Halton had come to mean a profoundly different educational paradigm from our beginnings in 1986 and from traditional views of education. In effect, eight years after the initiation of its 'odyssey', Halton was able to tie a sense of educational purpose to the insights gained from the work on school effectiveness and school improvement.

What emerged, more through trial and error than foresight, was an approach to organisational change which was more holistic or systemic, both conceptually and in practice. We found that schools and school districts are non-linear systems (Stacey, 1995) and that cause–effect relationships are not easily determined. We confronted innumerable political impediments, shifts in policies and personnel changes which confounded long-range planning. It became clear, as the effective schools project evolved, that it had to be woven into the very fabric of the system if our work was to impact on schools and classrooms. We therefore adopted the metaphor of the 'weave' as our guiding image for change in Halton. The remainder of this chapter, therefore, will illustrate our meaning by first addressing the emerging learning paradigm, which provides purpose to the Halton schools and school system, and then describing some of the strategies that have helped to 'weave' this sense of purpose into the fabric of the schools and system, and in the process begin to effect more authentic restructuring.

THE TRADITIONAL LEARNING PARADIGM

Barker (1989: 14) describes a paradigm as a 'set of rules and regulations that establish boundaries, and tell us what to do to be successful within those boundaries'. The prevailing school paradigm is outlined by Reich:

> [S]chools mirrored the national economy, with standard assembly line curriculum, divided neatly into subjects, taught in predictable units of time, arranged sequentially by grade, and controlled by standardised tests intended to weed out defective units and return for reworking.
>
> (Reich, 1992: 226)

This model of schooling, which emerged in North America in the late nineteenth and early twentieth centuries, was influenced by evolutionary theory. Society, which was largely of Northern European stock, used comprehensive common schooling as a vehicle to assimilate newcomers from Southern and Eastern Europe and Asia. This led to a school system, which, in the words of Purkey and Novak (1984: 11), 'labeled, libeled, sorted and grouped' children. A particularly useful device for sorting students into their appropriate places was the IQ test. One of the pioneers in the development of Intelligence Quotients (IQ) was Terman, who wrote:

> [P]reliminary investigation indicates that an I.Q. below 70 rarely permits anything better than unskilled labor; that the range 70–80 is preeminently that of semi-skilled labor; from 80–100 that of skilled or ordinary clerical labor; from 100–110 or 115 that of the semiprofessional pursuits; and above all these are the degrees of intelligence which permit one to enter the professions or the large fields of business. Intelligence tests can tell us whether a child's native brightness corresponds more nearly to the median. . . . This information will be of great value in planning the education of a particular child and also in planning the differentiated curriculum
>
> (Terman, 1922: 36)

Intelligence, therefore, was considered an unchanging trait which was normatively distributed in the general population. Some people were smart, some of average intelligence, and others were, by degrees, less intelligent. Intelligence, then, became that which was measured by IQ tests. This led to a very narrow definition of human intelligence and potential. Tests to a greater or lesser degree focused on what Gardner (1983) would call 'logical mathematical' intelligence.

This paradigm of intelligence led to the belief that learning is sequential; that it is an individual activity; and that it occurs best without the assistance of tools like calculators. A certain hierarchy of knowledge evolved which is reflected in contemporary secondary education. Thinkers use their intelligence; artisans use tools. Hargreaves *et al.* (1992) have described how this hierarchy of knowledge plays out in the marginalisation of music, visual arts, drama, technical subjects and business subjects in secondary schools.

Perhaps more insidious for many students is the decontextualised nature of much of what students are expected to learn. Getting the correct answer is more important than understanding the concepts behind the problem. Gardner suggests that students who learn at a surface level rarely gain the real understanding which comes through contextualised learning (Brandt, 1993).

The traditional school paradigm, therefore, came to mean the imparting of 'approved' knowledge through government guidelines, state-authorised textbooks, and standardised tests. Students were sorted according to ability to create more homogeneous groups. Special education legislation in many countries further exacerbated this sorting by creating new categories. Supported by detailed legislation, schools spent as much time ensuring compliance as they did attending to students. The evidence (Oakes, 1985; Hargreaves *et al.* 1996) indicates that this sorting process which has its roots in the early part of the century still divides students; not by intelligence, but by socio-economic class, race and ethnic background. Classes for students identified as gifted tend to come from higher socio-economic groups. In one large school board in Ontario, the assessed value of homes of students in gifted classes range from eight to 15 per cent higher than the average for the region, depending on the area. In contrast, students in vocational schools, in disproportionate numbers, tend to come from lower socio-economic groups and racial and ethnic minorities.

Teachers within this paradigm have come to be quasi-professionals, or less charitably, skilled trades people. Since students are the inputs in the educative process then the teachers' job is to mould them in accordance with the specifications (courses, hours, texts, tests) designed by educational experts to achieve the proper outputs which are measured by test scores. The proof of teacher and school effectiveness to many is computed in reading and mathematics scores on decontextualised tests.

If one assumes that students can be grouped homogeneously and dealt with in standardised ways, then one can externally prescribe the approach to teaching, and the teacher's job is to do, not to think. In other words, external agents attempt to deprofessionalise teaching by removing decision making. Staff development is not important in this model. In-service training for teachers is needed to ensure understanding of the 'way' to teach different groups of students. Supervision of teachers, therefore, becomes investigation to ensure compliance with external requirements. This paradigm for education worked well for many years. The evidence is fairly clear; the best students do very well (Bracey, 1991, 1992, 1993). In fact one might argue that we are prisoners of success. Our societies have been able to absorb young people with differentiated educational backgrounds. Industry required people with basic mathematics and reading abilities who could perform routine jobs in which punctuality and compliance were required qualities.

The unsuccessful in the traditional school paradigm found places in society and many have enjoyed the benefits of developed economies. This paradigm may have worked in 1966 but is not working in 1996 and will not work in 2006. The post-modern world requires a different model of schooling, one which is more in concert with the changing nature of economies and social structures.

We are moving out of the modern era with its dependence on factories, centralisation, bureaucracies and structure into a post-modern era in which 'economic, political and organisational and even personal life come to be organised around very different principles than those of modernity. . . . The post modern world is fast, compressed and uncertain' (Hargreaves, 1994: 8). We are also abandoning, whether we like it or not, the stability, security and certainty which have defined our lives. Like the 'age of enlightenment' of the eighteenth century, social forces have been unleashed which will profoundly redirect the course of human experiences in the twenty-first century. Our challenge as educators is to move our schools from a paradigm of learning which reflected modernity and is incompatible with the demands of a post-modern world to one which prepares young people to live and work in the twenty-first century.

THE EMERGING LEARNING PARADIGM

Among researchers and educators a new paradigm of learning is emerging:

> [T]he capacity for thoughtfulness is widespread, rather than the exclusive property of those who rank high, and our views of students are susceptible to change. Not only may students' capacities leapfrog our predictions but our cultural conceptions of skill and learning inevitably develop (or at least change) . . . learning at all levels involves sustained performances of thought and collaborative interactions of multiple minds and tools as much as individual possession of information.
>
> (Wolf *et al.*,1991: 49)

Everyone has a mind; these minds work in different ways. According to Gardner (1983) there are multiple intelligences. People are more proficient in some areas than others. In addition to logical-mathematical intelligence, he describes linguistic, musical, spatial, bodily-kinesthetic, and two kinds of personal intelligences, intra- and inter-personal. This is a much more democratic and inclusive concept of learning and intelligence. The challenge is not one of sorting the fit and the less fit but rather one of developing all of these 'minds'.

Research on school effectiveness indicates that ability is not fixed (Mortimore *et al.*, 1988) and learning research suggests that learning is not sequential. Students' ability can be modified by effective instruction. Learning is far more effective within a context (Berryman and Bailey, 1992). The popularity of cooperative education and work experience are reflective of this notion. The guidelines adopted by the National Council of Mathematics Teachers are also based on the premise that:

> knowing mathematics is doing mathematics and what students learn depends to a great degree on how they learn it. The emphasis . . . is on solving nonroutine problems in meaningful contexts.
>
> (Smith *et al.*, 1993: 4)

In addition to conventional basics there are new basics appropriate to a changing world. Reich (1992) contends that people who will succeed in a post-modern world possess the following four sets of basic skills:

- abstraction, the capacity for discovering patterns and meaning;
- systems thinking, to see relationships among phenomena;
- experimentation, the ability to find one's own way through continuous learning;
- the social skills to collaborate with others.

The compatibility between the new learning model, with its expanded definition of the basics, and the predicted demands of post-modern economies provide a compelling argument for change in schools.

Berryman and Bailey, in their study of what they call the 'double helix', that is, the needs of the new workplace and the imperatives of new approaches to learning, found that:

> our new understanding of both work and learning suggest very similar directions for reform. Strengthening the educational system so that it conforms more to the way people learn will also directly enhance the system to prepare students for the types of workplaces that are emerging in factories and offices throughout the country.
>
> (Berryman and Bailey, 1992: 44)

The Conference Board of Canada (Corporate Council on Education, 1992) in its outline of employability skills corroborates Berryman and Bailey's findings in its list of required academic skills. The Conference Board expands the conventional basics to include critical thinking, problem solving and technological literacy. The list also outlines personal management skills like positive attitudes, responsibility and adaptability. The skills list adds a set of teamwork skills which includes the ability to contribute to organisational goals and to work within a significantly expanded span of control. A cursory analysis of present educational practices suggest that schools are out of step with the needs of the larger society of the 1990s. Schools have become very effective in moving students up the educational ladder. The problem for many students is that the ladder is leaning against the wrong wall.

SCHOOL EFFECTIVENESS AND THE EMERGING LEARNING PARADIGM

The work on school effectiveness in Halton has created a knowledge base, as well as a climate which enhances the move towards the emerging learning paradigm. School effectiveness has helped us to design the 'right wall' for students. The effectiveness model is based on studies of schools which are effective for *all* students, not just those who rank high in society. It assumes that students are not standardised and that teaching is not routine. Within the effectiveness model, teachers need knowledge of child development, multiple teaching strategies, a variety of assessment strategies, as well as insight into children's learning styles. Teaching is as much an art as a science. Teachers in this paradigm are not just skilled tradespeople who must apply others' expert design, but rather autonomous decision makers who make multiple decisions to enhance the learning of each child, each day.

To perform at the highest professional levels, teachers must be empowered to become learners themselves through meaningful staff development programmes (Joyce and Showers, 1981; Hargreaves and Dawe, 1989). Fullan has stated that 'change in education depends on what teachers do and think – it's as simple and complex as that' (Fullan, 1991: 117). He also states: 'As long as there is the need for improvement, namely, forever, there will be need for professional development' (1991: 344). If we expect to change student learning, effective schools must attend to and invest in teacher learning.

For an organisation to survive and for teachers to grow professionally, the rate of learning within the organisation must be equal to, or greater than, the rate of change in the external environment (Garratt, 1987). To be effective, therefore, each school must become a learning community (Barth, 1990). The evidence to support this concept is fairly clear. A recent study of effective large-scale change in the United States reported that teachers who made effective adaptations to the students of today shared one quality: 'each belonged to an active professional community which encouraged and enabled them to transform their teaching' (McLaughlin and Talbert, 1993: 7).

The principal's role then, becomes crucial to an effective school (Fullan, 1985; Mortimore *et al.*, 1988; Rosenholtz, 1989; Smith and Andrews, 1989; Louis and Miles, 1990; Leithwood, 1992). The leadership necessary to initiate the new learning paradigm is a blend of instructional (Smith and Andrews, 1989) and transformational leadership (Sergiovanni, 1990; Leithwood, 1992). The latter style of leadership includes the pursuit of common goals, empowerment and maintenance of a collaborative culture, teacher development and problem-solving. These qualities are reflected in teacher-led professional development committees and staff-led school planning teams. Elsewhere (Stoll and Fink, 1996) we have criticised false dichotomies between managers and leaders (Bennis and Nanus, 1985) and transactional and transformational leaders (Burns, 1978), and proposed a more holistic approach to leadership which incorporates the essential competencies of instructional and transformational approaches into a conception which includes both the personal and professional dynamics of leadership. Built upon the perceptual tradition of psychology, the invitational image of leadership rests upon four pillars. Once again, the key investment is in the development and training of invitational leaders who supervise staff to ensure professional growth, rather than just compliance. The challenge for schools and school systems is to establish processes which weave together the various initiatives, while providing support for individual teachers and principals as they move towards a profoundly different learning paradigm.

THE WEAVE: A METAPHOR FOR CHANGE

Odiorne (1979) describes successful organisations as those which manage the planning process, and, more importantly, which engage the commitment of staff members to the organisation's directions. He describes these two management levels as management by anticipation and management by commitment. The challenge for all organisations is to weave these two management activities together to achieve the organisation's goals, while at the same time ensuring that individuals and groups at all levels of the system feel that their own goals are met. This seems to be a particular problem in educational settings. Just as a fabric is the result of the tight weaving of many different strands, it was our approach to try to integrate all system and school activities.

Management by anticipation

Neither centralisation or decentralisation works (Stoll and Fink, 1992). Efforts to effect change by destroying or undermining centralising authorities have been as unsuccessful as attempting 'top-down' change. Many current reform efforts throughout the world reflect a naive confidence in schools' ability to effect change without support. The most successful model seems to be 'top-down/bottom-up' (Stoll and Fink, 1994). At the system level, for instance, a Halton strategic plan wove together the work of the Effective Schools Task Force, major reviews of curriculum and special education and ideas from our links with the Learning Consortium (Fullan *et al.*, 1990), as well as various assessments and research projects, to produce broad policy directions from which schools could develop their individual school growth plans.

In 1988, three areas of activity were proposed in the strategic plan, to capitalise on the Effective Schools Project, ensure adequate attention to the teaching and learning process, and sufficient support for schools engaged in self development. These were:

- school-based planning
- an emphasis on instruction
- staff resources.

In 1993, this plan was reviewed and updated through a process which, over three days, involved all the stakeholders within the system as well as broad representation from parents, students and the community at large. The result was a reaffirmation of the 1988 directions, with the addition of a focus on involving the community much more closely in system and school decision making. The following items from the overall plan provide examples of initiatives directed toward the achievement of the new learning paradigm:

- curriculum that is defined in terms of learning outcomes and is more holistic and less subject-based
- learning defined by the achievement of outcomes rather than time spent in a classroom
- learning outcomes which are relevant and promote contextualised learning
- assessment of student performance integrated into the instructional process and based more on performance on real life tasks
- students grouped in a variety of ways, not just by presumed ability
- organisation of schools characterised by greater flexibility
- teachers who function as professionals and are encouraged by leaders who create a learning community
- system commitment to professional growth
- schools work within a 'top-down/bottom-up' network
- schools and school system that work closely with the local community to develop school policies.

At the school level, 'management by anticipation' has resulted in the school growth plan (Halton Board, 1988b). This planning model (Stoll and Fink, 1989, 1990; Fink and Stoll, 1992) has been well implemented (Stoll, 1991, 1992), and is designed to provide a systematic means of achieving continuous growth and development within a particular school.

As we have noted elsewhere (Stoll and Fink, 1994), more successful schools were characterised by:

1 A focus on shared decision making.
2 Coordination by a small group.
3 Emphasis on fundamental conditions to planning; that is, to develop a shared vision, to build a positive climate, to promote staff collegiality, and norms of continuous improvement.
4 Engagement in an on-going dynamic process.
5 Commitment to a few key goals.
6 Emphasis on assessment, monitoring, and evaluation.
7 Use of school effectiveness characteristics in the assessment phase.
8 Commitment to instruction.
9 Consideration of the school's unique context and culture.
10 Incorporation of older familiar features of the Halton culture, such as a well established supervision process.

These qualities appeared to be crucial to positive change within the Halton schools' culture. The school growth plans are a school-based version of the system's strategic plan. In this way system initiatives are woven into school planning and, conversely, school growth plans are annually reviewed to determine system-wide staff development initiatives and system activities.

Management by commitment

Elsewhere, we have described the nature and importance of system-organised staff development and leadership programmes in Halton (Stoll and Fink, 1988, 1989, 1992, 1996). These include peer coaching and mentoring schemes, leadership training workshops for school growth plan teams and a wide variety of institutes related to teaching and learning strategies, assessment, and the change process.

These programmes have been crucial to the change process because they provide staff with the knowledge and skills necessary to develop commitment to the new learning paradigm and to build their own change capacity. Equally important to that process of change is to weave 'older familiar features' into the change gestalt. From its inception in 1969, the Halton Board has placed a high value on the quality of leadership in the system. In its first year of operation, it initiated a leadership course which was open to all staff, regardless of role. In spite of financial difficulties over time, this programme continues to train Halton leaders.

In the early 1970s, the Halton system adopted an approach to the supervision of people in leadership roles called Education By Agreement (EBA). The vehicle for agreement on annual goals by system leaders, including principals and vice principals, was the Manager's Letter. Each person in a leadership role developed a Manager's Letter with the person to whom that person reported. The process involved the collaborative development of a statement of goals, indicators of success and activities to be pursued by the partners to the agreement. It was, to use Covey's (1989) phrase, intended to be a 'psychological contract'.

This process was reviewed in 1993 by a committee of principals, to integrate it into the effectiveness model. Each principal, therefore, continues to have a Manager's Letter with a superintendent, and each vice principal has a Manager's Letter with his or her principal. This personal growth plan contains a few 'high leverage' goals over a period which could extend from six months to three years. It contains goals related to:

- the expectations of principals and vice principals. These expectations were developed through continual discussion and negotiation with the principals' associations for elementary and secondary schools. Expectations reflect the research on school effectiveness, and personal and professional expectations of invitational leadership (Stoll and Fink, 1996) which are consistent with the type of leadership required as schools move to a different conception of learning.
- the principal's or vice principal's role in the implementation of the school growth plan. In this way, the principal's or vice principal's performance is woven into the school growth plan.
- the principal's or vice principal's own growth. In this way, each person's professional development is attended to by the system. The nature of leadership development programmes is heavily influenced by the needs identified in Manager's Letters. Supervisors of principals and vice principals are accountable for the professional growth of people who report to them.

The process is based on five premises (Halton Board, 1993). These are that each person has:

- a need to know clearly the expectations of the organisation; what constitutes good work
- a need for the freedom to choose how expectations will be achieved, and the removal of obstacles to effective performance when they exist
- a need for timely, constructive feedback on progress
- a need for training and guidance to develop the skills necessary to grow professionally
- a need for fair rewards based on performance.

The term 'Manager's Letter' is somewhat dated and perhaps misleading to the outsider. It is, however, meaningful in the Halton context, and an example of how traditional practices and language have been adapted to thread the commitment of system leaders into the fabric of the school and the system directions. Through negotiation between a principal and the principal's immediate superior in the organisation, the Manager's Letter becomes a statement of commitment by the principal to both system and school goals, and commitment by the person to whom the principal reports of specific kinds of support to assist the principal to achieve the agreed goals.

Similarly, Halton's procedures for the supervision of teachers (Cooperative Supervision and Evaluation – CS&E) were updated and melded into the effectiveness model. In 1976, the system established a Teacher Evaluation Task Force. By 1979, a model for teacher supervision and evaluation had been developed and, over time, was well implemented in the system. In 1991, as part of an Effective Schools Survey, a representative sample of Halton teachers was requested to respond to the following item: 'The administrative team uses the Cooperative Supervision and Evaluation (CS&E) process to assist in the improvement of instruction'.

Eighty-four per cent of elementary teachers surveyed agreed, thirteen per cent were uncertain, and only three per cent disagreed. Seventy-two per cent of their secondary colleagues agreed with the statement, 26 per cent were uncertain, and only two per cent disagreed. While reasonably well implemented and accepted, the need to make the process more relevant was apparent, however, because fewer teachers believed the process to be important (80 per cent of elementary teachers, and 64 per cent of secondary teachers).

A committee of teachers and one superintendent redrafted the previous document to compensate for weaknesses of the process. More importantly, the committee redrafted the expectations for teachers, which had been largely ignored in the past, to include insights gained from the school effectiveness literature (Rutter et al., 1979; Goodlad, 1984; Mortimore et al., 1988), the teacher effectiveness literature (Good and Brophy, 1991) and affective education (Purkey and Novak, 1984). Representatives for each school were shown a process to use in their school to ensure teachers had meaningful input into the process and expectations. In the past, representative committees developed the expectations and then used an in-service approach to implement the design.

Each school provided extensive feedback on the process and, particularly, on the expectations. The draft was recirculated to schools on three occasions and revised, which took almost two years. By taking the time and committing the effort, there appeared to be evidence that the renewed CS&E process had widespread acceptance within the system.

Performance appraisal systems walk a fine line between accountability to school boards and their public, and the professional growth of teachers. School board members often want to define principal and teacher roles in narrowly prescribed ways and delineate a review process which is punitive in spirit. A realistic approach to performance appraisals must have sufficiently high expectations to define a truly professional educator, and a process of performance review which is not only thorough, but perceived to be rigorous within the larger context of schools and school systems. The final Halton product received strong professional support as well as political affirmation.

The CS&E process requires each elementary principal to develop an agreement with each teacher every year. At the secondary level, principals develop Manager's Letters with department heads, who in turn contract through a Manager's Letter with each teacher in the department. The nature of these agreements depends on the age, experience, and goals of the individual teacher. Teacher goals will vary in depth and time commitment. Some will involve a Manager's Letter approach; others require classroom visitations and follow-up by the principal. The key word is cooperation. Goals are to be negotiated. If the principal has a serious performance concern, the procedure becomes more prescriptive and definitive to ensure 'just cause and due process'.

Perhaps the most significant part of this process is the emphasis on providing professional opportunities for teachers' growth. From dialogue between the teacher and the principal, a teacher's own professional growth plan is developed. This plan may include involvement in regional activities such as the many regional 'institutes' that are offered, or subject based in-service sessions (Stoll and Fink, 1990, 1992). The personal plan might also include the teacher's commitment to participate in various staff development activities within the school. These activities might include: mentoring and peer coaching schemes; collaborative planning of integrated curricula; paired classroom observation and feedback; in-service training provided by 'in-house experts'; and increasing discussions of educational issues, as well as teachers' educational beliefs and values. These are practised more widely in some schools than others. None the less, by 1991 the majority of teachers (90 per cent elementary and 86 per cent secondary) felt teachers in their schools were engaged in a wide variety of professional development experiences.

From a principal's point of view, the process provides an opportunity to involve the teacher in the school's growth plan. From a teacher's perspective, it has the potential to break down isolation, provide a vehicle to develop a personal growth plan and a connection to the larger school and system cultures. Once again, an attempt has been made to tie a traditional activity – performance appraisal – to the effectiveness model in a meaningful way.

While these strategies, described under the headings of 'Management by anticipation' and 'Management by commitment', are useful for organisational purposes, without a sense of moral educational purpose (Fullan, 1993) they can become inert or technocratic tools. This brings us once again, therefore, to the central premise of this chapter – school effectiveness for *what* purpose? School improvement for *what* purpose? School restructuring for *what* purpose? Public education is responsible for *all* the children of *all* the people. A truly public school cannot, and does not, discriminate based on gender, race, religion, physical or mental challenge, or the socio-economic background of its students. The mandate is to educate all children for a society in which knowledge is the currency of success. To effect the highest ideals of a democratic society, public educational systems must meet the test of non-repression and non-discrimination.

CONCLUSION

Guttman (1990: 17) describes repression as a 'practice or institution in its actual context that restricts (or impedes) rational inquiry'; discrimination as the exclusion of children 'from educational goods for reasons unrelated to the legitimate social purposes of those goods'. On this basis, such practices as tracking, decontextualised testing and grade retention must be challenged. Conversely, an education that promotes critical thought, problem solving, social and applied learning, and prepares all students, not just those who rank high, for the post-modern world, is much more in tune with democratic ideals. True restructuring or reform should promote democratic practices and discourage repressive and discriminatory structures and practices. All else is merely tinkering.

True restructuring must be informed by purpose and the common-sense knowledge of how *all* children learn 'the new learning paradigm'. The route to this profound shift in educational practice, which promises both quality and equity, is through the flexible application of what makes schools effective for children regardless of background, and the school improvement literature which helps schools and systems to effect change.

Schools and school systems need to weave their various activities, whether newly developed or traditional, into a gestalt which provides the best educational situation for *all* students. At the same time we must not become so enamoured of the system, method and strategy that we forget the profoundly moral business we are in. As Saul reminds us:

> One sign of a healthy Western civilization is that within a relatively integrated moral outlook – for example, agreement on democratic principles – a myriad of ideas and methods are brought face to face. Through civilized conflict the society's assumed moral correctness is constantly tested. This tension – emotional, intellectual, moral – is what advances the society. These contradictions are what make democracy work
>
> (Saul, 1993: 135).

By replacing the term 'Western civilisation' with the phrase 'the learning community' in this quote, one can capture the essence of a truly restructured school, i.e. a school in which the key stakeholders are continually engaged in processes which raise the philosopher's question, 'what is education for?'.

REFERENCES

Barker, J. (1989) *Discovering The Future: The Business of Paradigms*, St Paul: ILI Press.

Barth, R.(1990) *Improving Schools From Within: Teachers, Parents and Principals Can Make the Difference*, San Francisco: Jossey Bass.

Bennis, W. and Nanus, B. (1985) *Leaders*, New York: Harper and Row.

Berryman, S. E. and Bailey, T. R. (1992) *The Double Helix of Education and The Economy*, New York: Teachers College Press.

Bracey, G. W. (1991) 'Why Can't They be Like We Were?', *Phi Delta Kappan*, 7(2),104–17.

—— (1992) 'The Second Bracey Report on The Condition Of Public Education', *Phi Delta Kappan*, 74 (3), 104–17.

—— (1992) 'The Third Bracey Report on The Condition Of Public Education', *Phi Delta Kappan*, 75(2), 104–17.

Brandt, R. (1993) 'On Teaching for Understanding: A Conversation with Howard Gardner', *Educational Leadership*, 50(7), 4–7.

Burns, J. M. (1978) *Leadership*, New York: Harper and Row.

Corporate Council on Education (1992) *Employability Skills Profile*, Ottawa: Conference Board of Canada.

Covey, S. (1989) *The Seven Habits of Highly Effective People*, New York: Simon and Schuster.

Fink, D. and Stoll, L. (1992) 'Assessing School Change: The Halton Approach', paper presented at the Fifth International Congress for School Effectiveness and Improvement, Victoria, BC.

Fullan, M. G. (1982) *The Meaning of Educational Change*, Toronto: OISE Press.

—— (1985) 'Change processes and strategies at the local level', *Elementary School Journal*, 85(3), 391–420.

—— (1991) *The New Meaning of Educational Change*, New York: Teachers College Press.

—— (1993) *Change Forces: Probing the Depths of Educational Reform*, London: Falmer Press.

Fullan, M., Bennett, B., Rolheiser-Bennett, C. (1990) 'Linking Classroom and School Improvement' *Educational Leadership*, 47(8), 13–19.

Gardner, H. (1983) *Frames of Mind: The Theory of Multiple Intelligences*, New York: Basic Books.

Garratt, B. (1987) *The Learning Organization*, Glasgow: Collins.

Good, T. L. and Brophy, J. (1991) *Looking in Classrooms* (6th edn), New York: Harper and Row.

Goodlad, J. (1984) *A Place Called School*, New York: McGraw Hill.

Guttman, A. (1990) 'Democratic Education in Difficult Times', *Teachers College Record*, 92(1), 7–20.

Halton Board of Education (1988a) *Putting it All Together: Planning for School Effectiveness*, Burlington, Ontario: Halton Board of Education.

—— (1988b) *Building a School Growth Plan*, Burlington, Ontario: Halton Board of Education.

—— (1993) *Performance Appraisal Procedures*, Burlington, Ontario: Halton Board of Education.

Hargreaves, A. (1994) *Changing Teachers Changing Times: Teachers' Work and Culture in the Postmodern Age*, London: Cassell.

Hargreaves, A. and Dawe, R. (1989) 'Coaching as Unreflective Practice', paper presented to the American Educational Research Association, San Francisco.

Hargreaves, A., Earl, L. and Ryan, J. (1996) *School for Change: Reinventing Education for Early Adolescents*, London: Falmer.

Hargreaves, A., Fullan, M., Wignall, R., Stager, M. and Macmillan, R., (1992) *Secondary School Work Cultures and Educational Change*, Toronto: Ontario Ministry of Education.

Holly, P. (1990) 'Catching the Wave of the Future: Moving Beyond School Effectiveness by Redesigning Schools', *School Organisation*, 10(2 and 3), 195–211.

Joyce, B. and Showers, B. (1981) 'Transfer of Training: The Contribution of Coaching', *Journal of Education*, 163(2), 163–72.

Leithwood, K. A. (1992) 'The move toward transformational leadership', *Educational Leadership*, 49(5), 8–12.

Louis, K. S. and Miles, M. B. (1990) *Improving the Urban High School: What Works and Why*, New York: Teachers College Press.

McLaughlin, M. W. and Talbert, J. E. (1993) *Contexts That Matter for Teaching and Learning*, Palo Alto: Center for Research on the Context of Secondary School Teaching.

Mortimore, P., Sammons, P., Stoll, L., Lewis, D. and Ecob, R. (1988) *School Matters: The Junior Years*, Somerset: Open Books (reprinted in 1994 by Paul Chapman Press, London).

Murphy, J. (1992) 'School Effectiveness and School Restructuring: Contributions to Educational Improvement', *School Effectiveness and School Improvement*, 3(2), 90–109.

Oakes, J. (1985) *Keeping Track: How Schools Structure Social Inequality*, New Haven: Yale University Press.

Odiorne, G. (1979) *MBO II: A System of Managerial Leadership for the 80s*, Belmont: Pitman Publishers.

Purkey, W. W. and Novak, J. (1984) *Inviting School Success* (2nd edn), Belmont: Wadsworth.

Reich, R. (1992) *Work of Nations*, New York: Vintage Press.

Rosenholtz, S. (1989) *Teachers' Workplace; The Social Organization of Schools*, New York: Longmans.

Rutter, M., Maughan, B., Mortimore, P., and Ouston, J. (1979) *Fifteen Thousand Hours: Secondary Schools and Their Effect on Children*, Somerset: Open Books (reprinted in 1994 by Paul Chapman Press, London).

Sashkin, M. and Egermeier, J. (1992) 'School Change Models and Processes: A Review of Research and Practice', paper presented at the Annual Meeting of the American Educational Research Association, San Francisco.

Saul, J. R. (1993) *Voltaire's Bastards: The Dictatorship of Reason in the West*, Toronto: Penguin Books.

Sergiovanni, T. J. (1990) *Value-Added Leadership: How to Get Extraordinary Performance in Schools*, Orlando: Harcourt Brace Jovanovich.

Sizer, T. R. (1986) 'Common Sense', *Educational Leadership*, 42(6), 21–2.

Smith, S. Z., Smith, M. E. and Romberg, T. A. (1993) 'What the NCTM Standards Look Like in One Classroom', *Educational Leadership*, 50(8), 4–7.

Smith, W. F. and Andrews, R. L. (1989) *Instructional Leadership: How Principals Make a Difference*, Alexandria, VA: Association for Supervision and Curriculum Development.

Stacey, R. (1995) *Managing Chaos: Dynamic Business Strategies in an Unpredictable World*, London: Kogan Page.

Stoll, L. (1991) *Perceptions of Implementation of the School Growth Planning Process in Halton Schools*, Burlington, Ontario: Halton Board of Education.

—— (1992) *Perceptions of Implementation of the School Growth Planning Process in Halton Schools*, Burlington, Ontario: Halton Board of Education.

Stoll, L. and Fink, D. (1988) 'Educational Change: an international perspective', *International Journal of Educational Management*, 2(3), 26–31.

—— (1989) 'An effective schools project: the Halton approach', in D. Reynolds, B. P. M. Creemers and T. Peters (eds), *School Effectiveness and Improvement: Proceedings of the First International Congress for School Effectiveness and Improvement, London 1988*, Cardiff: University of Wales, College of Cardiff; Groningen: RION.

—— (1990) 'Organization for Effectiveness: The Halton Approach', in J. Bashi and Z. Sass (eds), *School Effectiveness and Improvement: Proceedings of the Third International Congress for School Effectiveness and Improvement, Jerusalem, Israel*, Jerusalem: The Magnet Press.

—— (1992) 'Effective School Change: The Halton Approach', *School Effectiveness and School Improvement* 3(1), 19–41.

—— (1994) 'School Effectiveness and School Improvement: Voices from the Field', *School Effectiveness and School Improvement*, 5(1), 149–77.

—— (1996) *Changing Our Schools: Linking School Effectiveness and School Improvement*, Buckingham: Open University Press.

Terman, L. M. (1922) *Intelligence Tests and School Reorganization*, Yonkers-on Hudson, NY: World Book Company; quoted in D. Wolf, J. Bixby, J. Glenn and H. Gardner (1991) 'To Use Their Minds Well: Investigating New Forms of Student Assessment', *Review of Research in Education*, 17, pp. 31–74, Washington: American Educational Research Association.

Wolf, D., Bixby, J., Glenn, J. and Gardner, H. (1991) 'To Use Their Minds Well: Investigating New Forms of Student Assessment', *Review of Research in Education*, 17, Washington: American Educational Research Association.

Chapter 11

Schools of the Future
A case study in systemic educational development

Tony Townsend

CONTEXT AND BACKGROUND OF *SCHOOLS OF THE FUTURE*

When the new Liberal government was elected in late 1992, after more than a decade in opposition, it set in train the most radical change to an education system in Australia's history. Victoria had entered the brave new world of education. It was the culmination of a transformation from education as it had previously been undertaken for more than a century into something completely new, one that might have been described by Drucker, who, in his most recent book, *Post-Capitalist Society*, argued:

> Every few hundred years in Western history there occurs a sharp transformation . . . Within a few short decades, society rearranges itself, its world view; its basic values; its social and political structures; its arts; its key institutions. Fifty years later, there is a new world . . . We are currently living through such a transformation . . .
>
> (Drucker, 1993: 1)

Yet it would be inappropriate to suggest that the transformation only started in 1992. Better, it might be seen as the culmination of something that had been going for more than two decades. In any discussion about school restructuring in Australia, the Karmel Report of 1973 is the logical starting point. The Report to the Commonwealth Government by the Interim Committee for the Australian Schools Commission, entitled *Schools in Australia* (Karmel, 1973), was described by Caldwell (1993: 3) as 'arguably one of the most influential documents in school education in the last twenty-five years'. It was here that the issues of equality, devolution and community involvement were first presented as part of a national educational debate, one that was to change the face of Australian schools dramatically for the first time in a hundred years.

Ever since the Karmel Report, Victoria has been Australia's flagship for many of the moves towards a fully decentralised system of education. The tentative first steps proposed by the 1975 School Councils Amendment to the 1958 Education Act, where school councils accepted some of the responsibilities for managing the finances and facilities of the school and advised the principal on issues of school policy, to later moves which included school council responsibility for determining school policy and selection of the school principal in the 1980s, have now developed into the *Schools of the Future* programme, which has many similarities to various models from the UK, the USA, New Zealand and Canada, but perhaps pushes the boundaries of school self-management even further than those countries have done.

At the time of the 1992 election, two separate, but related, concerns were identified as problems for Victorian education. They included both quantitative and qualitative aspects of education. The new government first argued that the education system was over-staffed and over-funded in comparison to other education systems in Australia, to the extent that there could be severe cutbacks in expenditure and staffing without affecting the quality of student outcomes; and second, the quality of education for all students could be improved by bringing substantial decision making, about staffing, about resource allocation, about curriculum, back to the school level.

The first part of this two-pronged adjustment of education in the state came with a substantial downsizing of the educational enterprise. Cutbacks in state funding to education had started in the mid-1980s with the then Labour government, but the dimensions of the cutbacks increased substantially. Since 1992 nearly 300 Victorian schools have been closed, and sold, and the teaching force has decreased by almost 20 per cent. Central office staffing was reduced by nearly 80 per cent and the regional offices and school support centres all but disappeared. While schools lost some teachers, which created an increase in the teacher–pupil ratio, they were the least hardest hit in the restructuring exercise. Thousands of teachers were offered, and took, departure packages.

The second part of the adjustment came with the new policy for the governance and operation of schools in the state, which was called the *Schools of the Future*. This was the Victorian government's blueprint for the delivery of quality education into the next century and has been progressively developed over the past four years. It has involved a considerable policy shift from the previous way in which government education was managed and structured and will involve a considerable commitment of resources over a number of years to implement the plan properly.

DEVELOPMENT OF THE PROGRAMME

The *Schools of the Future* is not a meaningless slogan, but a complex and comprehensive view of school management from both the systemic and local viewpoints. Just as it would be inappropriate to make judgements about an octopus on the basis of one of its tentacles, it is also inappropriate to look at the various dimensions of the *Schools of the Future* programme in isolation from the others.

The programme, which is almost certainly the most radical of the moves in Australia at the moment, changes the relationship between schools, the Directorate of School Education (DSE) and government. Not only is there now a contract between the individual school and the DSE (the school charter), upon which school funding is based and accounted for, but many of the support services (from teacher professional development to school cleaning services) previously provided by the DSE will no longer be available, and schools will have to contract with individual providers for them, either singly, or in conjunction with other schools.

The focus of the new structure of education is the self-managing school, and the underlying rationale for this structure comes from the 'commitment to the view that quality outcomes of schooling can only be assured when decision making takes place at the local level' (DSE, 1994a: 2). Three hundred and twenty-five schools from over seven hundred applicants were selected as part of a pilot programme which commenced in January 1994, and further groups were added at six-monthly intervals until, currently, 99 per cent of government schools are registered for the programme.

Key features of the *Schools of the Future* programme (Peck, 1996: 3) include:

- The school charter is the school's vision for the future. It is also the key planning and accountability document which serves as the formal understanding between the school community and the DSE. High levels of autonomy and accountability for each school are expressed through the school charter.
- To complement the charter, the authority of school councils as governing bodies has been expanded to include responsibility for the selection of principals, the employment of non-teaching staff, and the use of teachers on short-term contracts for particular projects.
- Each school council reports to the community through a comprehensive annual report focusing on educational achievements.
- An independent school review process that reconsiders and renews charters takes place every three years. This process assists schools to monitor and improve the performance of their students.
- Each school principal selects a teaching team.
- The principal has the responsibility to foster the professional development and personal growth of teachers.
- The school community decides on the best use of its resources through a one-line global budget which allows for local flexibility.

ELEMENTS OF *SCHOOLS OF THE FUTURE*

The school charter

The key feature of the *Schools of the Future* project is the school charter, which is the major accountability document between the school and its community (for the achievements of its students) on the one hand and the school and the Directorate of School Education (DSE) (for the proper expenditure of state resources) on the other. Each school develops its own charter which establishes a set of agreed expectations (conforming to DSE guidelines) that provides direction for the school. Through the school charter, school communities have the opportunity to determine the future character, ethos and goals of the school.

The school charter is developed by the school council in consultation with the community and with support provided by the principal and staff. The charter, which operates for three years, but could be amended where required, is signed by both the principal and the president of the school council, and a representative of the DSE. It includes (DSE, 1994b):

- a description of the school's philosophy and future directions
- its goals and the priorities identified as requiring further development
- how it intended to deliver the eight state mandated curriculum areas and any other special enrichment activities specific to that school
- codes of practice for school council members, principals and staff
- a code of conduct and the discipline approach used for students of the school
- details of the processes used for monitoring and reporting student performance
- a prediction of student numbers and an indicative budget for the period of the charter
- a statement that the school agrees to operate within the terms of the charter and to agree to take all reasonable steps to ensure the school meets its goals within the available resources.

The critical features of the charter are the school goals and priorities, which relate to curriculum, school environment, management, resource allocation and monitoring performance. Each goal is accompanied by indicators which enable achievement of that goal to be measured. The priorities are based on planned and continuous improvement, which requires a school to analyse its performance and, using the results of this analysis, to generate priorities for improved student performance. Schools report annually to the DSE and their local community on their performance in achieving their goals and priorities. Every three years a review is conducted at the school, in conjunction with the Office of School Review, to assist with the development of a new charter.

Accountability

The accountability structure of Victorian education includes both systemic and local accountability processes. At the systemic level the DSE has established a Board of Studies to provide curriculum leadership and assistance to schools on a statewide basis, and an Office of Schools Review to support the attempts of individual schools to raise the quality of their teaching and learning. The Board is responsible for course development and accreditation, course evaluation and assessment of student performance (including school completion and certification). The Office of Schools Review is responsible for the coordination and management of the accountability processes, particularly as they relate to the development and review of school charters.

At the school level, school councils have the authority to determine the educational policies of the school within the framework of the school charter, are responsible for maintaining the school plant and grounds, employ non-teaching staff and contract the services of teachers for particular projects. They are accountable to their local communities, to whom they report through their Annual Report, and to the DSE, through which independent auditors ensure that the financial dealings of the school conform to the appropriate guidelines.

As a further component in the accountability process, the Learning Assessment Project (LAP) was developed by the Board of Studies and first implemented in primary schools in 1995. Twice during the course of a student's time in primary school, his or her progress will be assessed against statewide standards in the 'key learning areas'. At the secondary level, all students involved in the final year of VCE studies are obliged to sit for a General Achievement Test (GAT) as a means of providing a check on the distribution of student grades for school-based Common Assessment Tasks within the certificate. Should the school's VCE performance fall within the tolerance range of that school's performance on the GAT, then the results for the VCE assessment will be confirmed. If not, the VCE results will be externally reviewed.

Curriculum

The Board of Studies developed a Curriculum and Standards Framework (CSF) for the eight key learning areas (Mathematics, Science, English, The Arts, LOTE, Technology, Studies of Society and Environment, and Health and Physical Education) which guide the development of curriculum from preparatory grade through year 10. The frameworks contain two components; curriculum content (in seven different levels to be attained over eleven years of study) across the various strands of activity within the key learning areas and the learning outcomes for students for each of those levels.

The Board of Studies is also responsible for the Victorian Certificate of Education, a two-year (years 11 and 12) completion certificate, which had been introduced some years earlier by the previous government. The VCE provides a wide variety of subjects for students to enable them to undertake studies for either university entrance and/or employment. It contains a series of common assessment tasks (CATs) to be completed by all students undertaking a particular subject to ensure common achievement measures across the system. Some CATs are assessed at the school and others through external examination, but a state-wide moderation system is used to ensure parity for all students' work.

The School Global Budget

The *Schools of the Future* has implemented a new basis for funding government schools in Australia, called the School Global Budget. This is a formula-based funding model which consists of a base element for all schools, together with an equity element based on the characteristics of the students enrolled. It provides funding for all school-based costs, including staff salaries and on-costs, operating expenses and school maintenance. The School Global Budget consists of two components: a core component, based on each school's student population; and an indexed component, based on the special learning characteristics of the students. This initially created some controversy, not only because of differences of opinion about what the basis of equity might be (for instance, what the indexed difference might be between a 'basic' grade 3 student, a grade 3 student who could not speak English and a grade 3 student with severe physical or intellectual disabilities), but also the difficulties that emerged in determining the base rates for a primary student and a secondary student. Some argued that more resources than previously allocated should flow to primary students to ensure that the basic curriculum was well covered and well learned. Others felt that secondary students should attract far more resources because of the level of support required for learning at higher levels.

The School Global Budget includes six components (DSE, 1994c):

1 Core funding, which would comprise at least 80 per cent of the total budget (with additional core funding for early childhood).
2 Additional funding for students with disabilities and impairments.
3 Additional funding for students at educational risk.
4 Additional funding for students from non-English speaking backgrounds (NESB).
5 Additional funding for rurality (depending on the size of the school and isolation) to guarantee staffing and a range of curricula in these schools.
6 Additional funding for priority programmes such as:
    Science and technology

Professional Development
Instrumental Music
Languages Other Than English (LOTE)
Physical and Sport Education
Arts in Australia.

In September 1995, when the calculations for the 1996 Schools Global Budget were outlined, a substantial amount ($52 million over two years) was allocated to the *Keys to Life* programme to ensure adequate literacy standards were obtained by all primary students. This translated into about $20 for each primary student each year. However, when it came to the more difficult concept of socio-economic disadvantage, a complex formula was required:

> The minister has accepted the recommendations of the Caldwell Committee that a new index be developed to allocate resources for students with special learning needs (referred to as 'students at educational risk' by the Caldwell Committee).
>
> For 1996 this index was based on the following student characteristics:

> - proportion of students receiving the Educational Maintenance Allowance (EMA);
> - proportion of students speaking a language other than English at home;
> - proportion of Koorie students;
> - proportion of transient students.

> To prevent targeted resources from being spread more thinly, an eligibility threshold will be established. On a statewide basis, this threshold will allow 30 per cent of students with combinations of the above characteristics to be eligible for this category of funding.
>
> (DSE, 1995: 7)

Schools would be ranked according to their proportions of each of these types of students and the amount of money allocated would be dependent upon the school's ranking and the total money to be allocated.

Three issues are raised by this process. First, the process of deciding how the money identified for 'students at risk' is allocated needs to be fair and open. The formula, developed by the Education Committee of the DSE, seems to be at the cutting edge of work related to the notion of resources following students, and is both fair and open. Second, there must be some way of ensuring that the money allocated to particular students gets to those students. Verbal advice indicates that, when schools are reviewing their charters after the first three years of operation, a requirement for receiving additional monies for some students will be that the school identifies in its charter how this money will be spent on improving the outcomes of the students for which it is intended. Third, no matter how fair the formula for allocation of funds might be, unless the total quantum of funds is sufficient, the disadvantage will continue. In fact, whole schools may be disadvantaged as they internally try to ensure an equality of learning outcomes for all of their students.

Using new technologies

Considerable finance has also been set aside to improve the technological capacity of the *Schools of the Future*, both in terms of administering the school and in terms of curriculum delivery. Since financial and personnel responsibilities have been devolved to schools, there was a necessity for each school to interface with the central computer in a meaningful way. This was accomplished by issuing all schools with an integrated and standardised computer hardware and software system (Computerised Administrative Systems Environment for Schools – CASES), and by using CD-ROM as means of publishing official documents.

In late 1994, the Interactive Satellite Television (ISTV) programme was established. Two thousand five hundred Victorian government and non-government schools with newly installed satellite dishes started to receive centrally produced programmes such as Science and Technology Education in Primary Schools (STEPS) and Primary Access to Languages by Satellite (PALS). Students could interact directly with the programmes' presenters using either fax or telephone. Professional development programmes for teachers and general access for other community groups were also made available through this new technology.

In late 1995, a new $20 million initiative, *Classrooms of the Future*, was announced. Aspects of this programme included all schools having access to the Internet, professional development in new technologies for teachers, the establishment of a DSE Internet address, a second channel on the ISTV, 400 schools involved in the *Global Classrooms* project and the identification of seven (later 14) 'navigator schools'. These schools were allocated additional resources to establish methods of using the new technologies. In secondary schools, these included upgraded computer laboratories and, for primary schools, laptop computers for teachers, sets of laptops for students, and better communication systems for teachers and parents. The government announced that it was their goal to have one computer for every four students by the end of the decade. Unfortunately, there was no indication of where the finance for more than tripling the current stock of school computers would be coming from.

In 1996 a new initiative, called *Digital Chalk*, was announced. It was hoped that people from education and the entertainment arena would work together to develop computer software that both educates and entertains, with the particular aim of keeping children who are potential dropouts in schools. These initiatives, together, represent a substantial commitment by the Victorian government to using new technologies as educational tools.

Professional development and support

All of these changes have involved considerable commitment by the DSE to professional development for principals, teachers and school councillors. All schools had a six-month induction programme to ensure they were ready for their new responsibilities. Professional development for principals included issues related to the global budget, leadership and management, administrative staff have undertaken programmes improving their understanding of the new computer system and the global budgeting process (including personnel management), teachers have been involved in programmes related to curriculum leadership in response to school charters, and school councillors have been given programmes to help them to understand the implementation of *Schools of the Future*, particularly with reference to the development of school charters.

The support structure for *Schools of the Future* was created through the development of 60 positions of District Liaison Principal (DLP), 58 of which were located in regions across the state while the other two positions were in the Change Management Branch of the Central Office. Each DLP works with a group of about 30 schools in a collegiate, rather than line-management, fashion. The role of the DLP includes acting as a change agent, providing advice and assistance to principals, assisting with professional development, and ensuring that schools have access to student services and curriculum support staff. In addition, a small number of support staff are located in each of two metropolitan and five country regions.

Ongoing support for principals, including leadership training, mentoring and coaching, with experienced principals supporting junior ones, and planning for a successor, have helped to establish the longer-term future of leadership in schools. The teacher Professional Recognition Programme (PRP) has also provided enhanced training opportunities for teachers. The aims of the programme (Peck, 1996: 6) are:

- to provide a working environment that encourages and rewards skilled and dedicated teachers
- to encourage the further development of an ethos that values excellence and high standards of achievement
- to provide formal feedback on a teacher's performance so that appropriate career development may occur through professional development and other means.

However, some concerns have been expressed by Teacher Unions that future salary increases for teachers have been conditional upon teachers joining the teacher recognition programme. The main basis of their concern is twofold. First, as the principal of the school determines which teachers, if any, are to receive promotion, nepotism may occur, and second, that any promotions must be paid for from within the global budget of the school and so there may be a tendency to hold back promotions to save the school money.

RESEARCH INTO *SCHOOLS OF THE FUTURE*

A further feature of the *Schools of the Future* programme has been the conduct of research that will enable data to be collected about the programme's progress. A number of studies have been directly supported by the DSE, including research into Early Literacy as part of the *Keys to Life* initiative, research assessing the impact of the *Schools of the Future* policy on school effectiveness, including outcomes for students, and research into the School Global Budget.

Perhaps most significant of the DSE-supported projects is a longitudinal study, 'Leading Victoria's Schools of the Future' (Thomas *et al.*, 1993, 1994, 1995, 1996). Commencing in 1993 and continuing until December 1997, it considers the purposes, processes and outcomes of Victoria's *Schools of the Future* programme, particularly as it affects the role of the principal in this development.

The study considered such things as the principals' perceptions of themselves, their work and the *Schools of the Future* programme; differences between female and male principals; characteristics of the schools in the study; reasons why particular schools applied to be a *Schools of the Future*; and perceptions of various problems and issues facing these schools in the future. Subsequent intakes have been asked the same questions, and the first group of principals has had the opportunity to reflect on the programme. Given the evidence of these reports we would have to say that, at this stage, principals remain concerned about many aspects of the *Schools of the Future* programme.

Despite the Committee's conclusion that 'principals are now becoming comfortable with the new framework for leadership and management for government schools in Victoria' (Thomas *et al.*, 1996: 57), a close analysis of the evidence does not really support this conclusion. For instance, of the 48 questions considering positive aspects of the programme (confidence that objectives and purposes will be attained; extent to which expected benefit has been realised in school; improvement in areas of school charter), in 43 of them the mean score in 1995 was lower than it was in the first survey in 1993, and there had been about a 10 per cent decline in the overall mean.

Conversely, of the thirty issues that considered the magnitude of the problems encountered thus far, in twenty-six of them the mean score in 1995 was higher than it was in the first survey in 1993 and the overall mean had increased by around 10 per cent. In the same period, the workload for principals had increased from a mean of 56.8 hours to 59 hours per week, with 60 per cent now working more than 60 hours per week (up from 48 per cent) and job satisfaction had decreased from a mean of 5.3 (on a scale of 1 to 7) to 4.6.

There was substantial concern about almost all issues relating to resources (including human resources). Issues such as time available (mean of 4.5 out of 5.0), principal workload (4.7), staff workload (4.4–4.6), expectations of further changes (4.0), staff morale (3.9), available resources (3.7), staff numbers (4.3), budget cuts (4.4) and equitable distribution (3.8) are all identified as being of substantial concern. The committee identifies this as being an 'arguably unrealistic expectation that there would be more resources' (Thomas *et al.*, 1996: 8).

Also, an ongoing study of more than 400 parents, teachers and school councillors (Townsend, 1995) showed that there were concerns about some aspects of the programme for parents, school councillors and school staff. Although more than 65 per cent of parents and school councillors felt that the *Schools of the Future* would provide schools with the opportunity to provide students with a broader education, only 31 per cent of teachers agreed. In addition, 50 per cent of parents, 47 per cent of school councillors, and only 20 per cent of teachers felt that the *Schools of the Future* programme would lead to an overall increase in the quality of education. Finally, 44 per cent of parents, 47 per cent of school councillors, and only 24 per cent of teachers felt that the *Schools of the Future* would promote achievement for students from different backgrounds.

The results of these two studies must be disturbing to the promoters of the self-managing school concept and indicate a need for government, the system and schools to work together to overcome the concerns of the stakeholders in education. Despite the rhetoric that argues that resources can diminish without affecting quality, there is a concern that the resource reduction has fallen below the critical level at which quality can be sustained.

EVALUATION OF THE PROJECT

The *Schools of the Future* programme is really a new step for Australian education. Not only has the government determined that all Victorian government schools will become self-managing, but the structures of education are changing so rapidly that teachers and parents have barely assimilated one change when another is put forward. In many ways, the changes seem to create a series of paradoxes for education that must be resolved over the next few years.

Some argue that there is greater devolution of some powers to schools, on the one hand, but more regulations and controls, on the other. It seems almost as if the functional activities of schools and the administrative centre have been reversed. In the past, the centre has been the overseer of school staffing and finance, while the schools, through school councils, were responsible for their own educational policy and teachers were heavily involved, with the assistance of curriculum frameworks, in the development, implementation and assessment of curriculum. Now schools are responsible for funding, through the global budget, and staffing, but the government has been heavily interventionist in the development of policy and the Board of Studies has taken responsibility for curriculum and assessment.

Caldwell identifies the rationale for much of the decentralisation in Australia by arguing:

> Forces which have shaped current and emerging patterns of school management include a concern for efficiency in the management of public education, effects of the recession and financial crisis, complexity in the provision of education, empowerment of teachers and parents, the need for flexibility and responsiveness, the search for school effectiveness and school improvement, interest in choice and market forces in schooling, the politics of education, the establishment of new frameworks for industrial relations and the emergence of a national imperative.
>
> (Caldwell, 1993: xiii)

On the other hand, some see it as simply a means to cutting costs. Smyth, in his response to the *Schools of the Future*, argues:

> One of the noticeable (indeed, even remarkable, or is it?) features of the move towards the self-managing school phenomenon around the world, is its occurrence in contexts of unprecedented education budget cut-backs. Whenever there is a break out of self-managing schools, the notion is used as a weapon by which to achieve the alleged 'efficiencies' and 'down-sizing' of education.
>
> (Smyth, 1993: 8)

Others have expressed concerns that the funding cutbacks are actually preventing schools from taking charge.

Such commentators have argued that the resultant decision making left to the schools is to determine where the cuts will come from. With the arrival of compulsory testing of certain academic areas at certain grade levels through the LAP, with the compulsory introduction of the curriculum areas of Languages Other Than English (LOTE), sport and physical education, and with government support and financing of programmes in technology and multimedia, the concern is that some areas of the curriculum will be cut back, or even dropped altogether, as schools respond to these new imperatives. It could be argued that the Victorian government has provided school communities with greater powers of choice, but also considerably less alternatives from which to choose.

A third concern relates to the market approach that has been adopted.

Marginson (1994: 22) argued that, through the *Schools of the Future*, the government wishes to reconstruct three basic relationships. The first is the relationship between a school and its community where parents are considered consumers of education rather than partners in the process. The second is the relationship between schools and the government where management is devolved to the school but policy control is centralised. The third is the relationship between one school and other schools. Rather than all schools being encouraged to do well (with schools supporting each other in the process), schools are now competitors for students. The more one school succeeds the more likely schools in the same area will lose students to it. This may mean that the attempt to raise quality across the system through a market approach may well result in an increase in inequalities across the system, as some schools move consistently in an upward trend, leaving those with less marketability, less students and, consequently, fewer resources, far behind.

With the *Schools of the Future* programme, schools are now encouraged to promote their capabilities in the hope of attracting students and to seek sponsorship from community businesses to support them in their development. This is a far cry from just a few years ago when the vast majority of students went to the school closest to them and about 96 per cent of the total budget of the school was supplied by the government, with parent and community fund raising being the only external source of funds.

Recent research on school finances (Townsend, 1996) indicates that, in addition to the Schools Global Budget supplied by the Government, locally raised funds have become a significant contribution to the running of schools. A sample of Victorian schools from both urban and rural settings, and from both primary and secondary schools, shows the potential discrepancies that can occur between communities. In the sample of 25 schools, the amount of locally raised funds ranges from $122 to $665 per pupil per year, with an average of $302 per pupil. In terms of the government allocation, schools of similar size, locality and student background would receive roughly the same allocation from the global budget assessment, yet over the course of a student's six year career, some schools would have up to $3000 in additional resources per pupil than others.

Further concerns need to be addressed. The first relates to the speed and extent of change. The ink barely dries on one innovation when the next one comes along. As well as the savage personnel and support cuts that staff of schools had to face, they also have had to be involved in the development of school charters and codes of conduct, to assimilate new curriculum frameworks and standards, the learning assessment programme, new forms of teacher selection and new funding arrangements, and to undertake staff development for new responsibilities for a whole range of school-based activities that have arrived with the implementation of *Schools of the Future*. In addition, they have increased commitments to children in the classroom as student–teacher ratios have worsened and new curriculum areas have been added. Staff in schools have almost reached the end of their willingness to adapt.

The previous system of decision making saw education as a partnership between the staff and the parents. Much of this seems to have been undermined in favour of more power to the principal. Townsend (1994) found, in both Australia and the USA, that there was unanimous agreement from members of school communities that the most critical factor for the development of more effective schools was 'dedicated and qualified staff'. It is hoped that this critical group of people do not become so isolated from the process of decision making that many of the positive steps taken in the past two decades are undone.

CONCLUDING REMARKS

Despite all of the concerns that have been expressed, the move towards self-managing schools, through *Schools of the Future*, may provide us with the direction we need into the future. Given the right conditions and support, some exciting possibilities emerge from the self-managing perspective that *Schools of the Future* brings. Some schools will specialise in particular curriculum areas, to provide additional work in the arts, music or the sciences. Some may be schools that cater to particular student needs or ethnic backgrounds, with additional programmes designed to encourage particular outcomes. Some might opt to be year-round schools, with no additional work for any one person but a twenty-five per cent increase in productivity, and with increased leadership potential as well. Others might extend the school day or school year to enable children access to many of the new subjects that cannot be squeezed in at the moment, and still others might develop inter-generational activities, where parents and grandparents utilise the schools for their own purposes, but in doing so demonstrate to the children that education is a life-long process.

All schools will need to start utilising the facilities that every community has to offer as a means of enriching school programmes. Some might encourage the development of health and social welfare services within the school building, and in return children can be protected and kept healthy. Others might look at adult retraining programmes. These possibilities would take further thought in both the concept of school and the design of school buildings. Schools in the future have the opportunity to become fully functional community facilities, providing a variety of services on a year-round basis, thus developing a wider range of community support than many schools currently enjoy.

The *Schools of the Future* programme is in its infancy. There are a number of areas that have caused concern, but there are a number of others that bring hope. Perhaps the most critical issue in the near future relates to the responsibility of school leaders, from Ministers and bureaucrats to principals of schools, to support the efforts of teachers and local communities in their attempts at development, and to demonstrate clearly that the short-term concerns are far outweighed by the long-term opportunities.

REFERENCES

Arnott, M., Bullock, A. and Thomas, H. (1992) 'Consequences of Local Management: An assessment by Head Teachers', paper presented to the ERA Research Network, 12 February.

Bridges, S. (1992) *Working in Tomorrow's Schools: Effects on Primary Teachers*, Canterbury, NZ: University of Canterbury.

Brown, D. J. (1990) *Decentralisation and School-Based Management*, London and New York: Falmer Press.

Caldwell, B. (1993) *Decentralising the Management of Australia's Schools*, Melbourne: National Industry Education Foundation.

Campbell, J. and Neill, S. (1994) *Curriculum at Key Stage 1: Teacher commitment and policy failure*, London: Longman.

Collins, R. A. and Hanson, M. K. (1991) *Summative Evaluation Report: School-Based Management/Shared Decision-Making Project 1987–88 through 1989–90*, Miami: Dade County Public Schools.

Directorate of School Education (1994a) *School Charters Information Package for Consultation and Promotion*, Melbourne: Directorate of School Education.

—— (1994b) *Guidelines for Developing a School Charter*, (draft), Melbourne: Directorate of School Education.

—— (1994c) *The School Global Budget in Victoria*, Melbourne: Directorate of School Education.

—— (1995) 'School Global Budget Improvements', *Victorian School News*, 3(30), 7–8.

Drucker, P. (1993) *Post-Capitalist Society*, New York: Harper Business.

Elmore, R. F. (1988) 'Choice in public education', in W. L. Boyd and C. T. Kerchner (eds), *The politics of excellence and choice in education*, New York: Falmer Press.

Halpin, D., Power, S. and Fitz, J. (1993) 'Opting out of state control? Headteachers and the paradoxes of grant-maintained status', *International Studies in the Sociology of Education*, 3(1), 3–23.

Karmel, P. (1973) *Schools in Australia: Report of the Interim Committee for the Australian Schools Commission*, Canberra: Australian Government Publishing Service.

Livingstone, I. (1994) *The workloads of primary school teachers – A Wellington region survey*, Wellington: Chartwell Consultants.

Marginson, S. (1994) 'Increased competition will mean more inequality', *The Age*, 19 July, p. 22.

Peck, F. (1996) 'Educational Reform: Local Management of Schools', paper presented at the International Congress for School Effectiveness and Improvement, Minsk, Belarus, January.

Rafferty, F. (1994a) 'Alarm at growth of 60-hour week', *Times Educational Supplement*, 5 August, p. 1.

—— (1994b) 'Many more heads leave jobs', *Times Educational Supplement*, 2 September, p. 9.

Scheerens, J. (1992) *Effective Schooling: Research, theory and practice*, London, Cassell.

Sinclair, J., Ironside, M. and Seiffert, R. (1993) 'Classroom struggle? Market oriented education reforms and their impact on teachers' professional autonomy, labour intensification and resistance', paper presented at a conference on Education, Democracy and Reform, University of Auckland, 13–14 August.

Smyth, J. (1993) 'Schools of the Future and the Politics of Blame', public lecture sponsored by the Public Sector Management Institute, Melbourne, Monash University, 2 July.

Thomas, F. (Chair) *et al.* (1993) *Base-Line Survey of Principals in 1993* (Co-operative Research Project), Melbourne: Directorate of School Education.

—— (1994) *One Year Later: Leading Victoria's Schools of the Future* (Co-operative Research Project), Melbourne: Directorate of School Education.

—— (1995) *Taking Stock: Leading Victoria's Schools of the Future* (Co-operative Research Project), Melbourne: Directorate of School Education.

—— (1996) *A Three Year Report Card: Co-operative Research Project: Leading Victoria's Schools of the Future*, Melbourne: Directorate of School Education.

Townsend, T. (1994) *Effective Schooling for the Community*, London and New York: Routledge.

—— (1995) 'Community perceptions of the Schools of the Future', ongoing research project funded by the Research Committee of the Faculty of Education, Monash University.

—— (1996) 'Schools of the Future are gaining acceptance, but still have some way to go', unpublished report, Frankston, Victoria: South Pacific Centre for School and Community Development, Monash University.

Whitty, G. (1994) 'Devolution in Education Systems: Implications for Teacher Professionalism and Pupil Performance', discussion paper, Melbourne: National Industry Education Foundation.

Wylie, C. (1994) *Self managing schools in New Zealand: The fifth year*, Auckland: New Zealand Council for Educational Research.

Afterword
Problems and possibilities for tomorrow's schools

Tony Townsend

A recurrent theme for the justification of restructuring has been its perceived ability to deliver a range of qualitative improvements to education. Townsend (1996a: 3) argued that the decentralisation exercise should provide:

- an improvement in the effectiveness of decisions related to education policy at both the school and system levels
- improved school management and educational leadership
- provision of a more efficient use of resources
- improved quality of teaching
- the development of a curriculum more appropriate to future workforce and social demands; and (perhaps as the focus of all of those above)
- generating improved student outcomes.

It is appropriate that we make our judgements on the success, or otherwise, of school restructuring on these and perhaps other issues as well. We need to ask ourselves, what evidence has been provided to demonstrate the link between school restructuring and improved outcomes? As this book testifies, some schools have taken the restructuring exercise as a means for reviewing and improving their provision of education to children and local communities. But is it likely that restructuring will benefit all students at all schools? At this stage of its development, we might have to argue that the reality of school restructuring has not matched the rhetoric of those that have promoted it. There are still some problems with the implementation that need to be addressed if the promises and possibilities are to be fulfilled in the future.

THE PROBLEMS

The current restructuring movement needs to be understood as a component of large-scale change: to the economy, to social systems and to people themselves. Education and training are seen to play a vital role in the development of nations, and the linkage between education and employment is perhaps stronger than it has ever been before. Although there has been universal agreement on the need for improvement in student outcomes, there is far less agreement on how this might be achieved.

Has restructuring delivered on the promise of local control?

One of the features of the restructuring activity has been the way in which schools have been given certain decision making powers but have had others withheld. In Chapter 1, McGaw argued that there is some evidence to suggest that, while there is a clear trend towards decentralisation in many centralised national or state systems, there is the need for a clear rationale to be developed to clarify the reasons for that decentralisation and to identify what is to be decentralised. In Britain, it has been argued, 'governments have actually increased their claims to knowledge and authority over the education system whilst promoting a theoretical and superficial movement towards consumer authority' (Harris, 1993).

McGaw (1994) argues, as do Hargreaves and Hopkins (1991), that care needs to be taken that the 'devolution of responsibility' does not simply become a 'displacement of blame', particularly where transfer of responsibility is accompanied by a decreasing resource base. In the USA, school-based management 'has emerged at a moment of public sector retrenchment, not expansion. School-based resources and decision making have been narrowed, not expanded. School-based councils feel "empowered only to determine who or what will be cut"' (Fine, 1993: 696).

We have seen in this book that there are individual schools and whole-school systems that have embarked upon improvement efforts, all in different ways. In almost all cases, the critical decisions have been made at the school level. Yet there has been a reluctance on the part of governments to allow people at the local level to make all the decisions. There is still a concern that some people might make poor decisions. Chubb and Moe (1992) consider decentralisation through school-based management to be a potential barrier to true improvement. They argue that, of the three major forms of restructuring, decentralisation, accountability and choice, choice alone is the key to improvement. In the current wave of reform, accountability is controlled by those outside of the school, and:

> Local management of schools is a good idea, as far as it goes, because it seeks to enhance local autonomy, but it does this by keeping the traditional top-down system intact and decentralizing certain budgetary and decision making authority to the school level. Bureaucracy remains a problem – there are plenty of rules, for instance, that limit school autonomy and specify exactly how and when it is to be exercised. More important, the hierarchy of authority remains, full of politicians and administrators eager to expand their dominion over the schools. . . . In

this kind of system, the schools are only safe from political attack and control when they do not use their autonomy to strike out on their own.

(Chubb and Moe, 1992: 11–12)

They argue that, with true choice, schools 'run their own affairs as they see fit. . . . When choice is taken seriously [school-self management] is beside the point' (Chubb and Moe, 1992: 12). Not everybody is prepared to accept this level of self-determination but, so far, it doesn't seem that an appropriate balance has been reached.

Has restructuring improved educational leadership?

Perhaps the linch-pin for much of the restructuring effort is the principal, but devolution has not always been an easy road for principals to follow, or even to accept. Both Fullan (1991) and Chapman (1988) have identified that the role of leadership within the school became a more complex and difficult task in the 1980s as a myriad of changes beset the education enterprise. The current wave of restructuring, with the principal as the key operator, might be seen by some principals as a return to a simpler way of managing. However, the massively increased responsibilities taken on at the school level have raised the question of whether or not it is possible for principals to do it all themselves.

Sinclair *et al.* (1993) report that:

headteachers are no longer partners in the process of educating pupils – they become allocators of resources within the school, managers who are driven to ensure that the activities of employees are appropriate to the needs of the business, and givers of rewards to those whose contribution to the business is most highly regarded.

Halpin *et al.* (1993) suggest that the process of running a self-managing school, with the need to balance both curriculum and resources, can result in an increase in the distance between the teachers and the headteacher. This would suggest that the multitude of new responsibilities, and the competing perceptions of the priorities that may be held by teachers and principals, may have diminished the leadership value in schools where the principal is not a natural leader. It may also suggest that the ability of the principal to be an educational leader may rely on his or her ability to address the issue of diminishing resources quickly and successfully.

Are resources better allocated to, and in, schools?

Some educators had argued that, to improve the outcomes of students, more money was required by the school system. Again, in Chapter 1, McGaw argues that many of the recent restructuring activities, accompanied by simultaneous cutbacks in education, indicate a lack of faith in the impact of resources which resulted from the substantially increased dollars per student allocated to schools in the 1970s and 1980s, without any systematic research to indicate the benefits of those increased resources. Hanushek (1981, 1986, 1989, 1991) argued that there was little consistent relationship between educational expenditure and pupil achievement (Hanushek, 1986: 1161), which has been used by many governments to argue the case that they could increase the quality of student outcomes and decrease the expenditure on education simultaneously. A recent re-analysis of Hanushek's data (Hedges *et al.*, 1994) has suggested, however, that the conclusions drawn by Hanushek are not as watertight as was first thought.

There is also evidence to suggest that the level of expenditure on education has an effect on the numbers of students that remain in the system, and on their aspirations for the future. The Association of Californian School Administrators (1996) argues that there 'is a direct cause and effect relationship between student achievement and the amount of money states spend per pupil.' In lower spending states, few pupils see further education beyond school as an option, whereas higher spending states encourage more students to undertake the Scholastic Aptitude Test (SAT), which determines who will go on to college. In the USA in 1995, for each of the seven states with the lowest per pupil expenditure on education, less than 10 per cent of high school senior students undertook the SAT, whereas for the seven highest spending states the percentage of high school senior students that sat the SAT ranged from 47 per cent to 81 per cent.

It is likely that the difference in the percentages of students that remain in schools will have greater impact on students from poorer communities than it will for students from more well-off families. This raises the issue of whether education has a social justice component or not, and whether the restructuring activity can truly address it. The resultant arguments about resources following students through various forms of voucher systems and the need for parents to have open choice about the school their child will attend are more widely debated now than at any time since they were first discussed in the 1970s.

Recent research into vouchers and school choice, presented by Terry Moe from Stanford University and Richard Elmore from Harvard at the 1996 American Education Research Association conference in New York, has done nothing to resolve the debate. The Stanford study, which focused on vouchers, found that 'parents who use vouchers are highly satisfied with the schools they have chosen and believe the shift from public to private has been beneficial' (Henry, 1996: 1), but the Harvard study found that 'parents participating in choice programs in Detroit, Milwaukee, St Louis, San Antonio and Montgomery County Md, are better educated, have higher achieving children and are more involved in their youngsters' schooling than parents whose children remain behind in neighbourhood schools'. Of course, there is no inherent contradiction in these two findings, but there is the possibility that choice and vouchers may help to increase the gap between the students of those parents able to make appropriate choices (and have them funded) and those students whose parents, because of their own previous educational disadvantage, make the wrong choice, or who fail to choose at all.

Some educators are now arguing that it is not only financial resources that create the internal effectiveness in a school, but the sum total of resources, which includes time and commitment by the various groups within the school, that help to overcome any lack of financial support. However, Chapman posed two questions that must be considered as critical at the system level. 'How is it possible to evaluate schools when they have uneven resources? What is the acceptable level of unevenness in a public system of education?' (Chapman, 1991: 31).

Has restructuring improved the quality of teaching?

There is evidence to suggest that the increased responsibilities of teachers outside the classroom may militate *against* some of the characteristics of schools that we want to improve. Whitty reports: 'it may be significant that the relatively few classroom teachers who were interviewed by the Birmingham research team were far more cautious than their headteachers about the benefits of self-management for pupil learning and overall standards' (Whitty, 1994: 7).

It has been found, in almost all studies thus far conducted in the United Kingdom (Campbell and Neill, 1994; Rafferty, 1994a), New Zealand (Bridges, 1992; Livingstone, 1994; Wylie, 1994) and Australia (Thomas *et al.*, 1994, 1995, 1996), that the implementation of the self-managing concept has increased the workloads of both principals and teachers alike. Townsend (1996b) found that it was universally accepted by parents, school councillors and teachers that the workloads of the principal, school councillors, teachers and administration had increased since the Victorian self-managing school programme commenced. Such studies have been accompanied by reports of some deleterious effects, such as 'no overall improvement in standards but teachers have been driven to burnout' and the evidence of 'a steep rise in the numbers of heads and deputies retiring' (Rafferty, 1994b).

Teachers and principals suffering from the negative impacts of increased workloads and stress are less likely to be able to deliver those facets of school operations that bring about improved student outcomes. Whitty concludes that 'in the particular circumstances of contemporary Britain some of the positive educational benefits claimed . . . have yet to be forthcoming and that, far from breaking the links between educational and social inequality, they seem to intensify them' (Whitty, 1994: 13). It could be argued, for instance, that the increased workload on classroom teachers, in the areas of school decision making, charter development and external accountability, may take away some of the emphasis on things such as 'structured teaching' and 'effective learning time' which have been shown by Scheerens (1992) to be the school-level factors most closely linked to student outcomes.

Has restructuring improved the curriculum and student learning?

It is clear that one of the promises of school restructuring is the opportunity for people to work cooperatively towards the achievement of jointly developed school goals. This may involve both school-wide and individual professional development programmes to develop skills of teaching and curriculum development, and some form of teacher appraisal and subsequent recognition of people who have achieved certain levels of capability.

Yet the diminishing resources, and the need to market the school, may have lessened, rather than increased, the breadth of the curriculum. Townsend (1996c), in a study of the school charters from 154 Victorian schools, found that the goals and priorities of schools are becoming narrowly focused, despite the introduction of eight key learning areas that spanned the curriculum. Over 40 per cent of schools indicated Languages Other Than English (LOTE) as one of their priorities, with a further 21 per cent having mathematics/language as a priority, 15 per cent having science/technology/computing as a priority, and 8 per cent having sport or physical education as a priority. In comparison, social education was identified as a priority by only one school, and music not at all. It could be argued that these results were possibly influenced, not by the community's wish to focus upon them, but by the schools' response to government priorities. Each of the programmes mentioned had been identified as important by the government in some way, either by compulsory implementation (LOTE and physical education), by special funding (technology and computing) or as the focus of standardised testing (language, mathematics and science).

Few, if any, schools directly addressed issues that might have reflected the social conditions of their particular community, although three schools referred to improving parent involvement. Although up to 30 per cent of children in some schools were living in single parent families, up to 70 per cent in others came from multicultural or aboriginal backgrounds, and with others that had substantial numbers receiving an Educational Maintenance Allowance, being transient or having parents with no, or poorly paid, employment, not one school of the 154 surveyed had a priority to address the needs of students from any of these backgrounds.

From this it might be concluded that only when schools are given complete control over curriculum decisions and adequate resources to fund both government and community priorities will school-based management lead to a curriculum that reflects the local community as well as the society at large. Whitty (1994: 6) suggests that the local management changes in the United Kingdom have not altered children's learning in the positive way that might have been expected, with 34 per cent of head teachers in a study conducted by Arnott *et al.* (1992) thinking there had been an improvement, 31 per cent thinking there had been a regression and 35 per cent being unsure. In their on-going work on the impact of self-management on schools in England and Wales, Arnott *et al.* concede that, although the study is broadly positive, 'direct evidence of the influence of self-management on learning is elusive' (quoted in Whitty, 1994: 5). Bullock and Thomas (1994) found that just over one-third of headteachers agreed with the statement that 'as a result of LM [Local Management], more meetings are taken up with administrative issues which lessen our attention on pupil's learning'. In the USA, Elmore argued:

> [T]here is little or no evidence that [site-based management] has any direct or predictable relationship to changes in instruction and students' learning. In fact, the evidence suggests that the implementation of site-based management reforms has a more or less random relationship to changes in curriculum, teaching, and students' learning.
>
> (Elmore, 1993: 40)

In New Zealand, less than half the principals and teachers felt that the quality of children's learning had improved since the shift to school-based management (Wylie, 1994). As identified in Chapter 11, Townsend (1996c) showed that parents, school councillors and school staff were unsure of the value of the self-managing school in relation to student learning.

Bullock and Thomas (1994: 137), in their review of the Locally Managed School in Britain, concluded that although the proportion of headteachers making a positive assessment concerning improvements in pupil learning has increased somewhat over the three years, significantly this assessment has come mainly from those schools which have experienced an increase in funding as a result of self-management. 'Put simply, LM may have brought benefits to learning in schools where the financial situation is healthy. [But a] reduced budget could result in unwelcome consequences for children.' Bullock and Thomas refer to the concern expressed by some headteachers 'about an apparent shift in emphasis away from matters explicitly "educational" towards a situation where decisions are based more on financial considerations' (Bullock and Thomas, 1994: 143).

Conclusions

Some observers have considered that the decentralisation activity has been used as a means to improve student outcomes (an issue of quality), while others have considered that it has been used as a way of winding back the money spent on education (an issue of finance). The fact that the implementation of self-managing schools in a number of different countries has been accompanied by a slashing of the educational budget in each instance has done little to clarify this issue.

Tickell is wary of future developments within the current push to decentralisation. He argues: 'the maintenance of a line relationship between the principal and the central authority and the capacity of the authority to intervene in school operations may well provoke the allegation that governments are less concerned with genuine devolution than with strategic centralisation' (Tickell, 1995: 7). He suggests that decentralisation within the current context of a market-driven provision of education is starting to blur the distinctions between government and non-government schools, which may lead to the possibility that some schools within the 'public' system 'could decide to appeal to affluent (and discourage less affluent) parents by offering a narrowly academic curriculum and maintaining an authoritarian approach to student management. It might also decide to charge substantial fees which would serve as a further disincentive to low income families' (Tickell, 1995: 11). The possibility here is that 'good' schools might get better and 'poor' schools might suffer from progressively less access to resources and the support required to improve their profile.

This concern for the social justice aspect of education is also present when Peter Mortimore (1996: 18) makes these cautionary remarks:

> Some of the lessons [from school effectiveness and improvement research], however, are less obvious and turn on the overall educational goals of societies and on whether policy makers wish to give priority to the education of a small elite or to the majority, which will include the disadvantaged. If the priority is to sustain an elite, then it needs to be recognised that only in exceptional cases will disadvantaged students – sponsored by particularly effective schools – win through. . . . However, if the aim is to improve the lot of the majority and to lift *overall* standards in that quantum leap, then ways need to be sought in which highly effective compensating mechanisms can be created . . .
>
> A policy of lifting overall standards, however, means ensuring that educational spending is fairly distributed and, in some cases, directed towards those schools which serve the most disadvantaged students instead of the seemingly inevitable situation whereby the most resources tend to end up at the call of the most advantaged.

The evidence is not yet conclusive enough to suggest that any of these promises have been fulfilled. For every claim there is a counterclaim. One of the difficulties that must be faced is that restructuring, in itself, does not imply improvements in any of the areas referred to above. The best that one can hope for is that it may be one of the criteria that will improve education, but without skilled staff, committed parents and dedicated school leaders, coupled with appropriate levels of resources and training, there is no guarantee that the restructuring activity will bring about the qualitative improvements claimed.

The international move towards restructured systems of education has been, to a certain extent, a leap of faith on the part of the various governments involved. But there are good reasons why there is not the research evidence we require. In the first instance, school-based management, as the logical endpoint of restructuring, is a relatively new phenomenon. It is less than a decade old. Consequently, it would be difficult to find any substantial longitudinal evidence one way or the other. There has not yet been a single group of students which has progressed through the restructured school process of education from start to finish.

Also, a review of the literature clearly establishes that educational improvement relies upon the complex interaction of a number of factors and, as such, there is great difficulty in establishing a clear cause-and-effect relationship between the act of restructuring education and improved outcomes of any sort. Many other factors, including staff development, methods of resourcing, the actual decisions made and leadership style, all of which can exist in both a centralised system and a devolved one, and which can be implemented in different ways in either system, will impact on the final outcomes.

THE POSSIBILITIES

It can be argued that the lack of evidence of improvement in student outcomes does not, in itself, demonstrate the failure of school restructuring. In fact, the general acceptance of this form of management internationally indicates high hopes for future developments which may increase the possibility of improved student outcomes over time, by increasing local involvement, teacher status and professionalism and giving the school more control over its decisions and resources.

It could also be argued that there are many other features of school operations apart from student outcomes that can be improved by the move towards a more decentralised system. If these factors are improved and the effect on student outcomes is not negative, then the case for the value of restructuring can still be made. Further, a case can be made that, if student outcomes remain the same, but at considerably less cost to the public, then the move has been worthwhile. Productivity will have increased and this may be seen by many as a plus.

However, it must be clearly established that the restructuring process has not diminished student outcomes before we can make this claim. There is an absence of data in this area as well. What the research has found is that change brought about by restructuring schools cannot bring about improvement easily, nor can it occur without some initial confusion, doubt or conflict. Griswold *et al.* (1986), in their study of 116 effective school projects across the United States, concluded that the improvement process showed that initial stages of change involved anxiety and confusion, and on-going technical and psychological support were important to cope with change-induced anxiety. It could be argued that, in circumstances such as these, at least initially, the decision making process would be less, rather than more, effective. Perhaps it may be the case that we are currently experiencing the anxieties that accompany change at an early stage.

We need to ask ourselves what structures and systems are available to schools that get left behind, to those that might fall below what Reynolds calls 'basic organisational adequacy'. Who does the school in trouble turn to in a decentralised system when there are few or no support structures provided by the education system?

> Superimposing on schools a range of responsibilities such as managing teacher appraisal, starting school development planning and running ambitious improvement programmes is likely to result in the raising of the educational ceiling by competent persons in competent schools, but is also likely to result in the floor of incompetence being left increasingly far behind.
>
> (Reynolds, 1994: 17)

A number of issues emerge that need to be considered carefully, by education systems, by governments and by researchers. The first may be to establish a list of student outcomes, both academic and non-academic, that we might reasonably expect schools to achieve within a devolved system of education. The second is to promote international research that seeks to isolate the effects of restructuring from other factors which may impinge on student outcomes, such as class sizes, management styles, levels and types of school funding (fees, sponsorship, etc.) and how that funding is allocated (teacher salaries, professional development, curriculum, accountability), and to establish the correlations of these factors with student outcomes.

But perhaps the most important challenge is to change the nature of the educational debate. It is important that the basis of any changes to education must always be focused upon the on-going need for continuous improvement in the quality of education for students, rather than 'fixing' a failing system. Much of the debate on restructuring education has focused on the failure of schools fully to achieve what they set out to do. We can ask the same question of any system, of any business, of any individual. Is there anyone who has ever achieved everything they set out to do? If there is, then we could argue that such people or groups have set their goals too low.

This book has not made the assumption that there is anything 'wrong' with schools now, but has focused on schools, school systems and research that have attempted further to improve what schools have to do. As I have argued elsewhere:

Just as we expect an improvement over time in all other aspects of human endeavour, from developments in technology, to consistent economic growth, to world sporting records, we are right to expect that education is on a consistent upwards curve as well. When a new athletics or swimming world record is achieved, we acclaim the new holder, but it doesn't make the efforts of the previous holder any less meritorious.

(Townsend, 1996a: 50)

People currently involved in restructuring efforts could be considered as analogous to the surfer catching a wave breaking on the shore. They might remember the time when the sea was smooth, but now are faced with all sorts of upheavals that a breaking wave brings. Some will catch the wave and pick up speed towards the future, others will be dumped, and yet others will miss the wave altogether and be relegated to the thoughts of the past. However, the new generation of teachers, parents and students may be much more accepting of this new way of doing things, because they know of no different way of administering schools. Perhaps in five years or so, the sea will seem to be smooth again.

Of course, that suggests that the changes experienced in the past twenty years or so will cease, or at least abate for a few years. However, we have to consider the possibility that the next major revolution in schools might be the one that is just starting to move from the edge to the centre of educational thought, namely the large-scale transfer into computer-assisted learning. It may be that education will never have smooth seas again.

REFERENCES

Arnott, M., Bullock, A. and Thomas, H. (1992) 'Consequences of Local Management: An assessment by Head Teachers', paper presented to the ERA Research Network, 12 February.

Association of Californian School Administrators (1996) *Debunking Myths About Public Schools*, Sacramento, CA: ASCA.

Bridges, S. (1992) *Working in Tomorrow's Schools: Effects on Primary Teachers*, Canterbury, NZ: University of Canterbury.

Bullock, A. and Thomas, H. (1994) *The impact of local management of schools: Final report*, Birmingham: University of Birmingham.

Campbell, J. and Neill, S. (1994) *Curriculum at Key Stage 1: Teacher commitment and policy failure*, London: Longman.

Chapman, J. D. (1988) 'A New Conception of the Principalship: Decentralisation, Devolution and the Administration of Schools', in J. Hattie, R. Kefford and P. Porter (eds), *Skills, Technology and Management in Education*, East Geelong: Australian College of Education.

—— (1991) 'The Effectiveness of Schooling and of Educational Resource Management', paper presented to the OECD, Paris.

Chubb, J. E. and Moe, T. M. (1992) *A Lesson in School Reform from Great Britain*, Washington, DC: The Brookings Institution.

Elmore, R. F. (1993) 'Why restructuring won't improve teaching', *Educational Leadership*, 49(7), 44–8.

Fine, M. (1993) 'A diary on privatization and on public possibilities', *Educational Theory*, 43(1), 33–9.

Fullan, M. G. (1991) *The new meaning of educational change*, London: Cassell.

Griswold, P., Cotton, K. and Hansen, J. (1986) *Effective Compensatory Education Source Book. Vol. 1: A Review of Effective Educational Practices*, Portland, OR: Northwest Regional Education Laboratory.

Halpin, D., Power, S. and Fitz, J. (1993) 'Opting out of state control? Headteachers and the paradoxes of grant-maintained status', *International Studies in the Sociology of Education*, 3(1), 3–23.

Hanushek, E. (1981) 'Throwing money at schools', *Journal of Policy Analysis and Management*, 1, 19–41.

—— (1986) 'The Economics of Schooling: Production and Efficiency in Public Schools', *Journal of Economic Literature*, 24, 1141–77.

—— (1989) 'The impact of differential expenditures on school performance', *Educational Researcher*, 18(4), 45–65.

—— (1991) 'When school finance "reform" may not be a good policy', *Harvard Journal on Legislation*, 28, 423–56.

Hargreaves, D. and Hopkins, D. (1991) *The Empowered School*, London: Cassell.

Harris, K. (1993) 'Power to the people? Local management of schools', *Education Links*, 45, 4–8.

Hedges, L. V., Laine, R. D. and Greenwald, R. (1994) 'Does money matter? A meta-analysis of studies of the effects of differential school inputs on student outcomes', *Educational Researcher*, April, 5–14.

Henry, T. (1996) 'Are school tax vouchers worthwhile?', *USA Today*, 11 April, p. 1.

Livingstone, I. (1994) *The workloads of primary school teachers – A Wellington region survey*, Wellington: Chartwell Consultants.

McGaw, B. (1994) 'Quality, Equality and the Outcomes of Schooling: Key Issues', keynote presentation at the 7th Annual Conference of the International Congress for School Effectiveness and Improvement, Melbourne, January.

Mortimore, P. (1996) 'High performing schools and school improvement', paper presented at the 'Schools of the Third Millennium' conference, Melbourne, February.

Mortimore, P., Sammons, P., Stoll, L., Lewis, D. and Ecob, R. (1986) *The junior school project: Main report*, London: Research and Statistics Branch, Inner London Education Authority.

—— (1988) *School Matters*, Somerset: Open Books.

Rafferty, F. (1994a) 'Alarm at growth of 60-hour week', *Times Educational Supplement*, 5 August, p. 1.

—— (1994b) 'Many more heads leave jobs', *Times Educational Supplement*, 2 September, p. 9.

Reynolds, D. (1994) 'The Effective School', revised version of an Inaugural Lecture, University of Newcastle upon Tyne, October.

Scheerens, J. (1992) *Effective Schooling: Research, theory and practice*, London: Cassell.

Sinclair, J., Ironside, M. and Seifert, R. (1993) 'Classroom struggle? Market oriented education reforms and their impact on teachers' professional autonomy, labour intensification and resistance', paper presented to the International Labour Process Conference, April.

Smyth, J. (1993) 'Schools of the Future and the Politics of Blame', public lecture sponsored by the Public Sector Management Institute, Melbourne, Monash University, 2 July.

Thomas, F. (Chair) *et al.* (1994) *One Year Later: Leading Victoria's Schools of the Future (Co-operative Research Project)*, Melbourne: Directorate of School Education.

—— (1995) *Taking Stock: Leading Victoria's Schools of the Future (Co-operative Research Project)*, Melbourne: Directorate of School Education.

—— (1996) *A Three Year Report Card: Leading Victoria's Schools of the Future (Co-operative Research Project)*, Melbourne: Directorate of School Education.

Tickell, G. (1995) *Decentralising the Management of Australia's Schools; Vol. II*, Melbourne: National Industry Education Forum.

Townsend, T. (1996a) *School Effectiveness and the Decentralisation of Australia's Schools*, Melbourne: National Industry Education Forum.

—— (1996b) 'Community perceptions of the Self-Managing School', paper presented at the International Roundtable of Families, Communities, Schools and Students' Learning, AERA Conference, New York, April.

—— (1996c) 'Matching the goals of Schools of the Future with the demographic characteristics of their local communities', unpublished research project funded by the Australian Research Council.

Whitty, G. (1994) 'Devolution in Education Systems: Implications for Teacher Professionalism and Pupil Performance', discussion paper, Melbourne: National Industry Education Forum.

Wylie, C. (1994) *Self managing schools in New Zealand: The fifth year*, Auckland: New Zealand Council for Educational Research.

Index